Clark

Clark

clark.

Clark

Clark.

Clark

Clark

Clarks

Clarks

Clarks

Clarks

MADE
------ to ------
LAST

The story of Britain's best-known shoe firm

MARK PALMER

P
PROFILE BOOKS

First published in Great Britain in 2013 by
Profile Books Ltd
3A Exmouth House
Pine Street
Exmouth Market
London EC1R 0JH
www.profilebooks.com

1 3 5 7 9 10 8 6 4 2

A CIP catalogue record for this book is available from the British Library.

ISBN: 978 1 84668 520 0
eISBN: 978 1 84765 845 6

Typeset in Photina by MacGuru Ltd
info@macguru.org.uk

The Tor trademark shown here, named after Glastonbury Tor, the hill overlooking the Clarks
home town of Street, has always been identified with the company. It was registered as a
trademark on 28 February 1879, but had been used by Clarks for nearly fifty years before that.

Printed and bound in Great Britain by Clays, Bungay, Suffolk

The paper this book is printed on is certified by the © 1996 Forest Stewardship Council A.C.
(FSC). It is ancient-forest friendly. The printer holds FSC chain of custody SGS-COC-2061

In memory of my father

Contents

Illustrations

Text illustrations

Acknowledgements

THE HABIT of keeping full and proper records was common to many Quaker businesses – and the records at C. & J. Clark Ltd are remarkably full and proper. They are so detailed and prized so highly that during 2012 the whole collection was moved to a dedicated new building near the Clarks headquarters in Street, Somerset.

The Clarks archives are managed by Charlotte Berry and Dr Tim Crumplin, assisted by Shirley Stocker. I could not have written this history without their help and cooperation, and I am immensely grateful to them. Tim spent many years researching, sifting and chronicling the archives long before I turned up. He graciously shared his findings with me, and this book includes much of his detailed and largely unheralded work.

Past and present employees of Clarks have been unfailingly generous with their time, often going out of their way to dig out letters, documents and other items of interest. I have been struck by their vivid memories of life at Clarks and the obvious affection they have for the company and everything it stands for. David Heeley, who occupied senior positions at Clarks throughout his working life, spent many hours patiently explaining the difference between one end of a shoe and the other, and he introduced me to a number of people who played key roles at the company. Among those I would like to mention here are: Neville Gillibrand, Kevin Crumplin, Paul Harris, David Lockyer, Eric Saville, Robert Wallace, John Aram, Michael Fiennes, Dudley Cheeseman, Royston Colman, Andrew Peirce and Maurice Burt, who joined Clarks as a teenager in 1948.

Those connected indirectly with the business as consultants or through advertising, marketing and other related activities are also due enormous thanks. They include: Colin Fisher, Peter York, Alan Bracher, Mary Portas, Professor John A. Davis, Suzanne Stroh, Geoff Howard-Spink, John McConnell, Ian Paris, June Swann and Grant Gordon, from the Institute for Family Business.

Rebecca Shawcross at the Northampton Shoe Museum allowed me to rummage through documents in the basement of her building, which presented a fascinating insight into the shoe industry of the past. Many thanks also to Carol Howard, Paul Charles, Peter Ford, Jenny Coad, Kate O'Grady, John and Jayne Haw, Laura Powell, Angela Southern, Richard Houlton, the librarians at Friends House in the Euston Road, London, Edgar Smith, John Potts of the Clarks marketing department, Anthony Perillo, Sylvia Woon, and Dick Shilton, archivist at Millfield School.

John Clothier and Malcolm Cotton were both senior executives at Clarks in the 1980s and 1990s and, as a result, I pestered them with great regularity. At all times, they responded with good grace and were unquestionably honest in their assessment of what went right – and what went wrong – while they were in positions of responsibility. Members of the current board have also been extremely helpful, not least the chief executive, Melissa Potter, and the chairman, Peter Davies. I would also like to thank Melissa's two immediate predecessors, Peter Bolliger and Tim Parker.

The Clark family is a big one and I have had the privilege of getting to know many of them. Richard Clark and Harriet Hall have been my main points of contact and they have guided me along the way with a sure and enthusiastic hand. I have appreciated their wise counsel and their great knowledge of Clarks.

Roger Pedder, a former Clarks chairman who married into the family and was at the centre of some of Clarks' most turbulent days, gave up many hours to help me and I am especially indebted to him. Other family members who have provided welcome assistance include Hugh and Gloria Clark, William Johnston, Jan Clark, Ralph Clark, Lance Clark, Caroline Gould, Caroline Pym and Hugh Pym.

It has been a great pleasure working with Profile Books. Paul Forty improved the final product hugely, supported by Fiona Screen and Virginia

Wallis. And I want especially to thank Stephen Brough, who has overseen this whole project with great clarity and calmness. From the start, his skilled editorial advice and general guidance have been invaluable – and he never lost his sense of humour.

I would like to thank members of my own family. My cousin, Howard Palmer, clarified diligently the connection between the Palmers and the Clarks (we are distant cousins) going back to the late eighteenth century in Somerset; my son, Henry, helped with research and worked the Clarks photocopying machine with aplomb; my daughter, Olivia, was always quick to give an opinion on Clarks footwear, both past and present, and my two stepsons, Freddy and Monty, have shown an interest in Clarks beyond the call of duty, always keeping spirits high during my long absences from home. My father-in-law, Noel Harvey, read parts of my account as I went along and I appreciated greatly his thoughtful comments.

Finally, I want to single out my wife, Joanna, for whom weekends were pretty dull while I was engaged on the book. But she supported me with love and affection. She enriches my life and she has enriched this book.

Introduction

CONTINUITY IS NO GUARANTEE of success in business. Sometimes it can be a hindrance, a disincentive for making the changes required to modernise, propel a company forward or even transform it completely. Statistics bear this out, with research by the Institute for Family Business showing that only around 13 per cent of family firms survive to the third generation. It is therefore remarkable that the company now known as Clarks has survived well into its seventh.

But it has not always been a comfortable ride. This is a firm that came perilously close to bankruptcy within a couple of decades of its formation in 1825 and then found itself in an even more precarious position a few years later. On both occasions, the family firm was bailed out by cousins, friends and others with whom it shared a powerful Quaker bond. It then went on to become one of the biggest shoe companies – and one of the most famous – in the world.

Along the way, the Somerset village of Street, where Clarks has been based for nearly 200 years, grew into a town almost entirely on the back of the footwear-producing firm. From just a few pairs of home-made slippers in 1831, Clarks now sells more than 50 million pairs of shoes a year, has a turnover of almost £1.4 billion and employs some 15,000 people.

That the company started at all is thanks to a seventeen-year-old apprentice, who, aware that he was to receive little in the way of remuneration for working in his brother's sheepskin enterprise, hit upon an idea that would lead to the creation of an iconic British brand. The apprentice was James Clark, son of Joseph Clark I, a Quaker with a 'gift in the vocal ministry' who travelled widely espousing the teachings of George Fox, founder of the Society of Friends, and who would have been pleased if his son had done likewise.

James was born in Street in 1811, the youngest of three brothers. His oldest sibling, Joseph, was a yeoman farmer specialising in the corn trade; his second brother, Cyrus, was in the wool business. After an exhaustive Quaker education – during which he was deeply unhappy – James was meant to be apprenticed to a chemist in Bath, but successfully pleaded with his father to let him stay in Street and help Cyrus.

Cyrus had a talent for trade. By the age of twenty he had set up a wool and tanning business with a Quaker cousin, but soon broke away on his own to make rugs from the sheepskins rather than pulling off the wool for sale to textile merchants. James, in turn, was keen to find some practical use for the off-cuts of Cyrus's rugs and began working after hours with a large pair of scissors and some needle and thread. He produced slippers which were so warm in winter that people didn't want to take them off and so comfortable in summer that people wanted to keep them on. He also made sheepskin socks, which at the time were used by the shoe trade as inner linings to protect the underside of the foot from the insole.

James and Cyrus went on to form a partnership, variously producing rugs, mops, chamois leather, galoshes, gloves, leggings, angora hats, scarves, coats – and shoes. Cyrus was ten years older than James and though they were close and appeared to work well together it did not prevent an acrimonious battle between their respective families over Cyrus's will following his death in 1866, the outcome of which would play a part in determining whether the business died or thrived.

It was left to James's son, William S. Clark, to start turning things around. A towering figure who lived to the age of 86, William knew instinctively what people wanted to wear on their feet. But he also knew where his father and uncle had gone so disastrously wrong: by taking too much money out of the company rather than reinvesting it for future expansion.

William was one of the earliest shoemakers in Britain to introduce machinery into the production process, and he went on to establish C. & J. Clark both as a pioneer of new technology and as a champion of footwear innovation. He remained at the heart of C. & J. Clark and at the centre of life in Street for more than 50 years, and was followed by his brother Francis (better known as Frank), and then by his son Roger, his grandson Bancroft, another grandson, Tony, and finally by his great-grandson Daniel, all of whom served as chairmen of C. & J. Clark. Two more of William's children, Alice Clark and John Bright Clark, and many of his descendants and the wider family have played important roles in the company.

Shoemaking was in their blood, but they were also imbued with a strong sense of what is now called corporate social responsibility. In Street, a school was founded so that young men and women could combine working in the factory with continuing their education. A theatre was opened, a library was built, along with an open-air swimming pool and town hall. Playing fields were established for the benefit of all and low-cost housing was provided by the company for its employees. C. & J. Clark *was* Street.

Today, the company places a concerted emphasis on its 'enduring values' and has a strict code of business ethics which talks openly about 'caring for people' both within the company and outside of it. Through the Clark Foundation, established in 1959, it supports a number of charitable initiatives in the UK and abroad, including Soul of Africa, a not-for-profit organisation working in Africa to fight unemployment and change the lives of orphans and children affected by AIDS.

Clarks is a modern business with a long heritage. More than 80 per cent privately owned by family members, the company goes about its business with little fanfare, largely shunning publicity and mindful – even subconsciously – of its social and religious roots.

The headquarters of Clarks remains exactly where it has always been, in Street at the northern end of the High Street opposite the Bear Inn, a public house the company owned until a few years ago and which only was permitted to serve alcohol as late as the 1970s. The chief executive – one of only a few women in Britain in charge of such a large organisation – operates from a group of New York-style loft offices with striking views of Glastonbury Tor. The Tor was at one time the brand image of Clarks, and it is still used for Clarks sports shoes today. On the outskirts of town, the futuristic-looking distribution centre has room for 5 million pairs of shoes and dispatches footwear to all corners of the globe.

Clarks has a clearly defined structure. It is run by professional, outside managers, with a family shareholder council serving as an intermediary, a sounding board and as a democratically elected consultative body. This was put in place following years of in-fighting that resulted in the company coming within a few votes of being sold for £184 million in 1993 to a City of London financial consortium with no experience of the footwear industry.

At the time, almost every newspaper and media organisation urged the family to sell up. The *Daily Telegraph* predicted that the fate of Clarks would be the same as other Quaker companies – 'the Lloyds and the Barclays, the Cadburys, Frys, Rowntrees' – all of which had either gone public or been bought out. 'If the bid is rejected, Clarks future looks grim,' ran the paper's editorial on the morning of the vote.

The bid was rejected, but the future was far from grim. Left to its own devices, Clarks regrouped and discovered a new resolve. It brought in experienced business people who had their own ideas about the future and who were allowed to see those ideas through. But crucially, the company remained family-owned.

Over the next decade or so, Clarks began the painful process of closing down all the factories it had run in the West Country, in Ireland, in the United States and elsewhere across the world. The survival of the brand now depends on production overseas, primarily in Vietnam and China. However, each line of shoe is still designed by Clarks, distributed by Clarks, marketed by Clarks and sold either in the 1,156 Clarks shops, franchise stores, factory outlets and concessions and through the Clarks website, or in independent shops and department stores serviced by Clarks as a wholesaler.

Nearly half its sales come from outside the United Kingdom. North America is one of the strongest markets, selling only 10 million fewer pairs than in Britain, and every year there is further expansion into the Far East and India.

For many people in Britain, their first pair of shoes has been and still is bought from Clarks. This reflects the company's dominance of the children's market, where parents are encouraged to take their sons or daughters to a shop so that their feet can be properly measured and their shoes properly fitted. Selling 'First Shoes' – the branded range for infants under two – and back-to-school shoes for schoolchildren remains at the heart of Clarks' success and it is now possible to buy a version of the company's famous foot gauge so that parents can measure a child's foot before ordering online or visiting a store.

Footwear has never been an easy trade. The science of making shoes is complicated. In the days when all shoes used leather, there was the challenge of working with a non-uniform raw material. Because all skins have their own unique strengths and weaknesses, machine production was almost impossible until the middle of the nineteenth century. The human foot also poses challenges. Its shape is intricate and highly individual, requiring shoemakers constantly to experiment with new techniques. And then there is the fleeting shelf-life of shoes as they fall victim to the vagaries of changing fashions.

Clarks has never been afraid of experimenting. It was one of the first to adapt the sewing machine for shoe production; an early convert to offering a variety of width fittings; the first to design a shoe in 3D on a virtual last; and the first to use new materials such as polyurethane soling to replace leather. And although to begin with, Clarks took a dim view of advertising – along with other Quaker firms who thought it degrading – the company was soon producing imaginative 'showcards' using stars of stage and screen to endorse its products. Collett Dickenson Pearce, St Luke's and Yellow Door have all held the Clarks advertising account, the last headed up by Mary Portas.

The Desert Boot is one of Clarks' best-known lines. It has changed little since its heyday in the 1950s. It is a casual shoe created by James Clark's great-grandson, Nathan Clark, based on his experiences serving in Burma as an officer in the Royal Army Service Corps in 1941. Made of soft suede with a crepe sole, the Desert Boot resolutely refuses to be labelled and seems forever in fashion as a result. Everyone from Liam Gallagher to Bob Dylan to Tony Blair to the Jamaican rapper Vybz Kartel has been spotted wearing the Desert Boot.

There was no history of shoemaking in Street at the start of the nine-teenth century. But today, fortunately, there is a huge amount of historical material about Street's shoemaking. Quakers believed in keeping accurate records of their day-to-day business activities. Ledgers, letters, copy-books, financial papers and several personal memoirs make up only a small part of Clarks' extensive archives. There is also a shoe museum and a collection of 20,000 assorted shoes going back to the Roman Empire.

These records paint an extraordinary picture of a British business that has changed beyond recognition since its simple, rural beginnings – and yet the survival of Clarks and its evolution as an international global brand is largely due to its unchanging values and the family's fierce determina-tion to remain independent.

1

A little extra pocket money

STREET DOESN'T MERIT A MENTION in the Domesday Book. Nor does its ancient moniker of Lantokay, so-named in honour of a Celtic saint by the name of Kea. Rather, Street assumed the role of an appendage, an unthreatening satellite of rich and famous Glastonbury barely two miles away.

Glastonbury used to be very rich indeed. Prior to the Dissolution of the Monasteries, its abbey's status came second only to that of Westminster Abbey in London. Although Christian legend claims it was founded by Joseph of Arimathea in the first century, there is more general agreement that the abbey was established by the Saxons following their conquest of Somerset in the seventh century.

Their king, Ine of Wessex, was a local man who put the abbey on a sound financial footing and it is he who is thought to have erected a stone church which later formed the west end of the nave. In the tenth century, St Dunstan, the Abbot of Glastonbury, who became Archbishop of Canterbury in 960, enlarged the church, and the Normans continued its expansion, adding more and more magnificent buildings.

Such was its reputation that King Edward I and Queen Eleanor spent Easter there in 1278 and during that visit the king proposed holding his Assizes within the grounds, only to be informed by the abbot that this would violate the site's ancient privileges. The king backed down and held the Assizes in Street instead.

Many years later, in 1539, the incumbent abbot, Richard Whiting, was in no mood to hand over his community's worldly goods to a rampaging Henry VIII, for which he was rewarded by being hanged, drawn and quartered on Glastonbury's Chalice Hill. To make sure the message got through to other would-be dissenters, his head was impaled over the entrance to the abbey and his severed remains were distributed in towns throughout the county.

Glastonbury Abbey was subsequently looted by the king's cronies and the surrounding land passed to Sir Edward Seymour, Duke of Somerset, eldest brother of Henry VIII's third wife Jane Seymour. The duke, who later became Lord Protector when the young Edward VI succeeded to the throne, moved effortlessly into the abbey and then, to bemusement and a degree of muted admiration, he embarked on an ambitious plan to develop the textile trade in Somerset.

Around 1551, Sir Edward settled weavers and wool workers from the Low Countries into the abbey's domestic buildings and provided them with a pastor to look after their spiritual well-being. Many of the neighbouring villages – Street included – benefited from the duke's business strategy. A certain Robert Hiet was given the task of setting up a cloth factory in Street and trade prospered there right up until the late eighteenth century.

Centuries earlier, the Romans had come and gone, leaving behind bits and pieces from their villas, some interesting pottery and sections of a road, all of which can be seen today in the Somerset County Museum in Taunton. On view in the Natural History Museum in London is a collection of fossils found in Blue Lias limestone that were excavated from quarries near Street in the nineteenth and early twentieth century.

One of these is an ichthyosaur, a dolphin-like creature from the Jurassic period, which caused so much excitement that when the Street Urban Council was formed in 1894 it decided to make the ichthyosaur its emblem. Blue Lias itself was used for making doorsteps, window sills, kerbing and paving and was big business in the region until concrete proved to be an easier and cheaper alternative.

Street – in years past spelled variously as Streate, Streatt, Streat, Strete and Stret – is derived from the Latin *strata*, meaning paved road, and was so named because of the causeway, once part of the Exeter-to-Lincoln Roman Fosse Way, that was repaired in 1184 to transport stone from Street to Glastonbury Abbey after a fire had destroyed some of the monastic buildings.

By the turn of the nineteenth century, most men in the village and surrounding areas had to eke out a living from the land. In 1801, Street's population was little more than 500, roughly similar to other agricultural villages in the county. Labourers worked as shepherds, peat cutters, cider makers or general farmhands on fields along the Polden Hills and across the slushy flats of Queen's Sedgemoor and on towards the Vale of Avalon. Farming became a lucrative endeavour during the Napoleonic Wars, as Britain's blockade of the continent and strict protectionist rules ensured that there was no competition from outside the country at a time when grain was needed to sustain the war effort. Wheat and barley prices were ring-fenced and remained high.

The defeat of the French changed all that. Immediately, the price of grain plummeted and, although the Corn Laws went some way in protecting farmers, the good life was not quite so good any more. In Street, there was something of a polarisation: many working men drowned their sorrows in cider, while others immersed themselves in work.

Alcohol has some history in Street. The museum in Taunton has on display a tankard dating from the Iron Age that was found near Shapwick. It is constructed of wooden staves covered with sheet bronze, with an elaborate bronze handle. It looks well used. In the 1820s, the Street Inn – still in business today in Somerton Road, where the stocks were once positioned – was where you went to drink, and just up the lane at the Society of Friends' meeting house was where a small group of mainly teetotallers went to worship.

The Society of Friends, or Quakers, as they were known, were a sizeable force in Somerset, many having fled persecution in the mid-seventeenth century and settled into the countryside from towns such as Bristol and

Gloucester. Street's meeting house was an attractive detached cottage built in 1717 and one of its earliest members was a man called John Clark III, who had moved to the village in 1723 on marrying Ann Coaxley, who was also a Quaker. Like his father and grandfather, John Clark III was a working farmer, but, unlike his forebears, he managed to avoid imprisonment for his religious beliefs.

The persecution of Quakers in the seventeenth century was relentless. In the early 1660s, the legislative programme known as the Clarendon Code, after Charles II's Lord Chancellor Edward Hyde, the Earl of Clarendon, sought to re-establish the supremacy of the Anglican Church. The Quaker Act was passed in 1662, making it illegal not to swear allegiance to the king – something that Quakers would not countenance out of religious conviction. That same year, John Clark III's grandfather, John Clark I, fell foul of the act and was sent to Ilchester Gaol. Two years later, the Conventicle Act came into force outlawing non-conformist gatherings of more than five people. The act was repealed in 1689, but that did not stop John Clark II also spending time in Ilchester Gaol.

John Clark I had farmed on the Poldens and lived in the village of Catcott. He later moved to Greinton in the south of the county, where he died in 1697. According to the Society of Friends' records, he was an 'honest old man serviceable to the Truth in his day'. He must have been an heroically early recruit to the Quaker cause and, although there is no explicit evidence to confirm that he ever met George Fox, the Quaker founder, the likelihood is that he did, given that Fox spent a great deal of time in the West Country, one of the Society's foremost strongholds.

His grandson, John Clark III, was born in 1680. His marriage to Ann brought together two important farming families. The Coaxleys were the bigger landowners of the two, owning three farms, including one at Overleigh, where John and Ann set up home together. One year into their marriage they had a son, John Clark IV, who caused considerable anxiety when in 1750 he asked Jane Bryant to marry him – and she accepted.

Jane's grandfather, Thomas, had been involved in the Monmouth Rebellion against King James II and was hanged in Glastonbury after sentencing by the notorious Judge Jeffreys. That was not the problem, however. The concern for the Clarks was that Jane belonged to the Church of England, a disagreeable fact about which her fiancé was left in little doubt. 'If you marry this giddy girl of Greinton,' he was told by a Quaker elder, 'thee will bring thy father's grey hairs down in sorrow to the grave'.

John Clark IV's cousin, James Clothier, was also exercised by the romance. According to a family memoir, *Somerset Anthology*, written many years later by John's great-great-grandson, Roger Clark, Clothier put pen to paper, telling his cousin:

> I heard very lately by a certain friend the party was afraid that thou would go to the priest for a wife ... Thou mayst prevent it if thee will, and therefore I would have thee desert from proceeding any further with the giddy girl of Grenton [*sic*] at present, and waite, have patience, who knows that in time she may come to join the Friends.

John went ahead with the marriage and it proved to be a happy one, even though at first he was racked by guilt for saying his vows before an Anglican priest. At a monthly Friends' meeting in July 1755, John's contrite testimony was read out. 'That what I did was even then much contrary to my mind and what I do now (so far as being married by a priest) sincerely Condeme.'

This difficulty came to a positive conclusion when within a few years Jane began attending the Quaker women's monthly meetings – and in 1787 both she and John were appointed elders.

They had two sons and two daughters. Their eldest boy, Thomas Clark senior, lived and farmed at Overleigh until retiring to Bridgwater on the death of his wife, Mary Metford. Thomas was, according to Roger Clark's memoir, 'apt to have odd or eccentric notions' and had been known locally as 'Tommy Weight-Bottle' because he was reported to have paid his workers in part in cider, weighing the drink rather than measuring it in pint or quart bottles.

Joseph Clark I was John and Jane's second son. He was born in 1762 and lived all his life in or around Street, firstly at Friends Charity Farm

Hindhayes, the house that Cyrus Clark's father, Joseph Clark I, had built in 1807. This photograph was taken in the back garden in the 1880s by Cyrus's eldest son John Aubrey Clark and shows three of Cyrus's other children: Alfred (at centre in hat); Bessie (Sarah Elizabeth), seated; and (at right, seated in front of window) Thomas Beaven Clark. The standing woman is Bessie's companion, Mrs Walker; Bessie had been left an invalid by the typhus epidemic of 1852.

Street, then at Lower Leigh and finally at Hindhayes, a house he built in 1807. He married Frances (Fanny) Sturge, from Olveston, Gloucestershire, in 1794 and they had three sons, Joseph Clark II, Cyrus and James. Joseph took on the family farm, while Cyrus and James were to become the founding fathers of what would turn out to be one of the world's most famous shoe companies: Clarks.

The three boys' father lived until he was almost 70, and by the time of his death in 1831 he had become a pillar of the Quaker establishment. In his later years, Joseph Clark I was not a well man. He had suffered a stroke and walked with an uncertain gait, but he continued to preach, seemingly oblivious to his deteriorating health. According to Roger Clark, his audience at Friends' meetings found him 'quite unintelligible' and:

... in a family meeting such as Street was at that time, no one could be found to deal plainly enough with the dear old man, and it was finally left to a Q.M. [Quaker Meeting] Committee with Bristol Friends on it, set up for the purpose, to explain to him that his Ministry was no longer effective... [but] we remember him as a kind old man who, when we were taken to see him, would shuffle across the room to get us sugar plums, and to set the cuckoo clock a-cuckooing for our amusement.

During his long, devout life, Joseph Clark I developed strong bonds with several wealthy Quaker families such as the Gilletts, Players, Metfords, Sturges and Palmers. For Cyrus and James, his two younger sons, these were to prove important contacts over the next few decades

By the 1820s, Street's population had risen to 800, but it remained largely isolated from the main centres of business and only 60 or so people were still employed in the once busy textiles industry. London was a sixteen-hour carriage journey away, while Bristol required eight hours of riding, and it wasn't until the opening of the Glastonbury-to-Highbridge canal in 1833 that new businesses in Street began to get established.

Cyrus Clark was a 'most imaginative and lively personality with a penchant for trading and manufacture' says George Barry Sutton in his book *C. & J. Clark, 1833–1903: A History of Shoemaking*. Certainly, he was an industrious young man. In 1821, he had gained enough experience in fellmongering (the removal of sheep's wool from hides in preparation for tanning), tanning and woolstapling (the buying of wool from a producer, followed by grading and then selling on to a manufacturer) to form a partnership with his cousin, Arthur Clothier, whose family had been in woolstapling since the seventeenth century.

Cyrus was only 21 when he entered into this partnership with Clothier – and it turned out to be a short-lived collaboration. In 1825, they went their separate ways, with Arthur retaining the more profitable tanning side of the business and Cyrus concentrating on the fellmongering and woolstapling. Generally speaking, 1825 is therefore regarded as the year in which the company that eventually became Clarks was founded, even though the formal partnership between Cyrus and James did not happen for a further eight years.

It was also in 1825 that Cyrus married Sarah Bull, daughter of John Bull, a local glove manufacturer. They were to have four sons and a daughter.

One of the reasons Cyrus had no qualms about breaking up with Clothier was that he had developed his own sideline that was to prove highly successful. His idea had been to make sheepskin rugs from some of the skins instead of pulling the wool off. This was a process that swiftly lent itself to a variety of other consumer goods. For example, offcuts were made into strips that were ideal for mops, while softer skins were adapted to make chamois-leathers and housemaids' gloves.

James, meanwhile, received a sound Quaker education that included some years at Sidcot School, in Winscombe, North Somerset, a co-educational establishment founded in 1699 for the children of Friends. But he was an unhappy schoolboy. In fact, his whole education made him miserable. Before attending Sidcot, he had been sent away, aged seven, to a mainly girls' Quaker school in Bridgwater, where there was only one other boy boarder. As James described it in an unpublished autobiography written for the benefit of his children:

> Although I was not unkindly treated ... I cried myself to sleep every night and crying again when I woke in the morning till the vacation came. Sidcot was little better. I never met with more depraved characters, so utterly lost to all that was good, as some few of the older boys, who tyrannised and exercised the worst possible influence over their younger companions.

He left aged sixteen, and his father resolved to apprentice him to a chemist in Bath. James hated the idea.

> I begged so earnestly not to leave home, saying I did not care what business I was apprenticed to so that I could live at Street, that in accordance with this wish I was apprenticed to my brother Cyrus ... I was greatly pleased with this arrangement, for having all my life lived in the country I could not bear the idea of the confinement of city life, or indeed of any sort of confinement.

The founders of a shoemaking dynasty: brothers James and Cyrus Clark

And so, on 22 March 1828, the seventeen-year-old James went to work for his brother Cyrus. He also lived with Cyrus and Sarah in a house that had belonged to John Bull, Cyrus's father-in-law. It was next to the outhouses where Bull made his gloves – premises that later would become the first Clarks factory.

The terms of James's five-year apprenticeship were unequivocal. They are recorded in an informal history of the company written by James's eldest son, William S. Clark:

> I have the indenture of apprenticeship which provides that 'Cyrus Clark in consideration of a premium of £80 paid to him and of his giving him faithful service in every way will cause James Clark to be taught and instructed in the arts of a Tanner, Sheepskin Rug Manufacturer and Fellmonger'. James was 'bound not to contract matrimony while apprenticed' and 'shall not play cards, dice tables or other unlawful games ... Cyrus Clark engages to find James Clark sufficient meat, drink and lodging' and my grandfather Joseph Clark covenants to find his

son, James Clark, 'sufficient clothes, mending and washing and medical and surgical attendance'.

James seemed perfectly content with all of that. As William put it:

James Clark always remembered with gratitude the extreme kindness with which he was treated by him [Cyrus] and by his wife, my Aunt Sarah, the latter being more like a mother or an elder sister to him than a sister-in-law.

There was no mention of a stipend. But within a remarkably short period, there was no need for any such arrangement. Keen to earn some money and achieve a degree of independence from his brother, James asked Cyrus to let him have some of the short wool skins that were unsuitable for the manufacturing of rugs. He then came up with the idea of cutting those skins into wool-lined slippers. At first, he did the cutting himself and employed a man called Esau Whitnell, a skilled local shoemaker, to make the slippers for him. Whitnell, who walked with a heavy limp because one leg was shorter than the other, lived in a ramshackle thatched cottage close to the Toll Gate at the end of the village. James wrote:

Having no allowance of pocket money... my brother allowed me to get some slippers made of our short-wooled sheepskins, tanned with the wool on, and to cut out and prepare them for socks for ladies' and gentlemen's shoes ... the slippers were made up by a village shoemaker and after a time other sorts of wool-lined slippers were added, till eight or ten men were pretty fully employed on them, my part of the working being attended to after working hours.

The story propagated by H. F. Scott-Stokes in his 1925 book, *Clark, Son and Morland Ltd: Centenary Notes and Reminiscences*, is that Cyrus at first showed little interest in his brother's entrepreneurial flourish. Rather, he 'turned to the serious business of the factory and never gave the matter another thought'. In fact, Cyrus's private ledger shows that he was willing to give his brother long credit and some additional cash advances to expand his slipper business. Cyrus even began experimenting with different kinds of slippers and shoes himself, and in October 1831, while James was on a sales trip to Manchester, he wrote an enthusiastic letter to his brother:

> We have much improved the slippers. The plan we now adopt is to take a white skin rather long in the wool, and then skim the top off it, by this means we get it perfectly white. We then use that skin for the bordering. By this means we cover stitches and we have a beautiful fringe round each, so that those thou now hast are not a fair sample – and we do the same with the brown by choosing a handsome colour prime mat and skim off the black tips.

In the same letter, he encouraged James to seek out new ideas and not come back empty-handed from his travels – 'now if thou see anything which thou consider an improvement, either boots or shoes, buy it and bring with thee'.

James's first dedicated salesman was a cousin and friend from Sidcot School, Charles Gilpin, who went on to become the Liberal MP for Northampton. Gilpin at the time was an apprentice to his father, a woollen draper in Bristol. The deal these cousins brokered was that Charles could keep any profit he made from the sale of slippers as a means of supplementing his meagre income.

Increasingly, as James went about the country selling Cyrus's rugs, he found that there was growing interest in the slippers, which by now were known as 'Brown Petersburgs' or simply 'Brown Peters'. The name remains a mystery. In Kenneth Ponting's *Sheep of the World* there is no breed or type of sheep called Petersburg, although there were clear connections between the British and Russian courts in the 1830s, and trade with Russia was strong. The late John Thornton, an authority on old footwear, who in the 1980s was head of the Boot and Shoe Department at Northampton College of Technology, once suggested that the name could have been chosen simply because it was evocative of a cold climate.

Brown Peters were soon joined by other classes of slippers on James's showcard, and he also introduced lambswool socks, some hand-welted boots and a few shoes. James may have been occupied in his workshop, but he was also busy travelling, having gone on the road at the age of eighteen. The riding was arduous, but the drinking with fellow commercial travellers was clearly far more debilitating. At one point, he heeded Cyrus's advice and restricted himself to what he called a 'modest' four glasses of port after dinner, but by 1831 Cyrus and James were finding it 'difficult indeed to bear witness at the commercial table' and abstained from alcohol from there on.

The making of sheepskin rugs remained straightforward. Skins were tanned with the wool on them and, according to William S. Clark:

> ... the colour afterwards struck a dark brown with limewater ... afterwards the dressing of the skins with alum and salt was introduced and the skins were dyed in various colours.

Shoe manufacturing, on the other hand, was going through a huge transformation with the introduction of 'ready-mades' in addition to more expensive bespoke shoes. All shoes were made on a last – a shaped piece of wood or metal around which the shoe is built – but ready-mades involved a universal last rather than one made especially for a particular individual. And it was not until the 1850s that there was a clear distinction between left- and right-footed shoes in the ready-made market.

Exactly when ready-mades were first introduced is unclear, but, as George Barry Sutton noted, a firm of shoemakers in Northampton produced 2,500 pairs of boots for Cromwell's army in 1648 using a uniform last. Similarly, a shoemaker in London testified before a Parliamentary Committee in 1738 that he employed 162 people 'from eight to eighty' to produce footwear to supply the Plantations in Ireland and elsewhere overseas.

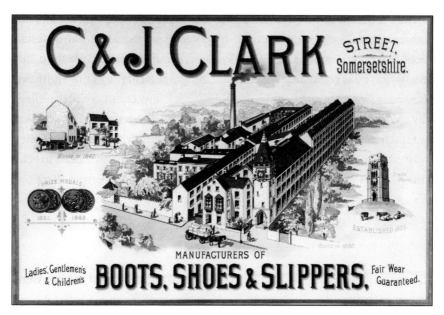

A Clarks showcard of 1890, showing the main factory site in Street at that time, as well as a small inset view of the works in 1840.

Unlike Northampton, which had a dedicated street of cordwainers (as shoemakers were known), and other towns known for their footwear, such as Norwich, Leicester and Kendal, Street had no pedigree in shoe production. Esau Whitnell was the sole shoemaker in 1829, but such was the energy of Cyrus and James that by 1841 there were 24 apprentices or junior shoemakers. Working conditions were cramped and not unlike the sweatshops of London, but it was these outworkers who changed Street from a sleepy village into a thriving town.

James Clark completed his apprenticeship in 1833, by which time he had saved £70. This was the year Cyrus and James officially worked out their business arrangement, setting themselves up almost as equal partners under the name C. & J. Clark, which would trade mainly in rugs, socks, slippers and shoes. The capital in the business amounted to £2,240, of which Cyrus's contribution was £1,170 – the net value of his rug and skin trade – and James's was £1,070. James raised £1,000 as the balance of his investment by mortgaging land left to him by his father, who had died two years previously in 1831.

Sales for the first six months of the partnership were £1,760. 4*s*. 1*d*. for rugs and £812. 8*s*. 5*d*. for shoes and socks. The net profit was £640.

2

Living beyond your means

QUAKERS TOOK A DIM VIEW of debt. It represented the irresponsibility they stood so implacably against. Consequently, the Society of Friends' monthly meetings stressed the words of Epistle 1754 – guidance emanating from headquarters in London of that year – about how they should be 'properly watchful' over fellow Quakers and 'early to caution all against running beyond their depth and entangling themselves in a greater multiplicity of trade and business than they can extricate themselves from with honour and reputation'. Being 'properly watchful' over others was a persistent theme within Quaker circles in the eighteenth and early nineteenth centuries.

Specific guidelines of this kind were relayed to clerks and read out at regional and local meetings. They were updated at irregular intervals in response to developments in the financial and industrial world. Applying the teachings of Christ to the workplace were essential, and in the event of money troubles, you were expected to seek advice from more experienced Friends – and to be candid about your predicament. For example, in the words of Epistle 1692:

All friends that are entering into trade, or that are in trade, and have not stocks sufficient of their own to answer the trade they aim at, be very cautious of running themselves into debt, without advising

The Friends' Meeting House in Street, built in 1850.

with some of their ancient and experienced Friends among whom they live.

Those who did incur debts were encouraged to wipe the slate clean as soon as possible. Failure to pay a debt was seen in Epistle 1735 as 'the great scandal and reproach of our holy profession' and Friends were warned to give 'timely caution to any such as either break their promises or delay payment of such debts, or otherwise render themselves suspected'. And woe betide those who were in debt but continued to enjoy the trappings of a comfortable life, 'it being exceedingly dishonourable for any to live in ostentation and greatness at the expense of others'.

Cyrus and James Clark grew up well-versed in these fundamental Quaker principles. And they would have learned at length about the character and behaviour of the Quakers' uncompromising founder, George Fox – who had happened to be apprenticed to a Nottingham shoemaker prior to his spiritual awakening in 1643.

Quakers were stoical in their response to provocation and persecution. In 1661, following the suppression of a violent Fifth Monarchist uprising (one of several non-conformist movements) led by Thomas Venner, Fox had issued the Peace Testimony, which officially committed the Society of Friends to pacifism and non-violence under all circumstances. 'The spirit of Christ will never move us to fight a war against any man with carnal weapons,' he wrote.

A turning point for Quakers came within months of the accession of William and Mary in the form of the Toleration Act of 1689, which was designed to be 'an effectual means to unite Their Majesties' Protestant subjects in interest and affection', according to Charles Braithwaite's respected Quaker history, *The Second Period of Quakerism.*

Fox died in 1691 – two years after this breakthrough – but had lived long enough to see positive results from his battles with Church and state, and a system was in place whereby Quakers knew what was expected of them, professionally and personally. Men and women should worship God directly and not through any intermediary, whether it be a priest or religious organisation. Personal religious experience was what counted. How you lived your life was more important than any prescribed system of belief and you were wholly responsible for your own actions. Redemption must be found on earth. The Kingdom of Heaven resided within the soul of all men and women, and was not merely a safe haven to which you were invited in the afterlife.

The closest Quakers came to a constitution or written code was the so-called 'Advices and Queries', which were circulated at the London Yearly Meeting. The overriding principle of these edicts was that Quakers should embrace the simple life. An allegiance of trust should always be maintained between Friends. They should work hard, support each other and be beyond reproach in their business affairs. Honesty was paramount. They must share any success with others, striving at all times for the common good.

By 1697, Quakers were enjoying considerable financial success. 'They have Grip'd Mammon as hard as any of their Neighbours; and now call Riches a Gift and A Blessing from God', scoffed one of their detractors,

Charles Leslie, in *The Snake in the Grass; or Satan Transformed into an Angel of Light*, published in London in 1697.

Some 150 years later, at least 74 banks had been founded by Quakers, their influence way out of proportion to their numbers, which never exceeded more than 30,000 in Britain except in the latter part of the seventeenth century. There is an argument that Quakers did well because they hailed mainly from middle-class families (and certainly Fox could be described as a man with access to independent means), but nothing can detract from their resourcefulness, innovation, graft and public-spiritedness.

Their progress became something of a business phenomenon. A Quaker, Edward Pease, was inspired to build the Stockton and Darlington Railway in 1814, which was to become known as the 'Quaker Line'. Railway ticket and stamping machines were invented by a Quaker, Thomas Edmonson, as was the timetable known as Bradshaw's Railway Times, created by George Bradshaw. The Reckitts, a Quaker family, went into the household goods business, while the Crossfields were soap and chemical manufacturers whose firm led eventually to the formation of Lever Brothers.

Bryant & May made matches; Huntley, Bourne & Stevens produced tins; Allen and Hanbury developed pharmaceuticals; and the Cadburys, Frys and Rowntrees all made their mark in the production of chocolate.

Several prominent biscuit companies also began plying their trade during the nineteenth century, most of them with Quaker origins: Carr's of Carlisle; Peek Frean; Jacobs & Co; and Huntley & Palmer, who were also affiliated to Huntley, Bourne & Stevens.

Those who brought the Quaker name into disrepute could be 'disowned' by the Society and there were occasions when the practice of Friends refraining from suing one another was suspended if 'Evil Persons' had proved 'base and unworthy'. Monthly meetings had the authority to 'speedily set righteous Judgment upon the head of the Transgressor'.

The guidelines were regularly updated and insertions added. In the 1783 Book of Extracts, for example, Friends were alerted to a 'most pernicious practice' that fell short of 'that uprightness that ought to appear in every member of our religious society', a practice that was 'absolutely

The interior of the Friends' Meeting House in Street, as it was in October 1955.

inconsistent with the truth'. This 'highly unbecoming' new menace was the availability of credit.

In 1833, both the 1738 Advices and 1783 Extracts were revised and became known as the Rules of Discipline, which themselves were tweaked in 1861 and divided into three main chapters: Christian Doctrine; Christian Practice; and Church Government. These helped Quakers keep their ambitions in check during the Industrial Revolution when wealth billowed from the chimneys of factories, mills and warehouses.

'We do not condemn industry, which we believe to be not only praiseworthy but indispensable,' stated the Rules of Discipline, which went on to reiterate that 'the love of money is said in Scripture to be "the root of all Evil"'. The Rules urged: 'Dear Friends who are favoured with outward prosperity, when riches increase not to set your hearts upon them.'

Cyrus and James Clark attended their local meeting house every Sunday, sitting in silence or listening to a Friend giving testimony. Their business was in its infancy and they would have been aware of their responsibilities, particularly the consequences of over-extending themselves. They only had to look at the plight of Elizabeth Fry, the famous Quaker prison reformer who had married Joseph Fry in 1800, with whom she had eleven children. Greatly influenced by William Savery, an American evangelical Quaker, Elizabeth had established a school in 1816 for the children of women serving sentences in Newgate Prison, Norfolk. She also arranged for instruction to be given to their mothers, especially in sewing and knitting; she organised Bible-reading and insisted that prisoners be divided into small, manageable groups, each under the watchful eye of a matron, who pressed upon her charges the importance of cleanliness in mind, matter and spirit.

Elizabeth became such a powerful voice that she was called to give evidence before parliament on penal reform, but for all her notoriety, her altruism, her contacts in high places and her towering international reputation (she had once entertained the King of Prussia at lunch), she suffered the humiliation in 1828 of seeing her husband's business fall into bankruptcy, which led to his immediate estrangement from the Society of Friends. Cyrus and James Clark were fortunate to escape a similar fate.

Rugs accounted for some 60 per cent of C. & J. Clark's sales in 1835, followed by footwear and mops, each approaching 20 per cent, and chamois leather making up the balance. Those figures would change dramatically over the next fifteen years. By 1851, footwear represented some three quarters of total revenue, with rugs down to a fifth and mops and chamois leather accounting for a tiny fraction of sales.

Chamois leather, which is soft and absorbent and leaves no streaks when used as a polisher, takes its name from the chamois, a goat-like mammal native to regions in central Europe, particularly the Carpathian mountains of Romania and the Tatra mountains in Bulgaria. From the nineteenth century onwards, however, most chamois leathers were chamois only in name. They were, in fact, made from the hides of deer, goats and sheep – and it is likely that those produced by C. & J. Clark were sheepskin. They were reasonably simple to make, requiring little in the way of machinery or equipment.

The non-footwear side of the business comprised a miscellaneous range of products such as ottoman covers, gloves and mops, and included woolstapling, fellmongering and the manufacture of rugs themselves. The mops were an effective way to use what would otherwise be wasted – consisting of a stick on to which were fastened strips cut from the leftovers of skins assigned for rug-making.

All respectable housewives had a good supply of mops. Seldom a day went by without women washing the floors inside their houses or the doorsteps and pavements outside – and if the neighbours were watching, so much the better. Mops occasionally had other uses. In the 1832 General Election, they came in handy during a brawl in Street on polling day between Whigs and Tories. The election had come shortly after the new Whig prime minister, Lord Grey, who succeeded the Duke of Wellington, had pushed the Reform Bill through parliament – an act that increased the number of MPs in growing, industrial cities at the expense of those in areas where fewer people lived, known as the 'rotten boroughs'.

This bill, designed to enlarge the suffrage by including more property owners, was seen as a crucial step towards parliamentary democracy and one which would usher in a wider electorate. As it happened, Grey himself came from a distinguished Northumberland family and his first cabinet consisted almost entirely of aristocrats. There was an irony to the bill's preamble. It spoke of how it was designed to 'take effectual Measures for correcting diverse abuses that have long prevailed in the choice of members to serve' in the palace of Westminster, and yet one of the first things Grey's government did after the act became law was to create two new dukedoms.

Voters in Street were mostly Whigs. In Wells and Glastonbury, they tended to be Tory. The nearest polling station to both towns was in

Ilchester. It was on the way back from the ballot box that a crowd from Wells stopped for refreshment at the Street Inn, where they were joined by men from Street, almost all of whom worked at C. & J. Clark. A description of this incident is included in *Clarks of Street, 1825–1950*, a wide-ranging history compiled mainly by Laurence Barber, a former archivist for Clarks, but with contributions from Clark family members and some senior Clarks employees:

> They were greeted with scorn and jeers by [the people from] Wells, and later with more solid missiles. Wells, armed with weapons from the inn, drove [the people from] Street up the High Street to the Factory gates, where a young lad named John Hooper, afterwards for many years well known as the factory carpenter, seeing their plight, handed out mop sticks through a window, and these, broken in half across the knee, soon furnished the shoemakers with effective staves.

Battle ensued, during which a man called Joseph White suffered a blow to the head and was laid unconscious. He was taken into Cyrus Clark's house to recover. Another man with the same surname but no relation, Josiah White, was Street's police constable and well-known as a Whig. He was also struck on the head, but brushed off the blow and then proceeded to cause mayhem. 'I'll teach 'ee who is constable,' he shouted, wielding his baton as he took matters into his own hands.

A few days later, the local magistrate, who was a die-hard Tory, acquitted the men from Wells, but handed out £200 worth of fines to the shoemakers from Street and fined Josiah White £10. The Whig candidate, who had been returned to Westminster and whose party won the general election, was so outraged at the treatment dealt out to his supporters that he paid all their fines out of his own pocket.

The number of men employed purely in the Clarks' shoe business began to rise each year, from one in 1829 to around 38 in 1841, according to the census returns. With ready-made shoes not requiring as much skill as bespoke footwear, Cyrus and James had little difficulty recruiting workers from nearby villages, especially those who had lost their jobs following the decline of the textile industry. In fact, with the exception of two Irishmen, the 1841 census showed that no shoemakers in Street, Glastonbury or Walton were born outside Somerset. Even in 1851, only 10 per cent of male shoemakers hailed from outside the county. But it was a young man's game: men under the age of 21 accounted for 39 per cent of Street's shoemakers in that same year.

Clarks was producing 60 lines of footwear in 1835, including for the first time a range of shoes for children. The pace of expansion took even James by surprise. 'We little thought that the slipper trade begun in such a small way would lead us into a large shoe business ... and greatly increasing the population of our village.'

In addition to sheepskin, a variety of other materials were used for slippers, while soles were also sold separately, though in declining numbers. Boots for ladies and men were the bestsellers. One ladies' boot was called the 'Ne Plus Ultra', which sold for 20 shillings (£1), a lot of money at the time, and two and a half times as much as the Clark brothers' second-most expensive boot. In fact, no boot or shoe would command such a price in real terms as the Ne Plus Ultra until 1921.

Ready-made footwear was sold to customers for 10 to 15 per cent less than bespoke. The main saving concerned the work of the 'clickers', or 'cutters' as they became known, who were the most highly paid individuals in the shoemaking process. Clickers were so named because the room in which they worked was silent apart from the click of their blades piercing the leather. Sometimes they were referred to as the 'gentlemen of shoemaking'. For ready-made footwear, clickers continued to cut out the upper leather, but in standard sizes rather than making new patterns for each individual order.

The clickers were based in the factory along with supervisory staff who checked the quality of shoes brought in every day by outworkers. The outworkers were divided between those known as 'makers' and as 'binders' (known also as 'closers'). The makers were men and boys, who were responsible for attaching the sole and heel to the upper. The binders were women and girls, who sewed together the pieces of leather that formed the upper. Binding involved two processes: the welt and the sew-round. Welting was far more common than the sew-round, except in the case of more sophisticated women's shoes. The maker would 'last' the shoe by tacking an insole to the bottom of his last and stretching the upper over it until its lower edges overlapped the circumference of the insole. Then he would tack the upper to the insole before a welting strip was laid along the perimeter. The welt and the overlapping portion of the upper was hand-stitched or sewn to the insole, at which time the tacks could be removed. The outsole was then stitched to the welt. A steady hand and patience were the prerequisite qualifications of the all-important makers, or at least that was what the men, anxious to remain better remunerated than the women, were quick to stress.

It was also the job of the makers to finish the shoe ready for sale, which involved paring the sole and heel edges, waxing, colouring and polishing – and then sanding, colouring and polishing the bottom of the sole and the top-piece. Such was the strict division of labour between the sexes that, if you lived in Street, it was common to ask on hearing that a baby had been born whether the child was a binder or a maker, rather than a boy or a girl.

The sweatshops of London were notorious at this time, but conditions in Street were not always much better. Shoemakers worked and lived in backshops with ladders leading through the scullery to the first floor where much of the labour took place. It was cramped and dirty. The conditions are described by Brendan Lehane in his book *C. & J. Clark: 1825–1975*:

> Sometimes whole families worked together to make enough in a week
> – a pound or so – to pay for necessities; not that they needed much, for
> several cottages kept pigs and most grew their own vegetables. Wives
> learned to rock their babies' cradles with their feet while they stitched
> uppers – 15 stitches to the inch – to earn, if they were nimble, 1½*d*. an
> hour. Eldest sons learned early to assist in their fathers' trades. With

his pincers, knife, hammer, awls, tacks and rivets of brass or wood, the man of the house made the complete shoes. In winter, they worked round the light of one central candle.

The system worked well, and for the first few years of the partnership, productivity kept up with demand. Sales tripled between 1832 and 1836. The Invoice Recording Book 1834–1836 shows that, even though transport options were still limited, Clarks shoes were spreading to parts of Britain and the British Isles that other companies weren't reaching. There were no trains at this time between Bristol and London, or from Bristol to the north of England. Goods were sent by wagon, pack-horse, barge or sometimes by ship. Even so, the Clark brothers' shoe business was trading well in Northwest England, the Midlands and other areas of the country even further from Street.

In fact, in 1835, sales of footwear in what the firm called the home area (Somerset, Cornwall, Devon, Dorset, Wiltshire, Hampshire, Gloucestershire and Bristol) accounted for only 18 per cent of sales, while in Eastern England, no sales at all were recorded that year.

Far and away the biggest single market was Ireland, which accounted for some two fifths of Clarks total output in shoes and around a sixth of its rugs. The obliging Irish – at least until the Irish famine and the general economic depression of the late 1830s – were made up mainly of the merchant classes thriving in the larger ports following the easing of trade restrictions in 1780. Clarks attracted buyers in Dublin, Cork, Limerick, Waterford, Belfast and Clonwell, the last being a strong Quaker town.

James Clark married in 1835, after which Cyrus built him a house, called Netherleigh, next to the factory. This meant that the partners lived at either end of the workshop. James's wife was Eleanor Stephens, whose father was a linen draper and gifted china painter. Her mother was Amy Metford, daughter of William Metford, a Glastonbury Quaker who ran a knitting business specialising in stockings. James and Eleanor had four-teen children, twelve of whom survived to adulthood. Their third child was William S. Clark, who would later succeed the partners as chairman and who went on to become the firm's early saviour.

James and Eleanor had got to know each other three years before they married when Amy brought her daughter to stay with James's mother. James wrote how 'this visit brought me into intimate acquaintance with your dear mother and I felt very much attracted to her'. The following year, Amy made another visit to Street, during which James

> ... did not let it pass without declaring my desire that my fondest hope might be realised in obtaining her [Eleanor] as my partner for life and I can truly say that all my hopes and expectations have been far more than realised in the rich wealth of blessing that has been the result of that union.

The winter before their wedding was a difficult one for Eleanor. She endured a severe attack of inflammation of the lungs and her doctors advised against marriage in case it weakened her further. James would not hear of it.

> I thought then if we could only have 10 years of union I should have cause for deepest thankfulness, and for how much more have I been indebted to a loving Father who spared her to me.

A year after the marriage, Eleanor gave birth to their first daughter, Amy Jane, who lived only a matter of weeks. Eleanor then became unwell and James took her north of the border to convalesce, reaching both Edinburgh and Glasgow, where he managed to do some business at the same time. 'I opened a trade that has since become a large one; it was our first visit to Scotland', he wrote. Within months, total sales in Scotland accounted for 7.6 per cent of the Clark brothers' footwear business.

Meanwhile, thanks to contacts James had made in Liverpool during his earlier sales trips to that part of the country, some shoes and rugs

James and Eleanor Clark with twelve of their children at Netherleigh in 1858: (left to right) Eleanor Clark holding Mabel, James Clark, Amy, William, Fanny, Mary, Annie, Eleanor, Florence, Sophia, James Edmund, Edith and Frank. The Clarks were ardent supporters of the anti-slavery movement, and their clothing was made from cotton grown by free labour. The Free Produce Movement promoted a range of 'slave-free' goods such as sugar and cotton; this allowed consumers such as the Clarks to take direct action against slavery.

were sold to America and Canada, where, almost from the start, Cyrus had been keen to open up a sales front. In 1833, he wrote to his brother urging him to explore 'by what means we could send some shoes and soles to America'.

At first, Cyrus and James travelled widely, but then limited their trips to two or three a year. As early as 1830, agents were appointed on a commission basis and these men were later known as 'travelling salesmen'. The Clarks' London man was John Jackson, who was on commission of 8.5 per cent of the sales he made, a higher rate than that paid to salesmen working in the provinces.

Competition was intensifying. Mass production of ready-made shoes was growing apace in America, while in France, after the Napoleonic Wars, shoe manufacturing was a burgeoning business. Northampton, the heart and soul of the British shoe industry, was particularly hit by imports from

Europe. As early as 1829, the House of Commons heard about Northampton's 'want of regular employment and the low prices of wages'.

But these were difficult times across most sectors. When Queen Victoria succeeded to the throne in 1837, she found herself presiding over a decade known as the 'hungry forties', replete with famine in Ireland, widespread rural and urban poverty, and economic depression of a magnitude not experienced before in Britain. She was only eighteen when she became queen and her first prime minister, Lord Melbourne, whom she trusted and revered, was anxious not to alarm the young monarch by the country's precarious predicament. When Charles Dickens's *Oliver Twist* was serialised for the first time, Victoria asked her prime minister whether or not he would recommend the novel. As recorded by A. N. Wilson in *The Victorians*, Melbourne was scathing:

> It's all among workhouses and Coffin Makers and Pickpockets ... I don't *like* these things. I wish to avoid them; I don't like them in reality, and therefore I don't wish to see them represented.

At C. & J. Clark, production was increasing month by month, but this was stretching the business's resources. As George Barry Sutton described it in *C. & J. Clark, 1833–1903: A History of Shoemaking*:

> The 1834 Stock Account is notable for its lack of any reference to cash assets. The size of the net profit suggests that business had been extremely brisk and it is therefore not surprising that cash assets had been fully utilised in helping to create the large current assets shown in the account. The money due from debtors was a large sum which would all be required for the heavy outlays in the footwear trade during the following months. It soon became clear that at the business's present rate of expansion, and taking into account other heavy spring expenditures, alternative sources of cash assets must be looked to.

A large amount of cash was needed each autumn to acquire sheepskin, but money was also needed for the shoe business in late spring and early summer in order to produce enough footwear for the busy autumn period of sales. In January 1835, Cyrus, who had banked for ten years with Reeves, Porch & Co. in Wells, arranged an overdraft facility as a temporary measure while working on securing long-term loans. The businessman in him might have had few qualms with this strategy, but the Quaker beating in his breast was uncomfortable. In a letter to James, who was travelling in Ireland, he said:

> We are much heavier at the bank than I calculated upon and I do not see an end to our shortness unless we transfer (probably, replace) the bank debts by adding sufficient capital to fully meet these difficulties. I have been considering this matter and I have thought there is much difficulty occasioned by our having separate trades. I should therefore be willing, say for fourteen years, to unite the wool trade [which Cyrus had retained] with our business. We may then do little or much as circumstances may occur, that is when required we can shove our capital into our mat trade ... we ought to average £100 in sales a week and this I think we may do by pushing the last five months of the year. I see we must drive close and we must not spend a shilling that can be avoided until we have paid off some of these debts ... give this thy calm consideration.

Such a predicament might have made some people take refuge in liquor. But in Cyrus's and James's case, it coincided with their involvement in the Temperance Society, which was founded in 1832 by Joseph Livesey, a cheese-maker from Preston. James Clark believed he was 'the first to sign any Temperance Pledge anywhere south of Bristol' and Cyrus had taken great pleasure in smashing bottles of wine and liqueur that were then mixed in with mortar to build James's marital home.

The Quaker take on drink was unequivocal. A flyer endorsed by Livesey was entitled 'Drinking Is All Lost' and it aimed to shock. Consume alcohol, it said, if you are happy with the:

> ... loss of hard earned money; loss of food and clothing; loss of happiness; loss of home comforts; loss of mind; loss of health; loss of life.

You seek for pleasure in drink, and find ruin. You seek to drown your troubles, and you drown yourself.

It went on to explain how there is:

... no such thing as *wholesome* beer, or good cider, or *pure* wines and spirits. All these drinks deceive and mock you; rob and starve you. Don't take the first glass!

Early temperance societies were inspired by a Belfast professor of theology named John Edgar, who in 1829 poured his stock of whisky out of his window, claiming it would destroy any lingering bad spirits. Livesey, the Temperance Society founder, opened the first temperance hotel in 1833 and the next year founded the temperance magazine, *The Preston Temperance Advocate* (1834–7). In 1835, the British Association for the Promotion of Temperance was formed to save the working classes from drink and it went on to become one of the biggest mass movements in British history. By the late nineteenth century, one in ten people had pledged to avoid alcohol.

James was an early convert, as he writes:

When about 19 years of age I became a member of a Temperance Society – which led to the formation at Street of a Society on the Moderation principle and brought me into association with other Philanthropic work ... This proved a source of blessing and profit to myself, for which I have had cause to be very thankful, as it has brought me into association with many good and earnest Christian men.

Cyrus and James's stance against alcohol may have been admirable, but it was also practical. Its enforcement was one means by which the production of shoes could continue unimpeded by cider-induced, drunken brawling, which was a regular event in Street. The brothers were particularly concerned about the young apprentices, whose lives were made that much harder when their masters were on the bottle. The problem is described in *Clarks of Street, 1825–1950*:

Each shoemaker would employ apprentices who made threads, sewed on the soles and did other minor parts of the work while learning their trade. The system did not work badly when, as in the majority of cases, the masters were sober, steady men and kind and considerate to the apprentices, but when, as sometimes happened, the masters were given to drinking and irregular hours of work, the apprentices suffered great hardship. Such a shoemaker would 'shop' his work on Friday or Saturday, would be drinking on Sunday and again on Monday (known as 'Saint Monday'), would be quite unfit for work on Tuesday, and would only start in earnest on Wednesday or even Thursday in some cases. To get his week's work into two or three days, he would then work half of one night and the whole of the next. This meant of course that the poor boys, of twelve, thirteen and fourteen years of age, and even younger, were brought up to waste and idle the early part of the week and then made to work day and night the latter part, and sometimes kept at their toil by doses of what was known as stirrup oil.

Working hours in the factory were from 6 am to 7 pm, with an hour's break for lunch and half an hour each for breakfast and tea. On Saturdays, the day ended at 5 pm. One man, James Marsh, used to walk eight miles to work from Wells in the morning and eight miles back home again at night – and was reported never to have been late.

A year after Cyrus had written bleakly to James about the company's finances, a number of advances were secured. Stuckey's Banking Company came up with £500 secured on land owned by the two brothers and then two years later, in 1839, the bank made a second loan of a further £500.

At that time, Joseph and Cyrus were planning to expand their corn business and tried to persuade James to join them. The two older brothers were buying corn mainly from their cousins, Joseph and Charles Sturge, who were trading in Birmingham. According to the *History of the Business of C&J Clark Limited*, written by William S. Clark in 1914, James Clark

... thought the business far too speculative for their [Joseph and Cyrus] limited means ... he also considered that the growing business of C. & J.

Clark needed all the undivided energy of the two partners [Cyrus and James] and that it suffered through the greater part of Cyrus Clark's time and so much of his interest being absorbed in the corn trade, and he rather strongly pressed his brother to draw out of it.

Joseph and Cyrus would have done well to heed James's advice. In the winter of 1841–2, the net assets of both the corn business and the shoe company were not enough to meet the firm's liabilities. In addition, James had been borrowing money from the company for his own private purposes, a clear departure from Quaker ethics and in many ways inconsistent with his own high standards. This was something he conceded when writing to his children many years later in 1881: 'We were unfortunately tempted, whilst still working with a large amount of borrowed capital, to spend too much on our dwellings, and this eventually brought us into great straits.'

There is no evidence to suggest that the brothers fell out or even came close to falling out during the early years of austerity. It may have helped that Cyrus and James were markedly different characters. William S. Clark described his father James as 'of a more hopeful turn of mind' compared with Cyrus, but to those working with James

> ... it may have sometimes seemed as if he did not fully realise that such
> Divine help usually worked through human instrumentability [sic] and
> that such help should be sought to prevent getting into difficulties as
> well as to find a way out of them.

Cyrus was a worrier. At times, he was perfectly capable of seeing the problem and would speak mournfully about it – but he did not always implement a remedy. In June, 1841, he wrote to James, full of gloom:

> I am sorry to say it will turn out worse than I anticipated and worse
> with me than thyself. My own expenses have been *so very heavy* ... We
> must still retrench and I see plainly we must get quit of one of our two
> cutters ... we must lessen our stock at least £2,000, say from £6,000

to £4,000 – an abundant stock even then ... I don't wish to discourage thee but I thought it was better to write ... when thou hast read this letter burn it.

The losses in 1841 amounted to £1,400 and a year later the situation was little better. Stocktaking in April 1842 made clear that, after paying the interest on loans, there was precious little left out of the profits for future investment. The mood of encroaching despair was such that Isaac Stephens, a relative of James's by marriage, suggested to Cyrus and James that they should consider emigrating to Australia:

Much better it would be to leave while you have something to take out with you ... the times are so awfully bad ... and I would strongly advise thee – at all hazards – to get out of thy present business.

Cyrus began to entertain the idea and it was left to his wife, Sarah, to enlist the help of James to persuade him otherwise. At one point, she wrote to her brother-in-law, saying that Cyrus was looking to 'escape from the storm, wind and tempest'.

The national situation was just as grim. Poor harvests brought virtual starvation to some parts of the country, followed by riots in town and rick burnings in the countryside. In Street, a cry for help went out from C. & J. Clark towards the end of 1842 – and the Quakers rallied round. The chief benefactor was Edmund Sturge, a cousin and one of James's closest friends. He was instrumental in soliciting the generosity of others, including Joseph Eaton and Robert Charlton from Bristol and Jacob Player Sturge, another Clark cousin. George Thomas, a family friend from Bristol, came up with £750 and Thomas Clark, a first cousin of Cyrus and James who had made money from a wholesale provisions business in Bridgwater, contributed £400 and became a key figure in keeping Clarks solvent over the next twenty years. In total, loans of £2,950 were promised, but before accepting the money, the partners had to gain the approval of Stuckey's Banking Company, easily the Clarks' largest creditor.

These delicate negotiations were left largely to Cyrus to handle because

James was travelling. In August 1844, Cyrus wrote to his brother saying that he had provided the bank with full and proper disclosure and that Stuckey's wanted to know what the brothers were worth after paying their debts.

> I think I said £1,000 or £1,200, that is jointly. I let them know that Joseph had lost all [on the corn business] and that we had to make considerable sacrifices on his behalf.

The bank then gave Cyrus ten days to provide a written statement of C. & J. Clark's affairs and in September it agreed to the loans. Stipulations were attached. The bank insisted on being kept closely informed about the business's finances and the Friends who had lent money made it clear that they wanted Thomas Clark and Edmund Sturge to supervise all future annual stocktakings. This became a heightened priority after it was discovered that for two years Cyrus had not even drawn up a proper set of accounts.

Many years later, after Cyrus had died, James reflected:

> The years following 1840 to 1848 were very trying ones, a very increasing business and great shortness of capital. My brothers Joseph and Cyrus were engaged in the corn business, which led us into many difficulties from which we were only rescued by the intervention of my cousin Edmund Sturge and other kind Friends ... our business improved after 1848, our shoe trade steadily increasing.

There were indeed improvements and trade did steadily increase – although it also needed a further loan of £450 from Thomas Clark in 1848 to help with a cash deficiency. A year later, Thomas became a sleeping partner in the business and earned the respect – and gratitude – of both Cyrus and James. Thomas was married to a sister of Cyrus's wife and was eight years older than Cyrus, eighteen years senior to James. Born at Greinton and the son of a farmer, he served as an elder at Quaker meetings. In the 1840s, he had worked as an accounts supervisor at C. & J. Clark and so knew about the business. He was also a highly knowledgeable botanist.

During the five years Thomas remained a partner, the firm made net profits totalling £15,364. 15s. 5d., of which his share was £2,561. 3s. 2d., with the remainder split between Cyrus and James so that each received £6,401. 16s. 7d. This arrangement with Thomas continued until 1854, even though the company was in no position to repay the original £2,000 he had invested, let alone any of the additional £5,276 he had put in during times of emergency. Thomas was a benevolent contributor. At one point during 1854, he was asked to make a further urgent investment of £2,000 and although he did not have the cash, he secured a loan on land which he was in the process of selling. He even went as far as apologising to the partners for the 'inconvenience caused by his difficulties'.

Later that year, it was agreed that Thomas would be paid interest on his loans at a rate of 7.5 per cent a year, some 2.5 per cent more than the bank rate. Fortunately, between 1849 and 1854, the value of Clarks' total assets almost doubled from £21,700 to £42,900, sales increased from £20,000 to £31,600 and the average annual net profit was £2,800.

The earliest surviving price list is that of 1848. It comprises 334 items, with prices ranging from 13s. 6d. for Gentlemen's Pump Boots to 3s. 9d. for Ladies' Best French Morocco shoes to 1s. for Children's Enamel Seal Ankle Straps. And despite those difficult early years there were some notable triumphs and some moments of reassurance for the two founding brothers. At the Great Exhibition of 1851, C. & J. Clark was visited by royalty and the company was awarded medals for its galoshes and sheepskin rugs. Cyrus was in London to receive the awards, after which he wrote to James:

My Dear Brother,

I came up here at eight o'clock, had a little difficulty in passing my parcels, but succeeded, there being new rules since the 17th.

The Queen, the King of the Belgians, walking together, arrived soon after nine o'clock, two of the Royal Children, two of the children of the King of the Belgians, and Prince Albert.

They passed rather rapidly, it seemed more a matter of ceremony, scarcely any examination of the goods. They first came in from the centre, and then came a second time and passed the other side. The guide directed the Queen's attention to the curried leather opposite, and walked before the Queen backwards and crablike.

I had a gracious bow from her, and met her the second time, when I had a very decided bow; the gent, who went round with her, said: 'Model of a Factory', and the Queen said: 'Very pretty', but neither particularly looked at the shoes or rugs ... I found I had as good, if not more, notice than some of my neighbours, but there was no time, without appearing rude, to push one's articles into notice, so to conclude I have had a very courteous bow from the Queen and a conversation with Prince Albert.

3

Friends in high places

So many items in the balance sheet turned out to be worthless, and there was so much confusion in the way the capital accounts had been entered in the ledger that even after the decision to struggle on had been taken it was found that things were worse than had been supposed.

THAT WAS THE BLUNT ASSESSMENT of William S. Clark, James's son, writing in 1914 while reflecting on the period leading to the firm's second financial crisis in 1863, a catastrophe that would have proved fatal without the help, once again, of Quaker friends and cousins.

Business had picked up after the 1851 Great Exhibition and continued on an upward curve almost until 1859. These were the golden years of Cyrus's and James's stewardship of the company – albeit a stewardship that was largely overseen by outside investors and by the bank. In 1857, C. & J. Clark produced 234,000 pairs of shoes – far exceeding Cyrus's expectations back in 1840 when he said the company would be able to sell a maximum of 9,000 pairs in any twelve months. Turnover from 1851 to 1859 was on average five times what it had been in 1833, with shoes now representing three-quarters of sales. The average annual profit during that period was £2,683, compared with £1,230 during the years from 1843 to 1847. There was a doubling of sales between 1849 and 1858, spurred by demand for ready-made footwear, which was widely regarded as both modern and better value than bespoke. Business was also helped by the country's recovery from economic depression and the beginnings of the age of 'Victorian Prosperity'.

There were some false starts, one of which was the production of so-called 'elongating goloshes', for which C. & J. Clark had been awarded a Gold Medal at the Great Exhibition. Goloshes (the spelling changed to galoshes during the 1920s) were made from gutta percha, a natural latex produced from the sap of the tree of the same name. They were introduced to Britain in 1844 and greeted enthusiastically by manufacturers up and down the land. An encyclopaedia from the time said:

> The immediate effect of its discovery may be compared with that of the gold fields in California and Australia; and perhaps no commodity, except the precious metals, has been more eagerly sought after or more highly appreciated.

Cyrus and James were acutely interested in this 'discovery' because the price of leather was forever fluctuating and, moreover, it was becoming hard to achieve a uniform standard in leather. The quality of the hides was inconsistent and the leather sorters and cutters varied in their expertise. C. & J. Clark was selling a number of gutta percha products as early as 1848, prompting James to take out a patent on boots, shoes and clogs made with this new material, and such was the focus on gutta percha that in the 1851 census two employees of the company described themselves as 'gutta percha workers' rather than shoemakers.

But the elongated golosh – which could be put on without the need to stoop and with no straps to fasten – proved unsuccessful commercially as cheaper options flooded the market. And they never quite did technically what they were billed to do. Consequently, at one point in 1855, Clarks opened a dedicated store in London's Blackfriars Road on a three-month lease in order to shift surplus stock of goloshes by means of a closing-down sale.

The partners accepted that goloshes had become 'very heavy losers arising entirely from a fault in the gutta percha which after a few years

This aspirational 1851 showcard for goloshes features a suave salesman complete with foot-measuring gauge. Sadly, goloshes turned out to be an unsuccessful venture.

became so hard and brittle that it will stand no wear,' and by 1858 the company's price list featured no gutta percha footwear of any kind.

It was a similar story with vulcanised rubber – named after Vulcan, the Roman god of fire – when the company bought a half share in a patent for combining leather and rubber to produce an elastic material that did away with the need for buttons or laces. Between 1851 and the spring of 1855, C. & J. Clark acquired a massive £25,000 worth of vulcanised rubber – but to little financial benefit.

During this experimental phase, Charles Goodyear, the American whose name would later be associated with tyres, had become a friend of Cyrus and James and gave advice about the production of a new rubberised boot. Goodyear, who said there was no other 'inert substance which so excites the mind' as rubber, was a year older than Cyrus and had begun his own business career by opening a hardware store in Philadelphia. Cyrus and Charles would have met at the Great Exhibition when the American's wares were on display in a huge pavilion built from floor to ceiling entirely of rubber. Goodyear never opened a factory in Britain, but a company in France agreed to manufacture vulcanised rubber – with disastrous results, ending up with Goodyear being arrested by the French police in December 1855 and spending sixteen days in a debtors' prison.

Five years later, Goodyear was dead, leaving debts of $200,000, but he went to his grave firm in the belief that his invention would eventually pay off. And so it did, though not for his immediate descendants. None of his family, either at that time or in subsequent years, was involved in The Goodyear Tyre & Rubber Company, which was so named in Charles's honour. Despite his turbulent career, Goodyear, quoted in the January 1958 American edition of *Reader's Digest*, was philosopical:

> Life should not be estimated exclusively by the standard of dollars and cents. I am not disposed to complain that I have planted and others have gathered the fruits. A man has cause for regret only when he sows and no one reaps.

The Clarks also investigated doing business with the North British Rubber Company, which had been set up by Henry Lee Norris, an entrepreneur from New Jersey, and Spencer Thomas Parmalee from Connecticut, who had moved to Edinburgh in 1856. The unreliable quality of Norris's and Parmalee's vulcanised rubber ultimately put an end to any formal business arrangement, but the partners had showed once again their readiness to explore new shoemaking techniques.

William S. Clark joined the company in January 1855 at the age of sixteen. He had been educated at two Quaker schools, Sidcot, in Winscombe, and Bootham, in York, and spent some months studying chemistry at the Laboratory of St Thomas's Hospital in London under the tutelage of a Dr Thompson. His arrival in the business coincided with the first attempts at introducing machinery into the manufacturing process.

William S. Clark on leaving Bootham School, York, in December 1854.

William was determined to be a modern shoemaker. Which is to say that he regarded technology as the way forward – and he wanted to see an end to the outworker system. In effect, he wanted shoemaking in Britain to catch up with what was going on in America, where, because of a shortage of labour, the search for machinery to replace men had quickened. The earliest footwear machines to have been patented in the US are thought to be David Mead Randolph's invention for making riveted boots in 1809, followed a year later by Marc Isambard Brunel's invention for the nailing of army and navy shoes. But a far more revolutionary development was on its way, one which would bring about a surge in the ready-made market and create havoc for the bespoke trade: the sewing machine.

Cyrus and James may have been resistant to some aspects of modern business practice – and, as William pointed out, their accounting methods were lamentable – but shunning innovation was never something of which they could be accused.

C. & J. Clark's machine room began to take shape in 1856 when Singer &

Co., based in America, persuaded the Clarks to acquire one of their sewing machines on trial. Isaac Singer, a failed actor and farmer, had patented his creation in New York in partnership with Edward Clark (no relation to the Clarks of Street). Singer invented the first commercially successful sewing machine, and between 1851 and 1863 he took out twenty patents and sold his machines throughout the world. It was, however, the British inventor and cabinet maker, Thomas Saint, who had issued the first patent for a general machine for sewing in 1790 – though he may not actually have produced a working prototype. That patent describes an awl that punched a hole in leather and passed a needle through the hole.

The arrival of sewing machines had caused controversy. In 1834, Walter Hunt, an American, had built such a machine, but did not patent it because he thought it would cause unemployment. Ten years later, the first American patent was issued by Elias Howe for a 'process that used thread from two different sources'. His machine had a needle with an eye at the point. The needle was pushed through the cloth and a loop was formed on the other side. A shuttle on a track then slipped the second thread through the loop to create what was, and still is, called the lockstitch – at five times the speed of a fast hand-sewer.

Howe assigned the British rights to his patent to a corset, umbrella and footwear manufacturer called William Thomas of London – and then sued Singer for patent infringement in 1854 and won. Howe saw his annual income jump from $300 to more than $200,000 a year, and he amassed a fortune of nearly $2 million over the next twenty years or so. During the American Civil War, he donated a portion of his wealth to equip an infantry regiment for the Union Army and served in the regiment himself as a private.

Singers, as they were known, were worked by treadle and were cumbersome beasts that required a dedicated person to master them. In Street, it was William S. Clark who spent three months learning every aspect of their capabilities, before passing on his knowledge to a trio of technically-minded women, all sharing the same forename – Mary Wallis, Mary Ann Haines and Mary Marsh. They quickly became experts themselves. The Clarks then bought two further Singer sewing machines for £30 each.

Output increased dramatically. By 1858, over 50,000 pairs of uppers were stitched by machine, accounting for 23 per cent of total production. And by now there were more women in the machine room than there had been in the whole factory five years earlier.

At the same time, riveting was becoming commonplace, and C. & J. Clark was one of the first firms to sell hand-riveted shoes on a large scale. Riveting was especially good for thick-soled boots or shoes.

Sewing machines and riveting spawned new machinery at C. & J. Clark for many of the ancillary jobs previously carried out by hand. For example, in 1858, Samuel Boyce, a boot manufacturer in Lynn, Massachusetts – and a friend of James Clark – produced a device that cut soles to size. It was worked by a foot treadle and became one of the first machines imported from America for use in the British shoe trade.

An enterprising man called James Miles, of Street, took it upon himself to copy or adapt these American machines, selling them on to shoemakers up and down the country. Likewise, William S. Clark and John Keats, the factory foreman (who claimed to be related to the poet of the same name), jointly invented a machine for the building up and the attaching of heels to soles, mainly of boots. This involved enlarging the heels in solid iron moulds and then punching holes in them, into which rivets were inserted before being attached to the boots. There was considerable secrecy over this piece of equipment, for fear that rival firms in Northamptonshire and Leicestershire would hear about it.

Not everyone was happy. The introduction of technology led to strikes in some traditional shoemaking towns in the Midlands, but the Clarks persuaded their workforce that technology would lead to more, not fewer, jobs, and largely avoided disruptive labour unrest organised by what were known as 'craft societies' – a precursor to the trade unions.

Encouraged by William, Cyrus and James also turned their attention to lasts, acquiring equipment in 1855 that would 'secure good fitting boots and shoes ... made from the finest wood seasoned on the premises', as they described it on a price list sent out to customers that year. Their first last-making machine was bought from a Scottish supplier for £12. 10s., with a condition of sale that a man called David Garner would move to Street to be in charge of it. Garner was paid 33 shillings a week, but there were stipulations attached to his employment. He had to give up alcohol and attend church.

How long Garner survived in his job is unclear, but his machine was soon replaced by one that would, according to company records, 'turn a right or a left last from the same pattern, or a large or small last from the same pattern'. These were state-of-the-art creations because a large proportion of footwear, particularly in children's ranges, was still made without any distinction between right and left feet.

By 1855, the shoe business in Street was improving faster than the quality of life. The town's poor drainage and inadequate water supply had been highlighted in official reports. One review conducted by the Board of Health in 1853 – a year after a typhoid epidemic struck the southwest of the country – noted with alarm that the only form of drainage was an open stream running through the main street, into which almost all houses discharged their waste. It was persistently stagnant and smelt dreadful.

There were a number of deaths from typhoid, including that of Cyrus's son, Joseph Henry, who died aged nineteen, and James's second son, Thomas Bryant, who was only nine. James reacted bravely, describing his loss as a 'bitter trial', but one that 'was sent in mercy by our Heavenly Father to bring us nearer to Himself. None but those who have experienced it can know of the bitterness of such a trial'.

In its report, the Board of Health took a sterner, more pragmatic view:

> There is no public provision of water within the parish, the inhabitants mostly obtaining their water from wells, the water of which is generally of an extremely hard quality, and sometimes polluted by a leakage from cesspools.

The Board's report went on to cite the Public Health Act of 1848 and insisted on the setting up of a Local Board, comprising nine elected members, whose purpose was to monitor the sanitary conditions in the town.

In addition to typhoid, Street suffered from other diseases such as scarlet fever and measles. As Michael McGarvie described it in *Bowlingreen Mill*:

> Various causes were suggested for this including that the orchards with which Street was surrounded impeded the circulation of the air and so increased the dampness, or that the out-work system under which six to nine men worked together in a small room was conducive to illness. The real culprit was defective drainage and the pollution of the stream which ran along the High Street. C. & J. Clark's factory contributed substantially to this.

Blame was indeed laid at C. & J. Clark's door. The Board of Health's report found that the:

> ... refuse drainage and tan liquid of the [Clarks] factory is passed into the stream towards the lower end. The condition of the stream and of the various ditches is at times very offensive.

James Clark was quoted in the Report admitting that:

> ... the drainage liquor consists of the boilings of dye-wood, alum and muriatic acid ... liquor in which green skins have been soaked, and whether from the presence of animal matter in a state of decomposition, or of vegetable matter in a similar state, has a very offensive smell.

Feelings were running high. Cyrus chaired a meeting in 1852 at the Temperance Hall to explain to ratepayers the implications of the Board of Health's report, opening proceedings with a diplomatic aside that 'good temper always gained the advantage in argument'. Some pointed an accusing finger at the Clarks, prompting James, seated near his brother, to remind people of 'the deaths and illness in our own families'. The meeting ended more harmoniously than it had started.

James became a more active and devoted Quaker following the death of his son. At the family's morning meetings – which he insisted on, with no exceptions – he began praying out loud in front of his surviving children and would, as he put it, 'express a few words in the evening meeting' as well. This, James said, 'proved very formidable', but he was rewarded with a sense of:

> ... peace, which I believe always follows an act of obedience to our Heavenly Father. From this time I had frequently some brief communications to offer in our meetings for worship.

In 1856, four years after this personal tragedy, James was appointed a minister in the Society of Friends, something which 'led me more deeply to feel my responsibility and strengthening me by this proof that I had the confidence of my friends'. In the spring of 1860 – the year his eldest daughter, Mary, became engaged to John Morland, who later would take over the rug side of the business – he felt enormous pride when his wife was appointed an elder of the Street Friends' meeting house:

> A very precious, wise and useful Elder she proved to be ... no one can know how much I have been indebted to her for her wise, loving and faithful counsel.

Towards the end of 1853, Britain established formal ties with Turkey, which was at war with Russia. Lord Aberdeen, the prime minister in charge of a coalition government, described the 'state of tension' in the Crimea as 'undoubtedly great' but said: 'I persist in thinking that it can not end in actual war'. *The Times* went further, thundering that 'War would not only be an act of insanity, but would be utterly disgraceful to all of us concerned.'

But there was no sign of Russia backing down. Instead, its navy sank the Turkish fleet at Sinope, provoking a declaration of war by Britain and France on 28 March 1854. The resulting campaign in the Crimea was to be a war like none before it. For the first time, photography brought home the graphic horrors of battle and there were stories in the press as much about inefficiency and incompetence as tales of heroism and bravery. The work of Florence Nightingale ensured that the war pulled at the conscience of those not immediately caught up in the conflict, especially when it became evident that more soldiers were dying from disease than from fighting the enemy.

In Street, the Crimean War tugged at the conscience in a different way. Quakers were pacifists. They were duty bound not to interfere in the war effort – but they also felt called to alleviate the suffering of war's innocent victims. As William S. Clark wrote:

> The Government urgently wanted a supply of sheepskin wool coats to save troops in the Crimea from perishing with cold. As C. & J. Clark had a supply of skins that were suitable for this and that could not be got elsewhere in sufficient quantity they felt bound to make these coats but decided not to keep any profit for their own use.

That profit came to some £300 – a large sum at the time – all of which was used to build the British School in Street. Education was important to Quakers. George Fox himself had established two schools, one at Waltham Abbey, Essex, another at Shacklewell, in what is now part of the London Borough of Hackney. Fox said these institutions were to 'instruct young lasses and maidens in whatsoever things were civil and useful in the creation'.

The *Western Gazette*, a local newspaper covering Somerset and the West Country, picked up on the story of Clarks making coats for soldiers fighting the Russians but failed to inform readers of the not-for-profit motive:

> Our enterprising manufacturer, Messrs Clarke [*sic*] of this place, are preparing at the rate of 40 sheepskin coats a day for the army in the Crimea. The sheepskins are prepared with all the wool on and are intended to be worn by our men in just the opposite way that they are worn in general – the wool will be worn inside and the skin outside.

Elmhurst, the house that Cyrus Clark built for himself in 1856, photographed in 1860 by his eldest son John Aubrey Clark. In the foreground can be seen (left to right) Cyrus's daughter Bessie (Sarah Elizabeth), his wife Sarah Bull Clark, Cyrus, and (at far right) his youngest son Thomas Beaven Clark.

As the Crimean War reached the bloodiest of conclusions, C. & J. Clark was fighting its own battles. Heavy losses were incurred between 1859 and 1862, for which a number of reasons were cited, not least the manner in which Cyrus and James continued to take money out of the business for their own benefit. In 1856, Cyrus had built an entirely new house, Elmhurst, which a few years later he would use as security for further loans to the business. James, meanwhile, made such alterations and additions to Netherleigh that it almost doubled in size. This may have been a practical necessity because he and Eleanor had such a large family – but it did not help balance the books. At the same time, Cyrus agreed to build a house for the second of his three sons, Alfred, to mark his marriage in 1857 to Sarah Gregory, the daughter of Bishop Gregory.

William S. Clark wrote later in his memoirs that he regarded the brothers' withdrawals as 'altogether excessive' and said:

William S. Clark in 1861.

it would take long to trace out the causes of the losses ... much was due to inefficient management, leading to heavy accumulation of unsale-able stock. The reduction of capital through the withdrawals ... led to constant difficulties in meeting the liabilities of the firm.

The firm's accountant, James Holmes, did not help matters. He managed to 'lose' the stock accounts at the end of 1859, and when the books were retrieved a year later it was discovered there had been a net loss over two years of £2,679. 17s. 10d. Holmes would become a divisive figure over the next couple of years. Cyrus thought him indispensable; James regarded him as a liability.

Under the terms of the brothers' partnership, any withdrawals from capital were allowed only if both men agreed to them. As it turned out, every single withdrawal from 1849 – except for one – was made without joint agreement. Furthermore, taking a lead perhaps from his superiors, Holmes, who had negotiated a 5 per cent share in profits in addition to his salary, set about making withdrawals for himself in anticipation of any future profits. Closer to home, Alfred, Cyrus's son, was also receiving 5 per cent of expected profits after he joined the company as a travelling salesman.

It was becoming hard to see where growth could be forthcoming.

Trade to Australia and other colonial countries had dipped – but the partners persisted with their battle to win over Australia. In the early 1850s, the Clarks had sent footwear to Sydney, Adelaide, Melbourne and Brisbane, with positive results, especially in children's ankle-strap shoes and women's slippers. But by 1857, shipments had ceased completely and would not pick up again until 1859. Samples were sent to New Zealand in the hope that this would become a new frontier, particularly in Canterbury, where wealthy colonists were arriving 'cabin-class' rather than 'steerage' as had been normal for other immigrants. But results here were also disappointing. Consignments were dispatched to South Africa in 1861, but were not repeated and trade with America and Canada was proving difficult because of the restrictive tariffs. A goloshed boot with fur on the inside was made especially for Canada in 1859, but its rubber component was subject to 25 per cent import duty, making the price unattractive to Canadian consumers.

Financial imperatives at home meant that Clarks refused to offer extra credit to its customers in Australia, who in turn cancelled their orders. Australia had always been an outlet for surplus stock and Cyrus and James were keen to keep this market going for as long as they could. 'We do not quite like giving up altogether – it is buying experience,' said James, while admitting that trade with Australia was 'disastrous in the extreme'.

It was not promising in the UK either. In 1858, output was cut dramatically following overproduction during the two previous years. Staff were laid off and it would prove tough to replace them once business finally began to improve in 1864. Wages were rising, partly because other shoe companies were offering inducements to Street workers if they moved to a different part of the country. In a letter to a fellow shoemaker in 1860, James observed: 'We do not find our workpeople as tractable as they were 10 years ago, especially with any new work'.

On another occasion, company documents concluded that:

> ... since the introduction of sewing machines and riveting there has been such an increase in competition that the shoe trade has not been in a very satisfactory state.

But Cyrus and James remained steadfast in their commitment never to compromise on standards, striving, as James put it, to 'keep up the quality of our goods to make such as a bespoke shoe need not be ashamed of'. Producing ready-made shoes that had the look and feel of made-to-measure footwear was a fundamental plank of their strategy.

Consequently, Clarks showcards emphasised craftsmanship and tradition. One of the earliest, designed by Cyrus's eldest son, John Aubrey Clark, in around 1849, shows the factory as a theatre stage, framed by elaborate curtains and stone masonry taken from a parish church. 'Sewing of Every Pair **WARRANTED**' is the strap-line, with 'warranted' in bold and in capitals. Another, two years later, features a prosperous middle-class drawing room, complete with roaring fire and grand over-mantel mirror. Well-dressed ladies watch intently as a young boy has his feet measured, a second child waiting his turn. Their mother holds a shoe in her hand as if admiring a precious piece of jewellery. The showcard names all the provincial towns where the Clarks' shoes are sold by 'respectable dealers' – 77 of them in total. In London alone, there were 32 shops selling the Clarks' footwear.

Price lists and showcards were the ways by which Clarks kept in touch with customers. Showcards were designed to be on display in shops, advertising certain lines and alerting customers to what was new in the forthcoming season. The partners were clear about how they wanted to present their wares. While other Quaker firms – such as Cadburys and Frys – advertised in newspapers, C. & J. Clark never did. The partners thought

A showcard designed by John Aubrey Clark, Cyrus's eldest son, in around 1849.

newspapers represented the mass market and they did not wish to be spoken of in the same breath as chocolate or soap. The Clarks' strategy was to appeal directly to consumers without appearing to do so. According to *The Shocking History of Advertising* by E. S. Turner:

> They [companies such as C. & J. Clark] were quite certain that [advertising in newspapers] was ungentlemanly ... the ideal, the traditional way to do business was to surround oneself with a circle of customers and to cultivate personal relations with them; excellence of goods and word of mouth recommendation would do the rest ... the last thing to do was to chalk the firm's name on the sides of quarries or to inset furtive little paragraphs in the newspapers, in the contaminating company of truss-mongers, snuff-sellers, pox-doctors, body snatching undertakers and cut-price abortionists.

Good relations with those who sold Clarks footwear were given high priority, but at the same time the partners refused to budge on price, recognising the downward spiralling that comes when drawn into a price war. James made his position clear to shops in Scotland, when he wrote:

> We may lose by refusing to take off the 2.5 per cent they now want, but this course will soon make it a worthless trade and we think it would be wiser to come to an understanding if possible.

There were also occasions when the partners were prepared to forgo a sale if they thought it would compromise their Quaker views. A business in Shepton Mallet received the following letter in October 1853:

> We are duly in receipt of yours ... But we feel that we can not, with a clear conscience have anything to do with an article which we believe to be destructive to the morals and best interests of the people. You will therefore excuse our declining to execute any order for mops for your brewery.

Guaranteeing the quality of shoes but offering them at much lower prices in comparison with bespoke footwear remained central to the partners' plans. But there was still the issue of comfort. Bespoke, by definition, is custom-made. The shoe fits the foot because it is built around a unique, personalised last. The Clarks understood this and responded by offering a range of three fittings and half-sizes from one to seven. By 1855, all ladies' boots came in this range of sizes and fittings.

Style was important, too, with Clarks quick to pick up on what was proving fashionable and popular in Paris. The brothers were anxious to register specific designs with the Board of Trade and although other companies were allowed to copy them, they had to display the name C. & J. Clark prominently somewhere on the shoe. On a number of occasions, the full weight of the law would come down on companies failing to credit C. & J. Clark. In 1854, six Dublin firms were visited by solicitors on the suspicion of pirating C. & J. Clark's registered designs.

William S. Clark was consistent in his approval of his father's and uncle's stance on maintaining high standards, even in trying circumstances. As he wrote:

> The greatest care was taken that threads should be properly waxed, that there should always be four to five stitches to the inch and the wear of every shoe sent out was guaranteed. In any case, a shoe that did not give fair wear was replaced by a new pair if sent back ... The shoemaker's number stamped in the waist was always a clue to the careless maker. It was this combination of solidarity and style that built up the reputation of the firm.

There were serious and continual mismatches between output and sales. In 1855, for example, sales had been more than £2,000 greater than in the previous year, but output could not cope with demand. A year later, there was a further rise in sales but this time output had outstripped demand. The same thing happened in 1857, resulting in a surplus of stock worth £12,000. George Barry Sutton, in his book *C. & J. Clark, 1833–1903: A History of Shoemaking*, wrote: 'The indications are that in producing large quantities of goods in anticipation of future orders Cyrus and James had not bargained for the recession in demand which hit them and the rest of the country in late 1857.'

The yo-yo continued in 1858 when production fell by 23.5 per cent but sales did not dip by anything like as much. Consequently, opportunities were missed. And then in 1860, demand fell while production rose by 15 per cent. Evidently, the partners were finding it hard to judge the market. The start of 1860 had seen orders increase and it is likely that Cyrus and James developed an overly ambitious sense of where the trade was going. Suffice it to say that by the end of the year stocks were still rising. One explanation was that the partners wanted the factory to be working at full pace to avoid losing staff, who would be hard to replace. Another was that Cyrus and James were 'unable or unwilling to exercise anything but a very

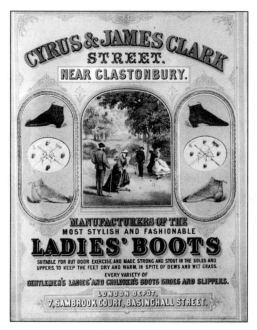

This showcard with its calm air of urbane sophistication gives no hint of
the financial turmoil that Clarks was going through in the 1860s.

loose degree of control over output levels', as Sutton put it.

Other areas of the business were hardly thriving. The brothers' farms,
which had officially merged with C. & J. Clark, had been losing money
consistently and chamois sales were too small to make a significant impact
on the overall financial position. In fact, William S. Clark discovered that
in 1862 only the sales of angoras, gloves and leggings (a new line) were
showing a net profit. It was also onerous how the price of leather and other
materials was rising year on year – and certainly faster than any increases
in the price of the company's shoes. James Clark wrote:

> We had great business troubles from the bad state of trade and shortness
> of capital. We passed through a time of great trial and were compelled
> to seek the help of our friends, who most kindly came forward to aid us
> in our difficulties.

That was an understatement. The years 1860–63 brought C. & J. Clark to the brink of bankruptcy. There had been a profit of £3,034 in 1861, but that was not enough to offset a combined loss of £2,680 for 1859 and 1860 and a further loss of £656 in 1862. Bank loans had reached nearly £11,000 and Thomas Clark, the cousin who had become a sleeping partner between 1849 and 1854, once more lent a total of £5,500 from 1858 to 1862. By June 1863, Cyrus and James would have no capital in the business at all.

Stuckey's Banking Company had begun to take a firmer line in May 1860, when the bank's secretary, Walter Bagehot – who went on to become the editor of *The Economist* and who wrote a celebrated book on the British constitution – received yet another request to increase the overdraft. His response was polite but clear:

> We can readily imagine that your trade has suffered from the circum-stances you mention, and that your stock of manufactured goods is larger than usual at this season in consequence. This however is a contingency to which all business is liable and shows the necessity of a reserve of capital to meet it, as I have frequently taken the liberty of pointing out to you when we have been discussing freely the position of your concern.

The partners did not appear to take much notice, prompting Bagehot to write again a few months later, pointing out that the company was continuing to disregard its maximum overdraft limit of £2,800. Such letters became more frequent. In March 1861, Stuckey's Banking Company said it would lend the Clarks no more money unless current advances were addressed, although Bagehot went out of his way to be encouraging:

> In reply to your observations respecting the securities we hold, and the confidence we have hitherto placed in you we can only assure you that there is no change in our sentiments regarding you in any respect. We have quite the same confidence in you and the same disposition towards you as we have had hitherto but as we told you when you were

here, the past course of your account for many years has determined us to definite restrictions regarding it in future.

Today, it is common for firms to hire management consultants in moments of crisis. In 1863, Thomas Simpson, a cousin by marriage to Cyrus and James and a great friend of the family, was asked to carry out an independent investigation and compile a financial report on C. & J. Clark. Simpson had run a successful cotton-spinning business in Preston, Lancashire, and had moved back to Street on his retirement to live with his mother-in-law, Martha Gillett. He was to become an important business confidant to William – as he had been to Cyrus and James. Indeed, it was Simpson who urged the partners in 1850 to implement a new system of accounts, writing to James saying it was 'the greatest want in your business'.

Simpson liaised with Thomas Clark in his investigation, first soliciting a promise from the partners that they would 'lay the full facts of their position before him'. It was to be an exacting and, at times, harrowing task. William wrote later how Simpson had intimated that had he known at the outset the full extent of the financial chaos he would have advised that the business be closed:

> While he looked on the case as almost hopeless he thought with the introduction of further capital and a complete change of management there was a possibility that the business might be saved ... it was never suggested that there was any wilful concealment from him but it took time to get to the real meaning and value of many items in the balance sheet, and affairs were in so critical a position that a decision had to be come to at once whether to go on or to stop and call creditors together.

Simpson's findings showed that over a fourteen-year period, Cyrus had withdrawn £17,890. 18s. 5d. and James £10,358. 3s. 2d. In James's case, it meant that already by 1860 his capital in the business had shrunk to a mere £1,157, while Cyrus was in debt to the tune of just over £10,000, a figure that Simpson increased to nearly £12,000 once he had factored in a bank loan Cyrus had secured on the deeds of his house, Elmhurst.

It was during this inquiry that Thomas Clark, who in 1863 was 69, was told that the firm was in no position to pay him the agreed 7.5 per cent on his loan. It would be reduced to 5 per cent with immediate effect. Thomas accepted the new rate and, with the encouragement of Simpson, supported the idea of persuading outsiders to loan capital to C. & J. Clark on a short-term basis. But there would be one clear proviso: Cyrus, James, and Cyrus's son, Alfred, must relinquish all responsibility for the day-to-day running of the business. Furthermore, the brothers would only be allowed to withdraw a combined total of £500 from the business in any one year. It was decreed that Cyrus's limit would be £200 a year and James's would be £300.

These strictures were long overdue. From 1849 to 1862, Cyrus, the worse culprit, withdrew on average £1,278 a year from the business when his average annual share of profits had been only £824. Such reckless behaviour meant it was harder for the partners to take a stronger line when the likes of James Holmes, the accountant, and Alfred, also sought to take money out of the business. As Sutton described it in *C. & J. Clark, 1833–1903: A History of Shoemaking*:

> In their financial affairs, the partners had displayed none of the qualities of determination and foresight which had characterised their achieve-ments in the fields of production and marketing. Whilst devoting a great deal of time and energy to securing outside monetary help, they had exhibited no competence in, and little interest for, the day to day administration of finance.

Simpson knew that only a complete change of management would throw C. & J. Clark a lifeline, and he knew that only the promise of new management would encourage friends and cousins to provide what is known today as a 'bail out.' And so, in addition to Thomas Clark, whose investment now stood at £13,000, seven other investors came forward, several of whom had helped rescue the company two decades earlier. George Thomas, a Quaker friend from Bristol, loaned £2,500 and Francis J. Thompson, who had helped Simpson in his financial review, offered

£1,300. Thompson, an ironmonger from Bridgwater, was a first cousin of Cyrus and James. His brother, Alexander, agreed to invest £500. Further help came from Charles and Thomas Sturge, who both gave £500, as did George Palmer and his younger brother, William I. Palmer, who were first cousins once-removed of James and Cyrus.

The Palmers, who came originally from Long Sutton, Somerset, were in the biscuit industry after joining forces with Thomas Huntley, their cousin by marriage. Huntley was born in 1803 in Swalcliffe, near Banbury in Oxfordshire. His father, Joseph Huntley, was a baker who moved to Reading in 1811 and established a bakery in 1822. George Palmer had, like James Clark, been to Sidcot School, leaving at the age of fourteen to be apprenticed to an uncle as a miller and confectioner.

Thomas Huntley and George Palmer became business partners in 1841, operating out of a small shop in Reading's London Road, directly opposite a posting inn where travellers waited to board their coaches or change horses. Huntley took care of the baking, while Palmer worked on developing the first continuously running machine for biscuit manufacturing. By the time the Clarks asked for financial assistance in 1863, Huntley & Palmer was producing 100 different varieties and the plant in Reading was the largest biscuit factory in the world.

With just short of £20,000 worth of loans in the bank, Thomas Sturge insisted that a trust deed be drawn up, signed by all investors, confirming that Thomas Simpson and Francis J. Thompson be appointed inspectors of the business and given executive powers to safeguard the future.

In a letter to a friend dated 30 April 1863, James admitted the situation was far worse than he had realised: 'I seem now clearly to see that we were only rescued when just on the brink of a precipice from which we could not have rescued ourselves'.

William S. Clark was only too aware of what was required. The promise of change had to be delivered.

The financial question being thus put on a more solid basis the inspectors [Simpson and Thompson] had to consider in whose hands the future management of the business should be placed ... They made very careful inquiries of those in responsible positions in the factory and searching examinations of the partners and their sons as to the part they had taken and their views as to the conduct of the business; a good deal of this naturally transpired in T. Simpson's full investigation of the state of affairs before he undertook to try to put things straight.

Modesty may have prevented him from adding that the 'careful inquiries' and 'searching examinations' led to only one overwhelming conclusion. William S. Clark, aged only 24, was to be handed full responsibility for C. & J. Clark on 31 May 1863, a position he would hold with unrivalled success for the next 40 years.

4

Make – or break

CHANGE CAME FAST. In fact, the turnaround was of such magnitude that even William S. Clark may have been surprised by the outcome. When he wrote about it many years later, he attributed much of the transformation of C. & J. Clark to his benefiting from seeing first-hand the inefficiencies of the previous era while working with his father and uncle. And now that James and, in particular, Cyrus (who was 62 in 1863 and in poor health) were no longer in charge of day-to-day affairs, William could set about making the necessary improvements unimpeded by intervention from the founders. Referring to himself in the third person, William wrote:

> Everything in the business had to be conducted with the most rigid economy ... W. S. Clark, having known only too well where some of the worst leaks had been under former conditions, though vainly striving to get them stopped, was very soon able to alter much that had gone.

The accounts told their own story. During the four and a half years from 31 December 1858 to the day William took control at the end of May 1863, there had been a net loss, whereas in the four and a half years starting 31 May 1863 and ending 31 December 1867, the business made a profit of £14,400. William, given to understatement, said these figures 'put a very different aspect on the state of affairs'.

Thomas Simpson continued in his role as an adviser, something William described as:

> ... invaluable, though occasionally his lack of acquaintance with the technical difficulties of the very complicated shoe business, so totally different to the comparatively simple process of cotton spinning [Simpson's business before his retirement], made it difficult for W.S.C. to carry out his [Simpson's] wishes.

High on both William's and Simpson's list of priorities was the repayment of the loans awarded to the company through a specially drafted Deed of Covenant. At the same time, it was evident that additional money had to be found in the latter part of 1863 and 1864 and yet again it was Thomas Clark – always known to the family as 'Cousin Thomas' – who stepped into the financial breach once more, sending William £2,300 to meet ongoing expenses. In addition, Stuckey's Banking Company, encouraged by the new management set-up, advanced £1,000 on the condition that the company's overdraft be reduced to £2,500 over the next two years.

In 1863, the total debt owed to fellow Friends amounted to £19,050. By 1868, it had come down slightly to around £18,000, but the subsequent four years saw it diminish considerably. Accounts in 1872 showed Friends' loans had been reduced to just under £3,750, while bank loans were £5,064 and the overdraft stood at a comparatively respectable £1,783.

That William threw himself into his new responsibilities with boundless energy and enthusiasm there can be no doubt. Factory hours in 1863 were 6 am to 6 pm, but the new chairman was putting in eighteen-hour days himself and took a mere fortnight's holiday in the first two years of his chairmanship. He recorded later that he had only two full-time foremen to help him in the factory – 'but poor ones at that' – during a period when he sought to end the practice of out-working and to stop the 'horror of the treatment of small boys in the home workshops'.

His weapon to achieve this was new machinery and his main lieutenant in this endeavour was John Keats. One particular process that exercised

William and Keats was finding a means of closing the uppers with waxed thread. No machine was capable of this because the wax in the thread habitually clogged the eye of the needle. Keats – whom William described as a 'very erratic genius in the machine room' – came up with the idea of using a hook in place of a needle. And it worked. This was especially crucial for the sales of heavy waterproof boots.

'Made strong and stout in the soles and uppers to keep the feet dry and warm, in spite of dews and wet grass' boasted an 1864 Clarks showcard. A patent for this invention – known as the Crispin machine, in honour of St Crispin, the patron saint of shoemaking – was taken out in 1864 in the joint names of William S. Clark and John Keats, and Greenwood & Batley, a company in Leeds, was commissioned to make and sell them under licence.

Adapting these machines to sew on the soles of boots was the next challenge. It was hoped that a variation of an invention by Lyman Blake would do the job. Blake, who was from Massachusetts in the USA, worked in the shoemaking business all his life, at one point joining Isaac Singer's company, Singer Corporation. By 1856, at the age of 22, he had become a partner in a shoemaking firm and two years later received a patent from the United States government for inventing a means of attaching the soles of shoes to their uppers. William and Keats had in fact seen the machine in action at the London Exhibition of 1862 – but had not been overly impressed.

William decided against its use – a decision he explained in his memoirs as being:

> … partly [because of a] strong objection to a chain stitch and partly because anyway the work was not satisfactory. The reason for this was at that time the horn was stationary and it was only by the introduction of the rotating horn not long after that that the machine became a success.

But the Blake Sole Sewer, as it was called, had proved hugely effective during the American Civil War and at the very least had convinced William that if:

... C. & J. Clark was to hold its own in face of constantly increasing competition it could only be by the adoption of these new American methods ... [and] as the Trade Union then had no foothold in Street they hoped the change might be made here without undue friction.

He was proved right – and wrong. Improvements to Blake's machine gathered pace, principally due to modifying its stitching unit. This involved the addition of a 'whirl' device which fed a loop of thread into the hook, copied from the original Crispin machine, but in a rare oversight, the 'whirl' had been omitted from that invention's patent. Blake's machine was too big to operate in the home of an outworker and required an over-head power source to operate the belt. This was fortunate from William's point of view because it quickened the process of gathering workers up into the factory.

William and Keats pushed on with their plans. They had success with a machine that burnished the edges of soles, a significant follow-up to James Miles's mechanised sole-cutter that trimmed soles exactly to size. They also invented a press for the building and attaching of heels, the first such machine to be used in Britain. On this occasion, rather than taking out a patent they simply operated it in secret without any fanfare – after reminding themselves that they were after all in the business of making shoes, not selling shoemaking equipment.

William nearly committed the company to screwing on soles as an alternative to both riveting and sewing after being introduced to an inventor who claimed to have developed a machine capable of fastening soles in that way. A special room in the factory was set aside for this inno-vative piece of equipment, but the delivery date came and went and when, a year later, the inventor – who was from Stalybridge in the foothills of the Pennines – said that he was ready to make the delivery, William wrote a thank-you-but-no-thank-you letter.

We fully indorse [sic] your opinion that boots and shoes must all be made by machinery before long but are not so sure that the public will not prefer having them sewed to screwed.

There were other frustrations in those early years of William's leadership. For all his long-term commitment to machine-made shoes, there was the short-term, uncomfortable truth that labour costs on boots made by machine were often one-third per pair more than had been predicted. In 1866, William wrote to Greenwood & Batley complaining of:

> ... a constant drain of expense upon us from which we have as yet reaped no advantage of any kind whatsoever, and none of the goods made hitherto have realised what they have cost us in wages and materials.

A few months later, he was more optimistic: 'We hope in time to make a paying affair of it, as we are still convinced there is something valuable at the root of the system'. By 1872, the 'something valuable' element became clearer with the adoption of a bent needle that allowed soles to be sewn while still on the last. This prompted William to declare:

> We are perfectly satisfied with the work ... we believe most of our customers sell it as hand work ... in fact, to give you our honest opinion, we are satisfied that no system at present before the public can in the long-run compete with it, and we are indifferent as to anyone else taking it up.

Cyrus Clark died on 14 December 1866 at the age of 65, only a few weeks after the death of his wife. There were no obituaries, but in *Clarks of Street, 1825–1950*, Cyrus is spoken of as 'warm-hearted' with an 'indomitable perseverance in carrying out any object on which he had set his mind ... no obstacle, or, as he would say, no "lion in the path" was allowed to stand in the way'.

His death led to an unseemly and unfortunate three years of wrangling between his brother, James, and Cyrus's surviving family, particularly his youngest son, T. Beaven Clark. James described it as 'passing through some of the deepest trials' of his life, which he only managed to negotiate with the 'loving support and sympathy of my precious wife'.

Two years before Cyrus died, he and James had renewed their partnership agreement whereby they or their heirs had equal shares in the profits of the company for seven years. Therefore, upon his death, half the profits of the business continued to be paid into Cyrus's estate and it was left to the two executors of his will to see that this happened. The executors were Jacob H. Cotterell and William I. Palmer, the Quaker cousin who worked in his family's biscuit business in Reading.

Some months after Cyrus's death, Cotterell also died, leaving Palmer as sole executor. Palmer was, according to William:

> ... anxious to wind up the trust affairs as far as possible and suggested that an agreed sum should be paid into the estate to cover the share of profits for the remaining years of the partnership and all claims there might be on the business for goodwill etc

It was agreed that negotiations should begin, with Palmer representing Cyrus's family and Thomas Simpson negotiating on behalf of James.

An agreement was reached for a payment by James of £1,500 as a goodwill gesture. In his account of this episode, William quoted Palmer as saying:

> If James Clark agreed to the terms he [Palmer] proposed as his brother's executor it would place him [James] in a position in which no one could find fault with him.

James signed his name to the settlement, but Palmer then informed him of Cyrus's wishes that accompanied his will, making it clear that he wanted his son, Beaven, to succeed to his share in the business. As William recorded:

> For reasons that seemed to him conclusive James Clark replied that after long and careful thought he had come to the conclusion that this was quite out of the question and there the matter rested.

A Clark family 'nutting' party under the oak tree at Kingweston in September 1870.

But it did not rest there. Beaven, who was employed in the business as a book-keeper, insisted that his family had 'an absolute right to a half share partnership in the profits of the business in perpetuity' and not just for the remaining five years of the partnership. James disagreed. He said that when the last deed of partnership was drawn up between the brothers in 1864, Cyrus had tried to insert a clause 'securing his family this half share, not in goodwill but in any further partnership' but had eventually backed down on the proviso that a line be included simply expressing his hopes that one of his sons would come in as a partner.

James, distressed and frustrated, was prepared to be generous to his late brother's family but would not give way on the matter of the future partnership. And William took exception to his father being accused of 'not doing his duty by his nephews'. The situation was weighing so heavily on William's mind that at one point he contemplated walking away from the business altogether. Certainly, that was the inference from a letter he received from Simpson, stressing that:

... you owe a great deal to your father ... and it will hardly look well that you should fly from the post of duty when trials and annoyances have to be met and overcome.

Arbitration ensued. Cyrus's family asked for a fellow Friend, Richard Fry, from Bristol, to act on its behalf; James sought the services of Lewis Fry (no relation to Richard), an eminent Quaker also from Bristol, who later went into politics. George Stacey Gibson, from Saffron Walden, a leading member of the Society of Friends on a national level, was asked to be an independent voice of reason.

Delicate deliberations took place at the home of Cyrus's and James's older brother, Joseph, and lasted a full day. T. Beaven Clark and his brother, Alfred, read out their statements, as did James and William. Alfred was speaking more on behalf of his brother than himself because he had been well looked after financially through his role in charge of the firm's London office in Sambrook Court, Basinghall Street, which was set up as an independent venture in 1863. Cyrus's eldest son, John Aubrey Clark, a qualified land surveyor who had played little part in the firm, remained silent.

Following that meeting, Simpson wrote to James on 10 June 1869 with encouraging news:

I duly reached home last night after a very satisfactory interview with cousin W. Palmer who said, 'if they [Cyrus's family] do not accept it now, I will have nothing more to do with it.'

And he sought to assure James that he was right to make a stand:

I have carefully read over the memorandums left by your brother [Cyrus] and although they deeply excited my sympathy and sorrow on his behalf, the perusal has only the more strongly confirmed my previous opinion on the whole question. Everything is stated in such a way as to give an incorrect estimate of the facts of the case and for the express purpose of exciting sympathy, but the false gloss cannot of course deceive me, as I know the facts too well ... if the proposition is now declined it would be wrong to take it up again.

But it *was* taken up again. In fact, it was a further five months before matters were brought to a close, during which time tensions between James's and Cyrus's respective sides of the family worsened. Simpson wrote to James on 22 June 1869 recommending it would be wise to 'have no further conversation with either Beaven [T. Beaven Clark] or Alfred or anyone else on their behalf on any subject at all connected with the negotiations'. He added:

Keep up your spirits for all may yet turn out better than you now expect. You have right on your side ... you have a wife and children who are your first duty, and their interests have for years been sacrificed to the interests of your brother and his family.

On 11 November 1869, James issued a signed statement that he hoped would assuage the growing resentment towards him from Cyrus's family:

The Arbitrators having expressed their opinion that the observations made by James Clark upon his late brother's conduct were of a more severe character than the circumstances warranted, and that some of such observations might be understood as reflecting upon Cyrus Clark's character, James Clark stated that he had never intended to make any reflections upon his brother's straight-forwardness and integrity and that he entirely withdrew any observations which might bear that interpretation.

Five days later, the arbitrators 'unanimously' decided that 'either some representative of the family of the late Cyrus Clark be admitted to a share in the said business or that a compensation for goodwill be paid to the estate of Cyrus Clark.' The amount was set at £2,250 – rather more than the originally agreed sum of £1,500.

William I. Palmer immediately wrote to James and pleaded with him not to make a hasty decision. James wrote back on 18 November 1869 saying that although the award was higher than he had anticipated he felt 'well satisfied' and was pleased to bring matters to a conclusion. He would opt to make the payment:

> It has been a great relief to me to be so entirely liberated, as only such an award could have liberated me, from a Partnership that has for many years been such a burden that I could not feel at all justified in leaving it on my children's shoulders.

Lewis Fry, the Friend who had supported James, told him:

> We were all very strongly impressed with thy candid and very honourable conduct in at once surrendering the agreement which had been signed. Hadst thou insisted upon it, as many persons would have done, I believe we should have felt that it would have precluded our making any award.

And Richard Fry, representing Cyrus's family, was similarly impressed, telling William: 'When thy father has carried out these terms no one can say but that he had done everything for his nephews that he could be expected to do'.

The immediate response of the nephews is not documented, but Beaven gave short shrift to James's subsequent offer that he might become a partner in the rug-making side of the business. William never expanded publicly on this for fear of 'the risk of injustice to James Clark's memory', adding how:

> ... time gradually restored friendly feelings with his brother's family. He always had cordial feelings towards them and deep regard and affection for the memory of his brother from whom he had received such unfailing kindness in his early days.

Palmer, who, although acting on behalf of Cyrus's descendants, had been thrown into the role of peacemaker, told James he hoped never again 'to have the misfortune' to be a sole executor 'in a business under similar difficulties'. Simpson, who had been bullish in representing James, was less magnanimous. He wrote to his client applauding his decision to make the goodwill payment rather than allow Beaven to be a partner in the business, adding:

> You have been sponged nearly dry by one thing or another on account of the family but I believe God will return it to you again in added prosperity, and your conduct throughout I consider to have been a very great honour to you whatever others may say ... I consider it [the award] to be an unjust one but it has to be abided by.

Despite the award, discordant rumblings continued. Bessie Clark, Cyrus's daughter, was under the impression that James never actually got round to signing his statement about not wishing to cast aspersions on Cyrus's character. James patiently wrote to her on 21 March 1870, stressing how his only desire had been to 'clear myself from the charge of having ever intended to cast any imputation on my brother's perfect honesty and integrity'. But Bessie was still not convinced. She thought James had not addressed directly the question of signing or not signing the document. James wrote to her again, spelling out his position even more clearly:

> I quite intended my letter of the 21st to confirm the paper I signed at the time of the Arbitration and I had no idea that it could be understood in any other sense.

Over the next few months, James wrote twice to his nephew and eventually, almost a year after the announcement of the settlement, Beaven responded in a conciliatory tone:

> Dear Uncle, I am extremely glad to receive the two letters thou has addressed to me and gladly accept them in the full sense in which I

trust they are written. I most sincerely thank thee for the expressions of regret they contain and for the frank acknowledgement of thy feelings with regard to my dear father ...

Beaven also conceded that he had been hasty in rejecting James's offer to get involved in the rug business:

I consider myself to blame for not speaking to thyself when I first heard of the state complained of as mutual explanations might probably have prevented the unpleasant misunderstanding which has occurred.

As it turned out, James and William decided later that same year in 1870 that the rug business would be separated from the shoe company. It was to be called Clark, Son & Morland, with James, William and John Morland, James's son-in-law, as partners. James and William had a quarter share each and John a half share. The headquarters was at Bowlingreen Mill, a tanning factory owned by James, which he had inherited from his father, though it was not long before the business moved to Northover, a nearby tanning yard bought especially for the purpose. Following the new status of the rug company, James wrote:

By the kindness of my friends, and the skilful and diligent management of my son, William, I was released from the great harassment I had endured for many years, working with insufficient capital entailing some years heavy losses instead of profit.

Cyrus's death and the subsequent fall-out came shortly after William's marriage at the age of 27. His wife, Helen Priestman Bright, was a year younger than him and they were to have six children, two sons and four daughters. Helen was the only child of John Bright by his first wife, Elizabeth Priestman. Bright – or to give him his full title, The Rt Hon. John Bright MP – was the much admired and hugely influential Liberal politician who, along with Richard Cobden, formed the Anti-Corn Law League.

An MP for 46 years, Bright was regarded as one of the greatest orators

Greenbank, where William S. Clark and Helen Priestman Bright
lived after marrying in 1866.

of his generation. His father, Jacob, was a Quaker who ran a cotton mill business in Rochdale and John remained proud of his radical religious roots. His first public speech was at a Friends' temperance meeting when he got his notes hopelessly muddled and began to break down in tears. The chairman told him to abandon his text altogether and just speak his mind. Which he did, gaining a rousing reception. His talent for off-the-cuff oratory never faltered from that moment on.

Bright was a strong supporter of the 1867 Reform Bill and is credited with inventing the expression 'flog a dead horse' which he used in the House of Commons, telling MPs that trying to rouse Parliament from its apathy on the issue of electoral reform would be like 'trying to flog a dead horse to make it pull a load'. He also coined the phrase 'England is the mother of all parliaments' while rallying support for a wider electoral franchise.

William and Helen began married life in Greenbank, so-named after the Rochdale home of John Bright. It was an old farmhouse on to which William had built two Victorian wings. The bay window was re-assembled from the Clarks showcase stand at the Great Exhibition of 1851. The family remained there until 1889, when William commissioned his favourite architect, George Skipper, whose main bulk of work was in Norfolk, to build a new house further away from the factory. This was called Millfield and is now part of the 1,200-pupil co-educational independent school of that name, which was founded in 1935. William and Helen were already familiar with the area around Millfield because in 1880 their youngest child, Alice, contracted tuberculosis aged six, and rather than send her abroad for the mountain air as so many tuberculosis victims were, they built a Swiss-style house called The Chalet, where Alice sat during the day and often slept at night. She survived.

The Chalet is now used as a chapel for Millfield School and is the oldest building on campus. Millfield House remained in the Clark family until the 1950s, with the school paying rent for its use. At first, it was where Millfield's founder, Jack Meyer, lived, before it became a boarding house for boys.

James and William formed a new partnership in 1873 and it was another seventeen years before James finally retired aged 79. Part of the agreement between father and son amounted to a job description of which most people can only dream: 'James Clark is not required to give more time to the business than is convenient or agreeable to himself'.

The capital within the company at the start of this new partnership was £9,505. 4s. 2d., of which James's share was £7,203. 3s. 9d. and William's £2,304. 0s. 5d. Profits were to be divided equally.

Crucially – and contrary to what had seemed possible only a few years earlier – by 1871 most of those who had loaned the company money in 1863 had been repaid in full. In triumphant mood, Thomas Simpson sent the deed governing the agreement between Clarks and its creditors to William, with a note saying: 'I should consign [the Deed] to the flames which has been the fate of all the other promissory notes'.

William no doubt felt greatly relieved. Honour had been upheld and the Quaker edict about living free from debt had been restored. William

Millfield House, designed in 1889 by the architect George Skipper as a family home for William S. Clark. It is now a boarding house for Millfield, a leading public school.

resolved never again to allow the company to operate without adequate reserves. He was also resolute in his commitment to reinvest profits whenever it was expedient to do so – and not take money out to build new homes or prop up struggling associated enterprises.

There were good years and there were less good years between 1863 and 1879, during the height of what is known as the second industrial revolution or the technological revolution. The development of the railway system allowed goods to be transported at an accelerated rate, but this had the effect in some parts of the country of saturating the market with products that could not be sold. This surplus in turn forced prices to drop as businesses tried to secure capital returns by making quick sales of their assets.

Clarks output remained strong. The company produced 78 per cent more pairs of shoes during the sixteen years from 1863 to 1879 than in the sixteen previous years, and in some years output actually doubled. In terms of numbers, Clarks produced 180,000 pairs of shoes in 1863. By 1903, that figure had risen to 870,000. And what was especially gratifying was the way the footwear industry in general, and Clarks in particular, defied the national economic mood. When the country was in

The main Clarks factory in Street in the late 1890s, seen from the High Street.
This view clearly shows the clock tower built for Queen Victoria's jubilee in 1887
and in the background the water tower (built in 1897) and the 'Big Room'.

the grip of recession in 1875 and 1876, Clarks increased productivity by 18 per cent.

William had made a point of saying in 1863 that he wanted to reduce the number of lines the company produced, but by 1896 there were no fewer than 352 different models of women's footwear alone. And whereas in 1863 Clarks produced more boots than shoes, this had evened up by the end of the century, with shoes representing some 50 per cent of total output.

Some of the more popular lines from early in William's career included: the 'Gentleman's Osborne' boot (1858); the 'Gentleman's Prince of Wales' shoe (1863); the 'Lady's side-spring' boot (1864); the 'Lady's Lorne Lace' boot (1871); the 'Lady's cream brocade side-laced' boot (made originally for the 1862 International Exhibition) and the Child's 'Dress Anklet' in black enamel seal, which had been designed by William himself in 1856.

Quality was sacrosanct. In 1867, William, clearly irked by what he felt were inferior shoes coming into the market at comparable prices to Clarks, wrote to a dealer saying:

> ... the quality of our goods is so entirely different from those of Crick & Sons [a Northampton firm of shoemakers] that ... we doubt if we could get up goods low enough in quality to sell where [theirs] have sold.

A little later, he explained to another dealer that 'ours is mainly a better class trade'.

For all his determination to end the out-work system, William had to accept that even as late as 1898 some 4,800 pairs of shoes were hand-sewn by more than 150 men operating from home in villages such as Long Sutton, Martock and South Petherton, and small towns like Wells and Shepton Mallet. Most outworkers still had at least one apprentice, who lived in and received his keep in return for work. Many of those apprentices came from Muller's Orphanage in Bristol.

Gradually, the so-called 'team system' that was proving so effective in America came to the fore in Street, culminating in the establishment in 1896 of 'the Big Room', a building measuring 240 ft by 120 ft that was divided into a number of 'rooms' but with no dividing walls. These open-plan departments comprised a Pattern Room for grading and design, a Cutting Room for the preparation of uppers, a Machine Room for closing the uppers, a Making Room for lasting and sole attachment, and a Treeing and Trimming Room for finishing.

Expenditure on new equipment was as low as £69 in 1877 – less than £5,000 in today's money – and it was only after 1878 that larger financial investments were made. Until then, William had concentrated on making sure the existing machinery was working to full capacity, but, surprisingly, in 1876, some twenty years after the first Singer sewing machine had been

The 'Big Room', seen here probably around the beginning of the 20th century. All
the major shoemaking processes took place within one large open-plan workshop.

introduced, only 80 per cent of the footwear produced by C. & J. Clark had
machine-sewn uppers.

Frustrations in perfecting machine-made shoe production were
compounded by Street's insufficient labour force. It was not unusual for
price lists to include an apology for production delays and promises that
such hold-ups were being addressed. Furthermore, workers' unrest was
festering. In 1867, the men operating the Crispin machine in the boots
department downed tools and demanded higher wages. This defiance
led to further apologies for production delays, with William telling his
customers that he had been persuaded to shorten the hours of the cutters
and Crispin machine hands – as well as increasing their pay. A double
headache.

Trade unions had been decriminalised in 1867 and the Amalgamated
Cordwainers Association became in effect the first shoemakers' union. But
it made little headway and in 1874 a new union was formed: the National

Union of Boot and Shoe Rivetters and Finishers, otherwise known as the Sons of St Crispin. This grouping soon established a network that helped workers throughout the country and provided such support as a funeral fund and sick pay. By 1887, it had 10,000 members. The Sons of St Crispin would change its name to the National Union of Boot and Shoe Operatives in 1898.

The union was suspicious when William brought in John Keats's father, William Keats, to help finesse the Crispin machine, and there were soon rumours of random strikes being planned. At one point in 1877, William felt it necessary to write to Greenwood & Batley insisting:

> It is a mistake to say that our factory was closed several times owing to disturbances. To the best of my knowledge this only occurred once – at the time of a strike which lasted two or three days just before W. Keats left us ... although a great many other matters caused ill-feeling towards W. and J. Keats, and it was heightened by a good deal of indiscretion on their part, and as a matter of fact in the strike referred to, and which was directed solely against them, the question of the sewing machine was never alluded to by the men. I quite believe that J. Keats may be right in thinking that a feeling against the machine was really at the root of the matter. I write this fully that you may understand that, as the men never raised any direct opposition to the machine, I do not honestly see that I could put the case any stronger.

There had been a further unsettling development in 1874 when a Clarks travelling salesman, E. C. Sadler, decided to exploit the shortage of jobs for hand-sewers by setting up a rival shoe manufacturing business in Street. He made this audacious move with the support of Edwin Bostock, a shoemaker in Staffordshire, and by 1877 E. C. Sadler & Co. was employing 300 people. Sadler paid his workers better than Clarks while at the same time copying many of the Clarks' lines, sometimes passing them off as made by C. & J. Clark. The competitive threat from Sadler's abated in the early 1880s when, citing union interference, it moved production to Worcester and in 1897 the business was closed.

The year 1880 was a pivotal one for C. & J. Clark. For the previous 24 months, the company had been spending large sums on new technology and the 'team system' was being slowly implemented. To help with the latter, a man called Horatio Hodges, the son of a former Street shoemaker, was recruited to drive through the changes. Hodges had experience of working in America and was, as William put it, 'thoroughly acquainted with the newest American machinery and systems'. But he may not have been so well acquainted with tactful man management and the need to find a common consensus. In *C. & J. Clark, 1833–1903: A History of Shoe-making*, George Barry Sutton wrote:

> Horatio Hodges was an unfortunate choice as the ambassador of progress ... He was a gifted machinery inventor and, as a local Salvation Army leader, made recruits. What he lacked, however, was the gift of understanding others of divergent views or of impressing them with his tolerance.

One of the many grievances against him was the way he tested the productivity of machines and then exaggerated their achievements. He was also unpopular for hiring boys because they were cheaper than men. The workers wanted Hodges out – and were prepared to go on strike until he was dismissed.

William flatly refused to sack Hodges and countered that only one boy had been hired in direct competition with a man. 'Pressure was brought to bear in many ways to give [the machines] up as failure' noted William in his private diaries.

Publicly, William made clear that if the men backed down, he would happily ensure they were secure in their jobs. But they weren't interested. A stand-off ensued, followed by an all-out strike in May 1880 that lasted not a couple of days, like the one in 1867, but the best part of two weeks. William took a hard line during the walk-out. He said no member of a trade union would be allowed back to work and then warned that if the strike were to continue, he would be compelled to move the whole business to Bristol.

On 22 May 1880, the *Western Gazette* ran a story headlined 'Strike at Messrs. Clarks Factory':

An unfortunate dispute is now going on here. It seems from what we can gather that a foreman has introduced machinery which the men say has reduced their earnings....The strike has since assumed a most determined character on the part of the rounders, riveters, finishers and the workpeople of both sexes in other branches of the trade .... There is now some talk of asking the firm to submit the points in dispute of arbitration and there is no doubt that great relief would be felt by all concerned on the strike if the matter could be satisfactorily adjusted.

Six days later, on 28 May 1880, the paper printed a breathless, long-winded response from C. & J. Clark:

Sir, We notice in your last week's newspaper an account of the difficulties with our workpeople ... they requested a meeting with us on Monday evening when we asked to have all their grievances submitted to us in writing that they might be fully discussed. We endeavoured to ensure that they had been mistaken in attributing their shortness of work during the past winter and other hindrances to the machinery and new system introduced in the factory and that other changes of which they complained were solely caused by a determination to improve the quality of the work turned out and that they had largely benefited from the increase in orders that had resulted from these improvements. We also pointed out that supposing all their grievances to have been well founded the straightforward course would have been to have brought them before our notice at the time they occurred and not to bottle them up and wait till the season of the year when they knew that a disturbance would cause us the greatest inconvenience and then suddenly threaten to strike unless we discharged our foreman adding that if we had been so cowardly as to yield to such a threat and thus commit an act of injustice it could not have been to increase their respect for us. The next day they decided to withdraw their demands and return quietly to work. We wish to take this opportunity to state that we think that great credit is due to them for the great order maintained during a fortnight of such excitement of feeling.

We are respectfully CJC

Once the strike had ended, William moved Hodges quietly out of Street, and he left the company altogether in 1887. This was the only all-out strike that Clarks encountered then or since. Later, William attributed the unrest to 'certain information that came to hand' but was sparing with the detail, saying only that 'all the difficulty at Street was caused by agents of the Trade Union who vowed that the machinery and system should be put an end to and used their utmost efforts to stop it'.

Kenneth Hudson, in his 1968 book *Towards Precision Shoemaking*, said William opposed the trade unions precisely because he:

... believed passionately in the importance of good relationships' [between employer and employee] ... He saw no virtue or value in discussion between representatives of capital and representatives of labour. Such meetings, he felt, made understanding and fair treatment less likely, not more.

William was something of a renaissance man. He was a keen reader and took a great interest in architecture and engineering. Sporty as a child, he remained a strong swimmer and skater throughout most of his life. But he also managed to find time to involve himself in almost every facet of local affairs. He was an Alderman in the County of Somerset and a magistrate; he acted as treasurer of the Western Temperance League and was chairman of the Central Education Committee of the Society of Friends. For 24 years he was a member of the local authority, first known as the Local Board, later the Urban District Council.

Quakers took seriously their wider commitments. They believed in the sacredness of human life and the acceptance of all people, regardless of gender or colour. As enshrined in the words of John Bellers in 1695, recorded in William C. Braithwaite's *The Second Period of Quakerism*:

> It is not he that dwells nearest that is only our neighbour, but he that wants our help also claims that name and our love.

The Quaker desire to create a convivial working environment would lead other Quaker families to build whole new towns on the foundations of their high-mindedness. In 1893, after Cadbury had opened a factory in Birmingham fourteen years earlier, it established a new community for the workers and their families that it called Bournville. This occupied a fifteen-acre site, ideally placed for rail and canal links, and everything was, as the company put it, 'arranged for well-studied convenience'. A founding principle at Bournville was that 'no one should live where a rose can not grow'.

Not to be outdone, Rowntree, Cadbury's big rival, acquired a twenty-acre site just outside York, and Reckitt, a Quaker company which produced household cleaning products, established its own model society near its factory in Hull. That is not to say that the entire workforce of these companies thought they were living a model existence. Generosity sometimes came with a price. The Rowntree family went as far as deploying supervisors to monitor behaviour to and from work and for a short period refused to employ single mothers.

Likewise, men who married their pregnant girlfriends were not entitled to the customary three-day, fully-paid honeymoon and those missing work through venereal disease did not qualify for sick pay.

Rules such as these were in keeping with Quaker thinking but, as James Walvin wrote in *The Quakers: Money and Morals*:

> ... what convinced Quaker magnates of their approach, was not so much the moral strength of their position but its commercial results: managing the labour force decently was good for business.

There was no question of depositing money in off-shore bank accounts or amassing excessive bonuses or taking the local community for granted.

Rather, the onus was on building up the community and investing in its future. At C. & J. Clark, there may have been a brief period of tension between management and workers over the introduction of new machinery, but the firm went out of its way to build an integrated society outside the factory. It bought large swathes of land on which workers could build their own homes, helped by loans offered by the company. A terrace of cottages, for example, on Somerton Road, built in the 1830s, had been bought by Cyrus Clark, and additional houses were acquired in Leigh Road and on the High Street. Property owned by Clarks in 1882 was valued at £6,524.

The company sponsored a Building Co-operative and land was let out cheaply for use as allotment gardens. George Barry Sutton quoted one employee as estimating that 30 per cent of Clarks' workforce owned their homes by the turn of the twentieth century. That sense of a wider community was further advanced in 1885 when construction was completed on the Crispin Hall, a cultural and community centre commissioned by the company. Like Millfield House, it was designed by George Skipper, and was big enough to seat 800 people. In addition, there was a lecture room, library, reading room and a geological museum, with a gym and billiards room added later.

Today, Crispin Hall – listed Grade II by English Heritage – is rented to community traders and charitable organisations, and the local Women's Institute holds its weekly market in the main hall every Thursday. The building was officially opened in 1885 by John Bright MP, William's father-in-law, who said:

> It has always been desired that the Factory and those connected with
> it should share the community life of Street rather than exist as a self-
> contained unit apart from that life.

There were annual factory outings organised by management. One, on 27 June 1885, involved a trip to Plymouth on a special train that left from Glastonbury at 5.30 am and arrived on the south coast nearly five hours later. The special fare was 4s. 3d. and was available to all those working at C. & J. Clark, Clark, Son & Morland, and the Avalon Leather

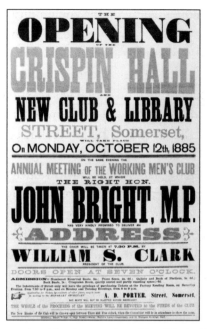

Poster advertising the opening of the Crispin Hall.

Board Company, which was set up by William S. Clark as an independent company (although he was the first chairman) for the turning of scrap leather into fibre board, which was used as part of a shoe's construction.

On this particular works' outing, the factory band accompanied everyone to Plymouth and the return train did not pull into Glastonbury until well after midnight.

The *British Trade Journal* of 1887 evidently thought highly of Clarks' general ethos, saying that it formed 'as industrious, temperate and intelligent a community as can be met with'.

In the same year that Crispin Hall opened, Clarks acquired the Bear Coffee House, formerly Jimmy Godfrey's Cider House – now the Bear Inn – directly opposite the factory. Once the transaction had been completed its licence to serve alcohol was immediately revoked. Then, in 1893, it was demolished and rebuilt under the supervision of the architect William Reynolds, a nephew of William S. Clark. It became known as the Bear Inn, but was granted a licence again only in the 1970s.

Crispin Hall, seen here in 1900, was provided by William S. Clark as a cultural centre for the population of Street. The hall is still in use for community and charitable events today.

Education was another priority. Cyrus's and James's mother, Fanny Clark, had been instrumental in founding the British School shortly after the start of the Crimean War, which then became the Board School. Later, William S. Clark built and personally financed for several years the Strode School, which was set up for boys and girls who had left full-time education at fourteen and were employed by Clarks.

Later, in the 1920s, a Day Continuation School was established for the benefit of boys and girls up to the age of sixteen working in the Clarks factory – but not exclusively so – as a means of extending their educational opportunities. Pupils would commit to one morning and one afternoon each week, their attendance being a condition of employment.

The advantages of working at Clarks were offset to some degree by lower wages compared with other shoemaking companies. Clarks was not a member of the Victorian Employers Federation, formed in 1885 to represent employers on issues of industrial and labour relations, and so it was exempted from negotiations with the unions over pay and conditions. A national strike in 1897, calling for a minimum wage, a 54-hour week, and, most notably, an end to child labour, had no impact on C. & J. Clark.

Advertisement card from 1926 for the Bear Inn (or Hotel) in
Street's High Street, opposite the Clarks factory.

Towards the end of the century, William relented over union represen-
tation, but still regarded it as a diversion. His main focus was on monitoring
output and sales – something both his father and uncle demonstrably had
failed to grapple with. William's original 1863 Summary of Stock Account
had analysed in detail the value of footwear output from 1851 onwards
and he did everything he could to eliminate the imbalance between output
and sales. As Sutton noted, somewhat complicatedly, in *C. & J. Clark,
1833–1903: A History of Shoemaking*:

> He enumerated the wage and material costs incurred annually, making
> sub-divisions to show expenditure on different classes of employees and
> components. These costs, hereafter called direct costs, were deducted
> from footwear output and sales to give 'gross profit on goods made' and
> 'gross profits on goods sold'. Other expenses incurred in the footwear
> trade, hereafter called indirect costs, were enumerated and deducted from
> each of the gross profit figures yielding 'net profit on goods made' and on
> goods sold. Finally, each item of costs, expenses and profit was expressed

as a percentage of both goods made and goods sold. This dual set of figures provided a comparison of costs with expected results, expressed in the value put on goods made, and with actual achievement expressed in sales.

This policy paid off. Between 1863 and 1904, there were only ten individual years when the number of pairs produced exceeded the number ordered. And while the founders never placed a great emphasis on the accuracy of their accounting, William insisted on preparing accounts half-yearly rather than just annually.

James Clark retired in 1889 and a new partnership was formed between William S. Clark and his brother, Francis Joseph Clark. Like William before him, Francis (always known as Frank) had been sent to the Quaker Bootham School in York, and had joined the firm at the age of seventeen in 1870. He was fourteen years younger than William. Within a short time, he was managing the cutting room and purchasing materials for uppers. Apart from one year studying at University College London, his whole career was spent in the family business. In July 1881, William wrote to his brother saying how he wanted him to:

> ... feel now more than ever ... thy full share of the burden of the business and ... that thy future position in the business must mainly depend on thy making thyself necessary to the business.

This partnership was to last fourteen years, concluding only when the business became a private limited company in 1903. During this period, the second-generation brothers ploughed more than four-fifths of profits back into the business, a level of reinvestment unheard of while Cyrus and James were partners.

The footwear market, meanwhile, was changing. Ready-made shoes were now the norm rather than the exception and the 1890s saw an influx

Frank Clark in April 1876.

of cheap shoes from America, Switzerland, France and Austria. Department stores – or, at least, buildings where a number of different shops sold their wares – were on the increase. C. & J. Clark, however, regarded its product as superior to anything found in a department store and continued to sell only to wholesalers and specialist shoe shops. Its shoes were given suitably establishment names: 'Lady's Morocco Oxford Lace' (1887); 'Boy's Derby Balmoral' boot (1887); 'Lady's calf kid Balmoral' boot (1887); and 'Lady's patent calf Langtry tie shoe' (1895).

Meanwhile, Ireland proved vexing. Cyrus and James Clark had enjoyed considerable success in a country that, back in 1836, accounted for 30 per cent of footwear sales and 20 per cent of rug sales. In 1877, William looked long and hard at the Irish figures and was not pleased by what he saw. He estimated that his salesman was spending nine weeks a year in Ireland, dealing with wholesalers in Dublin, Cork, Belfast and Limerick, and that the return, once you had factored in various discounts, was lamentable. William wanted to go direct to the retailer, effectively cutting out the middle man.

In May 1878, he appointed a new, roving Irish agent, instructing him to offer a discount to retailers of 2.5 per cent on payment of a bill settled within three months, or 5 per cent if the bill was paid in cash. These arrangements were a great deal more favourable to Clarks than when dealing with Irish wholesalers, who often received discounts of as much as 10 per cent. But within weeks, William told his new recruit that he would not be renewing his contract once it expired at the end of three months. Sales had been poor and to make matters worse there was now no going back to the wholesalers whom he had sought to circumvent.

Three years later, in 1881, Frank Clark travelled to Ireland and hit upon the idea of working with J. & S. Allen, which employed a team of salesmen selling a wide range of general goods. On the understanding that J. & S. Allen would carry no other firm's footwear, Frank offered Allen 5 per cent commission on sales. This didn't work either and by early 1884, J. & S. Allen wanted to end the agreement. Initially, William was keen to persist with it, suggesting that Allen should have direct access to stock in Ireland, but then he came to the same sorry conclusion. In February 1884, he wrote to Allen confirming how things had:

> ... turned out just as we feared ... and in consequence of giving you the agency we have entirely lost the custom of ... 4 houses ... who were, we believe, taking between them more of our goods than the total of your sales has since amounted to.

Later that year, it was agreed that yet another new salesman would cover Ireland, but that he would travel in the north of England as well and, crucially, he would sell rugs and fibre boards too. The result was not much better. Then, in 1890, Clarks came to an agreement with other footwear manufacturers – including A. Lovell and Co., in Bristol; Ward Bros, in Kettering; and Hanger and Chattaway, in Leicester – whereby a traveller would carry a full range of shoes from various manufacturers and the shoe companies would share the traveller's customers.

Not long afterwards, William wrote to A. Lovell & Co. complaining that 'we did not find the customers with whose names you furnished us generally such as we cared to open accounts with'. And in December 1891 he was telling Hanger and Chattaway that its goods were of inadequate quality to be shown alongside Clarks – and pulled out of that agreement too.

Elsewhere in the export market, caution was the policy, not least in Australia where Cyrus and James had enjoyed mixed fortunes in the past. Soon after he took control of the company, William wrote to Dalgety & Co., a firm of wholesalers in Melbourne, saying that he was considering sending new shipments to the country, but:

> ... the average results [in Australia] of the last few years have been so disastrous to us that on a principle that a burnt child dreads a fire, we are really afraid to take it up again.

Certainly, speculative shipments, which Cyrus and James had gone in for with disastrous consequences, were to be avoided, especially after the Australian legislature, keen to stimulate the home economy, voted in 1861 to impose tariffs on goods from outside the country. But in the 1870s and early 1880s Clarks made a push to secure big enough orders from Australian wholesalers to make it worth their while shouldering the burdens of shipping costs and customs duties. This slowly began to pay off, especially in Melbourne upon the appointment of an agent, Gavin Gibson. Even Sydney, which traditionally had not been a strong market for the Clarks, showed signs of life after a company called Enoch Taylor began acting on their behalf. In 1891, sales to Australia had reached £30,000, but these were followed by a worrying dip. Tension between agents – especially when the Clarks placed a greater emphasis on Victoria, South Australia and West Australia – combined with a limited range of footwear being offered to Australians saw sales plummet in the period 1893 to 1899. In fact, the years 1896, 1897 and 1898 showed no sales at all.

At one point, William's worst fears were realised when he heard from an Australian retailer complaining how he was never shown any samples of 'better class goods'. Clearly furious, William wrote to Enoch Taylor: 'He [the retailer] says the same as others, that you people practically only offer the ankle straps and a few other lines in the Melbourne market'.

There were, however, encouraging results in South Africa. William sent a salesman called Walter Seymour to the country in 1885. His brief was to visit all major cities, offering customers a discount of 5 per cent. Seymour was also carrying goods made by Cave & Son, of Rushden, from which Clarks received a commission of 3.5 per cent. After a slow start, Seymour enjoyed some success and by 1889 was making two trips to South Africa per year.

A year later, in 1890, William's eldest son, John Bright Clark, was diagnosed with tuberculosis. It was agreed that as part of his convalescence he would travel to South Africa. He arrived in Cape Town in September and it was not long before he had identified and hired a sole agent, E. C. Marklew, to represent Clarks in the whole of South Africa. Results were extraordinary. In 1891, Marklew achieved sales of just £43; a year later, that figure was £11,804 and in 1893 it had reached £16,099. By 1902, Marklew was shifting £46,551 worth of shoes, which was more than 30 per cent of C. & J. Clark's total sales. This meant that in 1902 South Africa was C. & J. Clark's strongest overseas market by some distance, followed by Australia and then New Zealand.

Sole agencies were now regarded as the way forward. In 1895, Max Vanstraaten was appointed the Clarks agent in France, Switzerland, Germany, Austria, Hungary, Holland, Belgium and Denmark. His company would receive 5 per cent commission on sales to retail outlets and 2.5 per cent on sales to wholesalers. Two years later, Oskar Wiener was hired on similar terms to look after South America.

T. P. Slim was taken on in New Zealand before, towards the end of the century, a man called John Angell Peck was appointed the sole agent in Australia and New Zealand. Peck became something of a role model for agents worldwide. Whereas sales in Australia and New Zealand in 1899 – the year of his appointment – were £3,948 in Australia and £213 in New Zealand, by 1903 they had reached £16,444 and £7,405 respectively. Peck remained in his post for 41 years, retiring in 1940.

A showcard for the home market in 1864 depicted a group of men and women playing croquet. 'Manufacturers of most stylish and fashionable Ladies' Boots' was the strapline. Underneath, in smaller print, was added:

'Every variety of gentlemen's, ladies' and children's boots, shoes and slippers'. In other words, the Clarks considered that their business made shoes for everyone.

But competition, especially from America, was intensifying and it was important that C. & J. Clark should stand out from other UK shoemakers. Certainly, one of the company's distinguishing features was its choice of fittings, something that had been pioneered and subsequently developed in the USA. As early as 1848, Clarks ladies' 'French shoes' were offered in three fittings (N, M and W, referring to narrow, medium and wide) and in every size and half size from one to seven.

Then, in 1880, a further four new fittings (B, C, D and E) were launched. This emphasis on shoes that fitted properly and comfortably had a big influence on the launch in 1883 of the Hygienic range. The idea was to stress the importance of health rather than style. Hygienic boots and shoes came with the implicit backing of the medical profession. As a showcard said: 'These boots do not deform the feet or cause corns and bunions but are comfortable to wear & make walking a pleasure'. Not perhaps the most sensual of recommendations, but sales were impressive none the less, with William declaring how the results had 'exceeded our expectations'. The Hygienic range eventually became the Anatomical range.

New styles were developing – the first 'ladies' high-heeled shoes' appeared in the 1877 price list – and strides were also being made with packaging and branding. The Tor trademark, so-named after Glastonbury Tor, the hill overlooking the town with St Michael's tower at its summit, was immediately identified with C. & J. Clark, the word 'Tor' clearly visible on the soles.

Shoe-shopping today has for many people become a heightened retail experience. Fun. Daring. Therapeutic, even. And part of that experience is enlivened by packaging – the boxes, the tissue paper, the carrier bags. Clarks saw the importance of this as long ago as the 1880s, when for the first time a pair of shoes could be bought in a box, at an additional charge of one penny on cheaper lines, or free if the overall cost came to more than 6 shillings. Then, in 1893, C. & J. Clark created its own carton-making department and almost all its shoes could be bought in boxes at no extra cost.

Total sales of Clarks shoes in 1900 had reached £140,000, of which around 60 per cent was accounted for by the home market. And Street, once a small village through which people would pass on the way to Glastonbury or further west, was a thriving town of almost 4,000 inhabitants –thanks entirely to a tiny slipper business that had grown to become an international shoe giant.

In 1879, twelve months before the strike at C. & J. Clark, Eleanor, James's wife, died. She had been ill for a number of years after suffering from congestion of the lungs. The final months of her life saw Eleanor mainly confined to the house and she was unable to go upstairs unaided. In summer, she would be taken in a pony carriage into the countryside, and James and she occasionally would stay a night with friends. Of his wife's death, James recorded that:

> ... it pleased the Master to take my loved one to himself ... words cannot convey an idea of the abiding sense of loneliness that has been my position ... since the severance after nearly 45 years of union.

However, three years later in 1882, James married Sarah Brockbank Satterthwaite, the widow of Michael Satterthwaite, a former physician and schoolmaster. He and Sarah, who was seven years his junior, were both active in the Quaker ministry in Street and in the USA. 'Heavenly Father had given her ten extra years of life to travel in America and another ten to marry James Clark' wrote James's grandson, Roger, in his journal dated 28 February 1903. By all accounts, James and Sarah spent 24 happy years together.

James became increasingly religious. Almost every morning at 7.30 am, he read the Bible at a small gathering of workers and in the course of one year during his retirement he made a point of visiting every Clarks employee in his or her own home. The Society of Friends' Annual Monitor of 1907 spoke of James's last few years as being a time when he 'accepted cheerfully and without a murmur' the restrictions of old age:

> To the end, his interest was keen in all passing events in the village in which his long life had been spent, in the Society to whose welfare so much of his time had been devoted, and in the wider political life of the country. His cheerful spirit, and gratitude for every little attention, were much appreciated by his attendants. If, as occasionally happened, a certain impatience in his natural disposition found expression in words, the humble apologies he would quickly make to those about him affected them deeply.

On 28 December 1905, James woke early and said to his family:

> I have given myself to the Lord tonight more entirely than I have ever done before, and he has promised me that His way shall be easy for me, and His burden light. And now I am wholly given up to the Lord.

A few weeks later, he started to weaken and on 15 January 1906, he said: 'If I should pass away tonight tell William especially I have nothing of my own to look to, nothing to trust in, only in Jesus!'

He survived until the morning, when his family gathered around his bed. 'I want to go to sleep' he said. Half an hour later, he was dead, the end coming 'so quietly that it was difficult to know when the gentle breathing ceased,' recorded Roger Clark. James was 95 when he died.

5

A business for the benefit of all

'OF COURSE I START WITH THE HEEL,' said Manolo Blahnik, the Spanish fashion designer and High Priest of the stiletto, in a 2010 interview with *Vogue*. 'Always! The heel is the most important part of the shoe, and the most difficult part. I have spent 35 years trying to make the perfect heel.'

In Street at the end of the nineteenth century, the debate was not so much about the height of heels as style versus comfort and the practicalities of combining both. Fashions were changing and younger members of the Clark family thought the company needed to move with the times. There was a danger of being left behind. For William S. Clark and his generation it was a case of coming to terms with the 'Belle Epoque' era, generally acknowledged as running from 1890 to 1914, when music, the arts and literature flourished, while the death of Queen Victoria in 1901 and the ascension to the throne of Edward VII was hastening the shift from Victorian formality to Edwardian frivolity. The new king enjoyed the company of women and was keen to see more of them. Hips became curvier, chests fuller, waists narrower.

Cometh the hour, cometh the much-celebrated hourglass figure, as bustles and heavy petticoats retreated into the sartorial distance. Women began joining men in the pursuit of leisure. They took up golf, croquet, fencing, riding and cycling – and needed to be shod accordingly. This called for an element of swagger to be introduced to the Clarks showcards, not least because America was stealing a march on many of its rivals in Britain.

Shoemakers on the other side of the Atlantic were experimenting in new, informal designs and offering them at temptingly low prices. Clarks was only too aware of this development because the company's Quaker connections in America gathered intelligence to feed back to Somerset. This link with the United States was further strengthened in 1900 when Roger Clark, William's second son, married a cousin, Sarah Bancroft, from Wilmington, Delaware, whom he had met during a sales tour of North America.

Roger had joined the company after leaving Bootham School in 1888 at the age of seventeen. At first, he worked in the counting house at Clark, Son & Morland, the rug business that was hived off from C. & J. Clark shortly after William took over as chairman. In 1890, Roger embarked upon two years studying dyeing and chemistry at the Victoria College in Leeds, but to little advantage because he suffered from severe eczema. Selling was one of his strengths and to this end he joined his brother, John Bright Clark, on a worldwide business tour in 1898.

John Bright Clark was four years older than Roger. He, too, had been educated at Bootham, returning to Street in 1884 after passing the London Matriculation Examination. He spent several years moving from one department at C. & J. Clark to another, including, at the age of nineteen, being taught the fundamentals of hand-sewn shoemaking from an outworker called Charles Maidment, who lived in Street's Cranhill Road.

Both John Bright Clark and Roger Clark were dogged by poor health. Roger spent periods of his early life in Davos Platz in Switzerland and at Nordrach in the Black Forest, Germany. In fact, he was so impressed by the healing properties of Nordrach that he became a great supporter and benefactor of an English version of this health spa, which was set up near Charterhouse in the Mendip Hills.

Roger was 'a sensitive man ... with leanings towards socialism and a classless Christian ethic, who had to come to terms with his own position as a born capitalist' according to Percy Lovell in *Quaker Inheritance, 1871–1961*. He was a great lover of Thomas Hardy novels, folk

Roger Clark wearing apprentice's working clothes at
Clark, Son & Morland in Glastonbury in 1888.

music, the William Morris arts and crafts movement, Pre-Raphaelite
art, Gilbert and Sullivan musicals and the plays of Henrik Ibsen, all of
which informed what Lovell called his 'genuine concern for the poor and
underprivileged'.

It was hoped that John Bright's and Roger's trip abroad would be good for
their health. They set out from Plymouth, calling in at Gibraltar, Marseilles
and Naples, and then sailed through the Suez Canal. Roger spent a fortnight in Cairo, later joining up with John Bright in Adelaide before they
both moved on to America. In September 1898, John Bright was called
back to Street to help in the factory following a tragedy. Joseph Law, a well-
regarded and highly talented foreman of the making and finishing departments, had died in an accident involving one of the factory lifts.

Roger, meanwhile, went on to stay with his cousins, the Bancrofts, in
Delaware, which was where he met Sarah, and within weeks they were
engaged. Such was the haste of their courtship that it was decided to keep

the engagement a secret from everyone except close family for six months. And the wedding would not be for a further eighteen months.

Sarah's father, William Bancroft, came from a family of Lancashire Quakers who had been successful in the cotton mill industry. They had emigrated to America in 1822, setting up a cotton manufacturing and finishing company in Rockford, Delaware, on the banks of the Brandywine river. In 1865, this business became known as Joseph Bancroft & Sons. William Bancroft's younger brother, Samuel, was made president of the firm, but also took an active part in politics, first as a Republican, then a Democrat. An avid collector of art, in 1890 he bought his first Pre-Raphaelite painting, Dante Gabriel Rossetti's *Water Willow*, and went on to amass the biggest Pre-Raphaelite collection outside Britain. After his death in 1915, his family donated his paintings to the Wilmington Society of Fine Arts, which is now part of the Delaware Art Museum. Sarah's mother, Emma, was also descended from English Quakers, but her ancestors had moved to America much earlier, in 1679.

Shortly before Roger asked Sarah to marry him, his mother wrote to his brother John Bright Clark and referred to a visit to England by the Bancrofts:

> They are all very nice people. He [William] very good and sincere, rather a character, very simple and friendly though very prosperous ... the two girls are very attractive.

After assessing his future son-in-law's potential, William Bancroft suggested to Roger that he should stay in Delaware and join the Bancroft family firm rather than return to Clarks in Street, an offer that was politely declined. 'They wanted me so much to go and live in America but I could not feel that that was the right place for me' wrote Roger in a letter to his aunt, Priscilla Bright McLaren, on 11 May 1899.

But not taking the job meant returning to England and living on a separate continent from his 21-year-old fiancée. In twice-weekly letters, Roger and Sarah shared their hopes and aspirations, agreeing on the importance of education, the emancipation of women, the fight against racism and the so-called 'new look' of Quakerism, described graphically by Roger as a turning away from the 'horrid old theory of sacrifice, substitution, propitiation, bargain-driving with Satan, and so forth'.

Their letters hinted at the challenges faced by the new generation of Clarks and how they would take the various businesses forward, while at the same time fulfilling their wider responsibilities to the community. But mainly the correspondence concentrated on a mutual desire to be together. Roger had already decided that he wanted them to live in Overleigh rather than Greenbank, William S. Clark's former house, where he said they could get away with only one servant and establish a 'really nice snug home'.

In a letter dated 27 April 1899, Roger wrote:

My own sweet love,

What a lovely letter thou has sent me. I cannot tell thee half the glad happiness it has brought me ... I read it alone after tea. Thou must not be sorry thou wrote that other letter; I would rather by far have thee brought so close to me as I feel that thou has been, by letting me share in thy perplexities, as well as in thy certainties; for we shall always share them when they come to us, n'est ce pas? Thou hast always been far too good to me, sweet. I must keep in mind not to be spoiled.

That summer, Roger appeared to be getting in touch with his rustic side, telling Sarah:

I should like to take my bath always out of doors. It makes you feel so akin to the earth to stand naked on the grass with the delicious sun pouring down upon you; and after pouring the water all over me from as high as I could reach, my whole being seemed to give itself up to the simple enjoyment of the divine reaction and glow over body and limbs.

A couple of paragraphs later, he reverted to the more mundane topic of work and reflected again on William Bancroft's job proposal:

I have been in the Boot Factory at a fresh job. I find it very hard to feel much satisfaction in taking up this new business; it is so complicated and full of detail. I am sure it would have been a fatal error to have attempted something similar in your mills at Rockford.

Sarah replied:

I should think the new business would worry thee. It would worry me dreadfully, even though I should like the learning, even the dull parts, but that too would weigh upon me when I thought of the wearisomeness of doing nothing else all one's life ... I wonder what the ambition of people who do such work can be. I should think it would kill all one's ambition. And the moment one looks forward to some better work one begins to worry for fear one will not succeed. Oh, there are many difficulties along our pathways, aren't there? But it is better so, of course.

The wedding eventually took place in the drawing room of the Bancroft family home in Rockford on 18 June 1900 and was attended by some 80 people. Roger's parents, William and Helen, had sailed to America a few weeks before the ceremony, keen to see as much of the country as possible. In particular, Helen, as if doing the bidding of her reformist father, John Bright MP, 'was always sniffing for evidence of colour prejudice and, not surprisingly, found ammunition in plenty' according to Lovell.

Sarah did not find the transition from Delaware to Somerset always easy, but maintained close ties with her family, especially her sister Lucy, who also married an English Quaker, Dr Henry Gillett, and lived in Banbury Road, Oxford. Then, two years after setting up home together in Street, Roger and Sarah's first child was born, a boy named William Bancroft Clark in deference to both the infant's grandfathers. From an early age, he was known as Bancroft.

The infusion of young blood at the top of the company was encouraged by William S. Clark and formally acknowledged in 1903 when C. & J. Clark became a private limited liability company, with nominal capital of £160,000, preference shares of £100,000 and £60,000 ordinary shares. Five directors were appointed, all of them for life under the Articles of Association. William, who was now 64 and beginning to suffer from arthritis, remained as chairman and his co-directors were his brother, Frank, and three of his children, John Bright Clark, 36, Roger Clark, 32, and Alice Clark, 29.

Of the directors, Frank was the biggest shareholder with around 20,000 Ordinary shares, followed by William (with 18,000), John Bright (12,000), Roger (4,000) and Alice (3,000). The remaining shareholders were William's three other daughters, Esther Clothier (1,000), Margaret Clark Gillett (1,000) and Hilda Clark (1,000).

Alice, who as a young girl had been sick with tuberculosis and who experienced poor health all through her life, joined the company in 1893 at the age of eighteen. She attended, briefly, a course in housewifery at Bristol, something that may have been lost on her given that she never married – although she was regarded as a great beauty – and went on to became an active campaigner for women's suffrage. After four years learning how the factory operated, she went to work for Thomas Lugton, a Clarks agent in Edinburgh's Princes Street, returning to Street as supervisor of the Machine Room. Later, she was responsible for the Trimming Room and the Turnshoe department, and was one of only a small group of women to reach a managerial position in industrial Britain at the start of the twentieth century.

The new, younger directors of what was now C. & J. Clark Ltd recognised that as a result of imports of cheaper footwear from America, many British manufacturers were turning their attention to what at the time was called the 'better class trade'. Shoemakers throughout the country were determined to raise their collective game and were prepared to implement aggressive ways of increasing home production. How to attract a 'better class of trade' was a conundrum. It was William who, in 1897, came to the realisation that C. & J. Clark should forge closer ties with

William S. Clark in May 1906.

London's fashionable West End, and at one point a suitably well-established shoemaker called A. McAfee was identified as a potential partner in the capital. McAfee was a bespoke shoemaker. The plan was that he would open a new shop selling shoes made by C. & J. Clark in addition to his own lines.

In a letter to McAfee in June 1897, William was forthright:

> The main inducement, in fact we might say the only inducement, from a business point of view ... has been that we thought it would be an advantage to our general trade to be kept more closely and constantly in touch with the highest class of West End Trade.

To this end, C. & J. Clark would commit up to £3,000 on this joint venture, receiving a quarter of net profits. In effect – apart from a shop in Bridgwater, Somerset, that closed in 1864 – this represented the company's first tentative foray into retailing. But it was not a path upon which

William S. Clark with his wife Helen and their children at Millfield, probably in the early 1900s. Standing, left to right: Roger, Margaret, John Bright and Alice. Sitting, left to right: Esther, Hilda, William and Helen with Fly the dog.

William was setting off with any great relish and within months the partnership ended.

The issue of C. & J. Clark and retailing would persist for decades. In later years, there were family members who thought the firm should have opened its own shops a lot earlier, others who believed the company was right to stick to doing what it did best – manufacturing shoes. Writing to John Keats in 1898 following the McAfee episode, William told of his fear of upsetting existing outlets where Clarks shoes were sold and his concern about cutting out wholesalers who supplied the retail sector:

> We are not at present prepared to cast all our present business to the winds and follow the example of Manfields and others in starting our own shops. The choice has to be between one and the other as if it got out that we were in any way going into the retail trade our present

The Clarks shoe business began when James Clark started producing sheepskin slippers in the early 1830s from the offcuts of his brother Cyrus's rugs. With Cyrus's support, this new line of slippers, known as 'Brown Petersburgs' or 'Brown Peters' (the slipper above is an accurate later reconstruction), prospered and led to other types of footwear, including lambswool socks. Below is one of the brothers' earliest known showcards for their fledgling range.

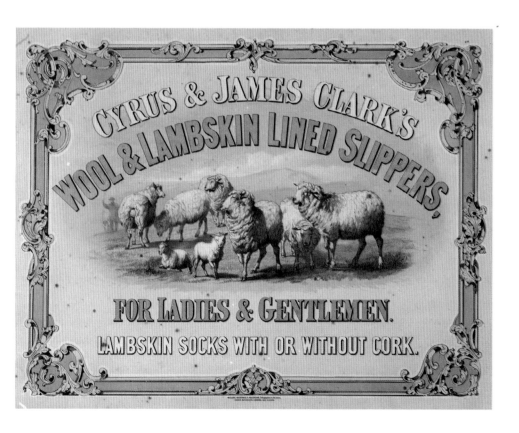

CYRUS & JAMES CLARK'S
WOOL & LAMBSKIN LINED SLIPPERS,
FOR LADIES & GENTLEMEN.
LAMBSKIN SOCKS WITH OR WITHOUT CORK.

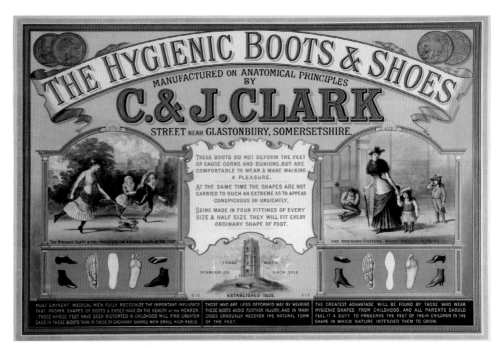

A showcard from the 1880s, proclaiming the healthy and beneficial properties of the Hygienic range – it eventually became the Anatomical range. At the bottom of the card is the iconic image of St Michael's Tower on Glastonbury Tor, which was to become the well-known Tor trademark. The trademark was gradually superseded by the Clarks brand in the 1930s, but it continued to be used on the bottom of shoeboxes until the 1970s, and it still appears on Clarks shoes today.

A 1925 centenary showcard with prominent Tor branding, one of several designed for Clarks in the 1920s by the American-born artist Edward McKnight Kauffer.

Showcards for Tor shoes from 1927 (at right – a design by the Austrian artist Mela Koehler) and 1928 (below – by Freda Beard), showing very different styles of design.

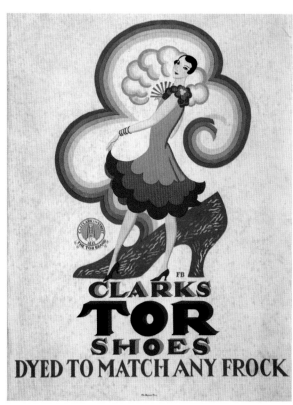

CLARKS
DANCING SANDALS

Mela Koehler's supremely stylish 1929 showcard for the new 'T-bar pump' dancing shoes.

CLARKS SHOES
FOR EASY ELEGANT WALKING

This 1932 showcard features strong and confident Clarks branding, but the longlasting Tor symbol still appears discreetly.

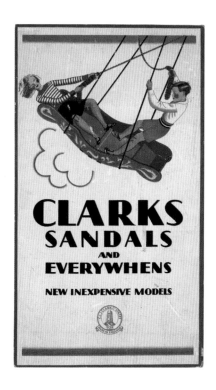

These four showcards for children's shoes (from 1932, 1933, 1934 and 1938) show rapidly changing styles of illustration and of typography for the Clarks name itself: the 1938 card shows an early form of the famous handwritten Clarks logo.

The 1940s saw a determined push by Clarks to associate its shoes with celebrities – particularly glamorous actresses. Many of the photographs were taken by John Hinde, son of the Clarks director Wilfrid Hinde, and great grandson of James Clark, including this 1945 image of Wendy Hiller, who was starring in the Powell and Pressburger film *I Know Where I'm Going*. Here she wears a pair of Prestwick lace-up shoes.

Wendy Hiller is the heroine of the new Archers film " I Know Where I'm Going," which has been written, produced and directed by Michael Powell and Emeric Pressburger. This picture was taken at Denham Studios by John Hinde during the making of the film, and shows Miss Hiller wearing Clarks Prestwick Lace Shoes.

MADE BY C. & J. CLARK, LTD. (WHOLESALE ONLY) STREET SOMERSET and by Clarks (Ireland) Ltd, Dundalk.

Photographer John Hinde uses the magnificent facade of Wells Cathedral as a backcloth to lovely Greta Gynt—latest star discovered by Two Cities films— Miss Gynt herself has discovered Clarks latest wood-soled sandals —the finishing touch to a carefree summer outfit.

Made by C. & J. CLARK, LTD. (wholesale only) and by Clarks (Ireland) Ltd., Dundalk.

Actress Greta Gynt, photographed wearing wood-soled sandals in 1945 by John Hinde. In the background is Wells Cathedral, near the Clarks home town of Street.

Margaret Lockwood, star of many successful films of the 1940s, was invited to tour the Clarks factory at Street with her daughter Toots in 1946. She is seen here with Toots in costume for her 1946 film of Daphne du Maurier's *Hungry Hill*. Clarks recreated period shoes for the film.

Anna Neagle, who starred in a stage adaptation of Jane Austen's *Emma* in 1945, photographed in costume by John Hinde. The advertisement notes that she wears a replica of a fashionable Clarks shoe of the period, and includes an image of the 1845 original.

A 1951 showcard for the classic Clarks footgauge. Many years later, Bancroft Clark, chairman of Clarks for 25 years and a major figure in the company's history, said that the footgauge was the idea on which 'the vast expansion in our children's business was founded'.

This 1953 showcard emphasises the crucial importance of offering a comfortable and correct fit – the cornerstone of Clarks marketing for nearly 200 years.

accounts would be closed. There is so much jealousy of these multiple shops.

George Barry Sutton wrote in *C. & J. Clark, 1833–1903: A History of Shoemaking* that the board wanted 'time to see which way the cat would jump' when it came to going down the retail path. The company was not alone in this. Most UK shoemakers operated in a similar way, selling via wholesalers or specialist shops. It was from foreign competition that the main threat came, with the Americans, in particular, making shoes and then selling them in Britain through specially opened shops.

In the same letter to Keats, William seemed to suggest that he was growing weary of the day-to-day stresses of running C. & J. Clark:

> There is also the feeling as far as I am personally concerned, that I want as soon as I can see the chance, to get out of business altogether – as I have told you before I have done my share and now I am nearly 60 I want to get free and not to launch out in fresh extension and development.

In fact, he did not relinquish the reins of responsibility for a further 27 years, remaining chairman until 1925, by which time his arthritis had confined him to a wheelchair.

Responding to the new demands of fashion required nerve. The company produced a poster in 1905 that originated from America, showing an attractive women looking at herself in a full-length mirror. Dressed to impress, she was seen lifting up her long skirt and admiring her shoes, replete with high heels and pointed toes. This promotion for Clarks 'Dainty' shoes was successful in America, but was regarded as too risqué for the British market, although it was later pressed into service in Australia and the Far East.

Tapping into the American way of doing things took on a fresh impetus when John Walter Bostock joined the company in 1908. Bostock, who was born in 1873, came from Staffordshire. The Bostocks originally were from Heage, Derbyshire, moving to Stamford and then Northampton.

Public procession to mark the opening of the Street waterworks, heading
along the High Street and past Crispin Hall on 18 June 1904.

Their connections with the shoe industry were even older than that of
the Clarks. In 1759, Walter's great-grandfather, William Bostock, was
apprenticed to a shoemaker and it was his son, Thomas, who in 1814 set
up a small business designing and making uppers, which he sent on to
outworkers for them to attach the soles.

Thomas Bostock had three sons, who went into partnership in 1840,
naming the company Thomas Bostock & Sons, of which Lotus Ltd became
a subsidiary in 1903. Lotus is today part of the Jacobson Group, whose
brands include Gola, Ravel and Dunlop. In 1904, at the age of 31, John
Walter Bostock, a grandson of Thomas, went to Boston, Massachusetts, to
open up an agency selling, among other things, leather for uppers, and C.
& J. Clark became one of his main customers.

Bostock was a moderniser. Throughout his career, he resisted the forces
of conservatism and was credited with an 'exhaustive knowledge of the

Frank Clark (at steering wheel) and Harry Bostock in a De Dion motor car, 1906. Harry Bostock was at this time the Clarks agent for New Zealand, and was instrumental in introducing his cousin, John Walter Bostock, to Clarks.

shoemaker's craft ... inventive brain, lively imagination and unswerving determination to succeed,' according to *Clarks of Street, 1825–1950.*

Bostock made a brief trip to Street in 1907 to show the management his glacé kid and upper leathers. 'During this visit we were so impressed by his knowledge that we arranged for him to come over again,' wrote Frank Clark's son Hugh. He came to Street a second time in July 1908 and within a year had accepted a permanent job as production superintendent. This put him in charge of the pattern cutting, upper cuttings, closing, making, finishing, production of new lasts and sampling. A big brief, in other words. He was the first non-family member to occupy such a senior managerial role and went on to become a director in 1928, only retiring in 1946.

Company documents show that Bostock was given considerable authority and that he exercised it without threatening those who had come into the business by virtue of bearing the Clark name. His remuneration in 1909 amounted to a fixed salary of £750, plus 10 per cent of all profits above £8,000. A further 5 per cent would be added to profits between £12,000 and £16,000, and an additional 10 per cent on profits in excess of £20,000 a year.

Many of his responsibilities impinged on departments headed by members of the Clark family, but it was with Hugh Clark, Frank's son, that he forged particularly strong links. Hugh had joined the company through the traditional route. After completing his education at Bootham and Leighton Park, a Quaker boarding school on the outskirts of Reading, he embarked on a four-year apprenticeship in 1904 at the age of seventeen. But finding a role for him was difficult, judging from a letter he received from his uncle, William, in June 1908 that spoke of securing:

> ... a more definite opening ... to give ... the opportunity of being of some real service in the business after ... rather wearisome years of preparation for it.

In fact, Hugh went on to occupy a number of senior positions, while also serving as a captain in the First World War, during which he was awarded the Military Cross for evacuating a French town under enemy fire. His first main role at C. & J. Clark was overseeing the building, engineering and electricians department. Later, he succeeded John Bright Clark as head of sales and was influential in the company's first forays into retailing.

Another influential figure singled out for high office was Wilfrid George Hinde, who was thirteen years older than Bostock and a grandson of James Clark. Hinde joined the firm in 1910 to work under John Bright Clark in the costings department and had special responsibilities for developing the 'factory system'. To this end, he was sent in 1912 to America, where he visited several shoe factories including J. Edwards & Company in Philadelphia, which specialised in high-grade children's shoes. This factory was managed by a man called Parrott, who happened to come from Somerset and was only too pleased to share his carefully defined work practices with young Hinde.

Parrott had made factory systems his hobby and was renowned for his

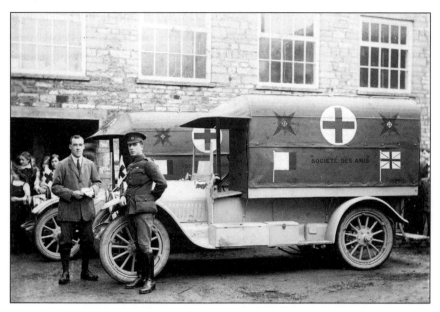

Hugh Clark (at left) at the Friends' Ambulance Unit in 1915, with his
father Frank Clark's Bianchi after conversion into an ambulance.

production timetables, which Hinde then adapted for use at Street. This
marked a new departure for the company. Until then, orders went through
the factory in rotation, but there was no daily or weekly timetable for each
department. When it came to costings, Hinde was meticulous. On one
occasion he was even keen to know how much money had been spent
repairing Frank Clark's Daimler, prompting Frank to remind him that any
work on the car was entirely due to it being used to transport customers to
and from Glastonbury train station.

Hinde, whose brother Karl also worked at C. & J. Clark, was seen as a
man of many talents. In addition to costings and factory systems, he was
instrumental in introducing 'standard lines', which in the 1920s would
lead to the first mass production of shoes – footwear using high-quality
materials but not requiring so many man-hours. Hinde also saw the value
of advertising, eventually working on C. & J. Clark's first campaign devised
by the Arundel Advertising Company.

Like Bostock, Hinde – who had spent time in prison as a conscientious objector in 1916 – was appointed a director in 1928 and remained with the company until 1947. Non-family members found it hard to reach such exalted positions. Richard Wallis Littleboy, who hailed from Birmingham, was one exception. He joined in 1904 and was put in charge of accounts, but was soon given additional responsibilities, not least the organisation of salaried staff. It was not long before he was a signatory on company cheques and he, too, was given a percentage share of profits.

Bostock was keen for other non-family members to secure similar promotions, but there was often resistance. In May 1911, he pushed for a man called William Wells to be made manager of the Machine Room, but the minutes of a directors' meeting noted that while there were:

> ... great advantages in giving promotion to those who have grown up in the Factory ... grave doubts [existed] as to whether he [Wells] has sufficient tact and organising power to handle a department containing 300 women and girls.

So Hugh Clark was given the job instead and Wells became his foreman.

The company was proud of its American influences. The 1906 Tor Shoes Catalogue trumpeted:

> ... the newest and best, the lasts and patterns having been perfected in the United States by the highest American skill procurable for money, care having been taken that the shapes should be exactly adapted to the requirements of our market.

But there were dissenting voices within Clarks about the speed of change and the pursuit of style, especially when it came to breaking into the fashionable London market.

One of the problems in London was that as a sales territory it was split between the regions – the Midlands, the South East and even the North – and served by dedicated travelling salesmen, who worked for a straight salary, plus expenses, and who were offered bonuses in good years. The travelling salesmen were held in high esteem, but there was disagreement between them and the board over commission. 'We do not work any of our home grounds by giving commission – we do not think it a satisfactory arrangement', said a 1908 directors' minute.

A year earlier, John Angell Peck, who had been so successful as an agent in Australia, was invited to Street to 'supervise the travellers', although the board noted that he was not enamoured of the prospect. Peck, keen for Clarks shoes to become more fashionable, insisted on setting up a dedicated showroom in London, and by January 1908 he found the premises he was looking for in Shaftesbury Avenue, on the corner of Soho's Dean Street. It would cost £130 a year in rent.

'When in London be sure to call at our Office and Showroom' said a leaflet sent to wholesalers, with a complicated map printed on it. Peck himself did not stay in London long, returning to Australia less than two years later. He was replaced by John Downes, a former buyer from Jones & Higgins, the noted department store on Peckham High Street, which had opened in 1867. Downes was offered a salary of £250 per annum, with commission of 1 per cent on any increase in turnover. The commission floodgates had opened and it was to prove a lucrative pool for all concerned, so lucrative in fact that in 1918 the board wanted to cap earnings, noting that some travellers were making more 'than any director of the company has ever drawn'.

Agents overseas, however, were enjoying mixed fortunes. Results in South Africa continued to be encouraging, with trade reaching £48,000 in 1910, compared with £28,052 in 1895, but South America proved more taxing. Peck travelled to Buenos Aires to discuss trade with Clarks' representative, Alex Zoccola, but the situation there was not helped when a partner of Zoccola's absconded with money. At one point, in 1911, the board noted that 'after many thefts – unreasonable claims – and difficulties in turning out the right stuff ... [it was decided] a mistake was made in ever going into it'. In fact, Clarks persisted in South America, as it did elsewhere, even sending a senior agent to Russia and Siberia to explore potential new markets.

The French were proving tricky. Or, rather, it was proving difficult to produce shoes that the French were willing to buy. Edmund Skepper became C. & J. Clark's agent in France and he was supplied with specially designed samples to entice retailers. An advertising campaign was launched, talking up the Clark name and pushing the Tor brand, but at a managers' meeting in 1911 there was concern about 'future trouble with other houses if we made a big success of the [French] advertising'. Those concerns cannot have been too great because a year later Skepper received new lines worth £1,500, with a further £1,500 of stock heading his way.

At first, sales in France picked up, but then Skepper asked if his retailers could be given 30 per cent discounts, with an extra 2 per cent on orders of more than three dozen pairs. By 13 July 1913, the board was told that Skepper 'reluctantly came to the conclusion he could not make a success of it'.

Elsewhere in Europe, agencies in Germany and Switzerland were increasing their turnovers and the market in Finland was growing. New agents were sought for Austria, Belgium and Holland, and, further afield, Joseph Law, who would later head Clarks' operations in India and the Far East, was sent to Burma (now Myanmar), Ceylon (now Sri Lanka), Java, India, Siam (now Thailand) and Sumatra.

Shortly before the First World War, *The Economist* published an article entitled 'The Victory of British Boots', in which it took British shoemakers to task:

> It was a surprising number of years before our makers woke up to the necessity of bestirring themselves ... they found that the secret of Yankee success lay entirely in style and finish, and on returning they set to work to imitate their competitors in those respects ... the significant fact should not be lost sight of that the great bulk of the improvement has occurred in the last five years, and when it is borne in mind that for 1912 the exports were worth very nearly 4 millions sterling, some conception can be formed of the splendid possibilities before the trade in the immediate future.

A parade in support of women's suffrage outside Crispin Hall, Street, in 1913. Alice Clark, one of only a small number of women to reach a managerial position in industry at the time, was an active campaigner for the women's suffrage movement.

The war would take its toll in Street. Unlike shoe manufacturers in Northampton and Leicester, C. & J. Clark failed to gain a share of government orders for soldiers' boots. Overseas sales suffered badly to the extent that by the end of the war – when C. & J Clark was producing a million pairs of shoes – a mere 100,000 of these were destined for export and it took nearly three decades for exports to double, reaching 200,000 pairs only in 1947. Overall, total volume sales fell dramatically from a 1914 peak of 1,013,000 to 541,000 in 1921.

William S. Clark remained chairman during the war years, but the two joint managing directors – his brother, Frank, and his eldest son, John Bright – took increasing charge. Meanwhile, Roger, William's second son, became the company secretary and Alice, William's daughter, was responsible for Personnel Management and the Closing Room.

Semi-retirement for William was filled with onerous duties outside the factory. From 1878 to 1922, he served continuously as a member of the Local Authority, sixteen of those years on the Local Board and 28 on the Urban District Council. And most of that time, he was chairman of both

William Sessions, an outworker in Street, photographed at work around 1917.

bodies, only relinquishing his post at the age of 83. On standing down from the council, he was praised for his enduring sense of duty. The citation read:

> We are grateful for all the recollections that we cherish of your public spirit, unfailing courtesy and kindness ... We remember your fearless advocacy of all you believed to be true and right. You never sought a fleeting popularity by disguising your principles, you gave freely and fully of your experience, and the fruit of your sound judgment and keen business acumen to the moulding and fashioning of the life and character of the Institutions of Street.

William had been a Justice of the Peace, president of the Glastonbury and Street branch of the British and Foreign Bible Society, treasurer of the Western Temperance League, Fellow of the Royal Meteorological Society, long-time member of the Somerset Archeological Society (now

A Dennis lorry used for transporting goods around the factory site and for regular runs as a charabanc to Glastonbury railway station, seen outside the main entrance to the Street factory around 1920.

the Somerset Archaeological and Natural History Society) and a governor of various schools. He had also developed a passion for poetry. Edmund Spenser's *Faerie Queene*, the first volume of which was published in 1590, was a particular favourite. He carried many of its verses in his head and used to recite them to his children when they were young.

William was regarded as a good communicator. Doubtless he would have approved of the formation, in 1919, of a Factory Committee or Factory Council or Works Council, as it variously was called. This in-house council comprised a combination of workers and management and its aim was to deal with grievances and consider any suggestions from the factory floor. In particular, it would come into its own during the depression years of the 1920s and 1930s, when work-sharing was introduced to avoid widespread unemployment. Further support for employees came in the form of clubs, such as the Street Shoemakers' Benefit Society, Street Women's

Interior of the library, designed by Samuel Thompson Clothier and paid for
by the Clark family, built in Street in 1924 and seen here in 1949.

Benefit Society and Street Women's Club. These organisations joined forces
in 1913 to become the Street Shoemakers' Provident Benefit Society, which
led to the founding in 1918 of a C. J. C. Savings Bank, which used its surplus
(profit) to make payments to members who were sick or retired.

Several years later in 1924, C. & J. Clark began circulating its *Monthly
News Sheet* as a means of communicating directly with the workforce. The
first issue, in August, made a point of stressing that the publication had
come about at 'the request of the new factory committee' and that it would
include 'items of news likely to be of general interest to those working in
the factory'.

That same year, a new library in Street, funded entirely by C. & J. Clark
and designed by William S. Clark's son-in-law, Samuel Thompson Clothier
(known as Tom), who designed many civic buildings in Street, was officially opened by Charles Trevelyan MP, who had recently been appointed
President of the Board of Education by Ramsay Macdonald, the prime

Alice Clark as a young woman in 1895.

minister who led the Independent Labour Party to victory in the 1924 General Election.

One of the loudest voices in favour of better worker welfare was that of William's daughter, Alice Clark. In 1914, she played a key role in setting up the Day Continuation School in Street, to which the company contributed half the costs. The school was intended expressly for boys and girls who had abandoned their education at the age of fourteen to work in the factory. Pupils would attend one morning and one afternoon a week. Alice, a resolute feminist, was thrilled at the prospect of young girls attending continuation school. She had been present, aged seventeen, at the formation of the Street Women's Liberal Association and served as its secretary for eleven years. She sat on the executive of the Union of Suffrage Societies, which meant she spent a lot of time in London meeting and cajoling MPs, for which she had the full support of her family and fellow board members in Street. Alice also served as chairman of the committee responsible for Quaker relief work in Austria at the end of the First World War.

At a meeting of the directors of C. & J. Clark in 1914, it was agreed that 'the possibility of arranging to let out children from 14 to 16 or 17 during Factory hours to attend classes was ... discussed and felt to be desirable'. This was conducted on an ad hoc basis, particularly during the First World War, when:

> ... it had sometimes been necessary to keep one or two away from the afternoon school, labour shortages prompting the suggestion that Mr Alexander the School Master might, weed out ... some of the older ones, especially any who do not care about school, or who are troublesome in discipline.

But sanctioning boys and girls to miss school was not something the board wished to encourage. It 'should not be a precedent to be resorted to easily again,' it concluded.

After the war, weekly attendance was increased to eight hours, or two half days per week for each pupil. This was in sharp contrast to what was happening nationally, despite the Education Act of 1918, which raised the school leaving age from twelve to fourteen and offered some form of continuation classes. In reality, many authorities, short of cash, were cutting back on education, leaving continuation schools solely in the hands of private companies. In 1921, a full-time qualified headmistress named Annie Bent was appointed to the Strode Day Continuation School, as the school had then become, and she was joined four years later in 1925 by a headmaster called William Boyd Henderson, known as Boyd Henderson.

Marvelling over the circumstances contributing to his employment, Boyd Henderson referred to there being:

> ... no advertising; no scanning of testimonials; no interview with the Governors. The fact that I was Millicent Falk's [a mutual friend of Henderson and Alice Clark] cousin seemed to be all the testimonial that was needed, and on that recommendation I was appointed.

In fact, Alice had been instrumental in the choosing of Boyd Henderson, believing that he shared many of her ideas and that he would embrace the school's liberal ethos.

His arrival was accompanied in 1926 by the adoption of the half-time system of twenty hours per week, which meant that if two children shared a job, one would be working in the factory while the other went to school. Pupils included workers from Clark, Son & Morland after 1926, in addition to those employed by C. & J. Clark.

As Roger Clark wrote in the foreword of William Boyd Henderson's *Strode School*, a short history of the school:

It was always the aim of W. S. Clark, of Alice Clark and of those following them that the school should never be a mere technical adjunct of the Factory, but rather that the children who left school at fourteen to enter the Factory should acquire a richer mental background, a wider culture, such as would serve through life to stimulate the intellectual powers and an interest in things worthwhile.

Henderson himself was passionate about the school's mission:

They [the pupils] are engaged in industry but yet they are continuing their education. But there is more than that. Entry in industrial life at whatever age it takes place is a revolutionary change in the lives of boys and girls. Previously they have been at a whole-time school mixing with companions of their own age. Now they are in a factory mixing with men and women. Previously they have been dependent on their parents for pocket money. Now they are wage earners whose pay packet makes a considerable difference to the weekly family budget.

Alice Clark's interest in what her brother Roger called 'things worthwhile' included writing a book, published in 1919, entitled *Working Life of Women in the Seventeenth Century*, which is still highly regarded today and was the subject of a discussion on BBC Radio 4 *Woman's Hour* in 1998. It was based on the premise that British women, especially those from the middle and upper classes, were more independent and therefore more liberated in the seventeenth century than they were in the nineteenth.

It was while working on her book that Alice was awarded the Mrs Bernard Shaw Scholarship to study at the London School of Economics. When she returned from London to Street in January 1922, she threw herself into her job, making the personnel management department a model for everything she felt important about factory life. She organised a system of records for each employee to ensure they were in the right job and adequately fulfilled in what they were doing. She checked the earnings of each worker and played a key role in setting up a company pension plan, with a trust to protect it. The pension scheme was launched in 1926 with £15,000 assigned for this purpose, with a further £10,000 added shortly afterwards. Over the next twenty years the capital would exceed £100,000.

Alice was absent from C. & J. Clark for long periods due to illness, a legacy of her childhood tuberculosis, and she became an increasingly ardent supporter of the Christian Science movement. 'The problem of evil, which the War had made more terrible than ever, was lying on her mind; and there was also her personal trouble of being several times disabled by illness' wrote her sister, Margaret Clark Gillett, in a special obituary pamphlet published by Oxford University Press shortly after Alice died.

> On both these lines she came to find an explanation which satisfied her in the doctrine of the Christian Science Church. The doctrine helped her; she felt herself liberated; she gained the experience of rising over what was threatening to conquer her. Thus she was enabled to bring light and courage to many others.

The article also sought to sum up Alice's thinking about the dispersal of company profits:

> She came to feel more and more strongly that a business should be run and profits apportioned for the benefit of all concerned in it. She saw that this would involve a limit being set to the rate of interest paid to shareholders on their capital, and she realised that there would be

Greenbank Pool, built at the wish of Alice Clark and paid for from her estate, primarily for the benefit of female bathers, seen here from the roof of the new post office on Whit Sunday, 1963.

great difficulty in rendering such a limitation effective, but she believed that a solution of this difficulty is essential if we are to find our way to juster [*sic*] social order.

Towards the end of her life, Alice resigned her Quaker membership, but she was often heard to declare how she 'could not swallow Mary Baker Eddy [founder of the Christian Scientists] whole'. Family members were sorry to learn of her religious defection, but Roger remained in awe of his sister's personality. In a letter to his mother-in-law, Emma Bancroft, in January 1927, he spoke of Alice's 'sweetness and calm', adding:

I don't know just what Christian Science can do for the body, but if it deserves any of the credit for Alice's spiritual poise and character it must have something in it ...

When Alice died at the age of 60, on 11 May 1934, she left a legacy to her youngest sister, Hilda, and also expressed a wish that a swimming pool be built in Street, primarily to be used by women and young girls, who were loathe to join their male counterparts bathing in the river, often naked. She set aside a gift of £5,000 for this purpose. Hilda fulfilled her sister's wish and the pool opened for business on 1 May 1937, attracting more than 36,000 people in its first summer. The annual subscription was 2*s*. for those over nineteen and 1*s*. for those under nineteen, with an entrance fee ranging from 2*d*. to 6*d*. a visit. It became known as Greenbank Pool, after the Clark family home of the same name, and remains a popular outdoor pool and public space today.

The Roaring Twenties heralded a new dawn for luxury and fashion goods, but among the majority of consumers there was no great appetite for spending hard-earned money on everyday shoes, even when the quality was high. The management of C. & J. Clark was only too aware of the problem, but not entirely sure how to remedy it.

John Bright Clark was open with the workers about what he saw as some of the pressing issues facing the new generation of management. Writing in the first issue of the *Monthly News Sheet* in August 1924, he said C. & J. Clark was proud of its high-quality Tor brands, but:

> ... unfortunately there is a limit to the demand for goods of the Tor brand standard in this country, and it must take a long time for it to increase enough to cover our capacity for output. The management are considering the possibility of introducing a cheaper grade of ladies' shoe to meet the public demand.

He went on to highlight the downside of this strategy and then did his best to end on an optimistic note:

A postcard showing factory workers arriving at the Street factory main entrance in 1925.

Competition for these lower grades is very keen and it may prove impossible to meet it in a factory burdened with the costs necessary for the present high grade of production. The management are exploring every possibility of reducing costs by mass-production and other ways, so as to secure some large business on these lines, but they cannot as yet say whether their efforts will be successful. It is not proposed to make any lines that will not do us credit or give reasonable satisfaction, but care will have to be taken to keep them distinct from existing lines, so that business done on them may be extra and not in the place of what we might otherwise be doing. For this reason, these lines will not carry the Tor brand trade mark and we shall endeavour to keep the design distinct and use different grades of upper material.

Trepidation was in the air. And, as if to compound the anxiety, William S. Clark had a massive heart attack in August 1925, from which he would never recover. Unable to walk more than one or two steps without help, he spent the last months of his life in bed or in an armchair. On the morning of 20 November 1925, he appeared more engaged than he had been for several days, asking his son, Roger, for details of the new Club and Institute Committee, of which William had been re-elected president the day before. He was also keen to know of any developments at the latest meeting of the Western Temperance League Executive.

William died later that morning in what was the centenary year of the founding of C. & J. Clark. He was 86. A flag was run up a pole on top of the clock tower at the factory and flown at half mast. The announcement about his funeral, scheduled for three days later, included two verses from Spenser's *Faerie Queene*, beginning with William's favourite opening line: 'And is there care in Heaven?' His widow, Helen, who followed the cortège in a wheelchair, wanted a band to lead the procession, but not just any band. She chose the local Street Prize Band, which played Chopin's 'Funeral March'.

The turn-out in honour of the man described by the *Central Somerset Gazette* as 'the father of the town' was like nothing seen before in Street – or since. One published account said:

> The usually busy village was full of silent waiting crowds, no throb of engines from the factory, shops shut, blinds drawn, men, women and children waited in the slant November sunshine as if for a royal procession.

Roger Clark wrote how it was:

> ... a grey soft afternoon with gleams of sun and the music quite extraordinarily beautiful and moving and it had a wonderful uniting effect on all that long procession – of which one could not at any time see the end.

The service was held at the Society of Friends' meeting house at 3 pm and he was laid to rest in the burial ground beneath the boughs of a huge cedar tree, his grave framed by white chrysanthemums and roses. As his oak coffin – with several wreaths on top of it, including one from the Factory Council – was lowered into the ground, the hymn 'Abide With Me' was sung.

From there, the band struck up once more, playing Beethoven's Funeral March, and the crowd made its way to Crispin Hall, where a thousand people managed to squeeze into the main hall, with many others waiting outside. Dr Henry Gillett, a cousin from Oxford, explained that the service would follow Quaker traditions: 'At a time like this when a Friend is missed from among us we recognise that there is strength in silence, communion of sympathy, deeper than words.'

But there were words. Speaker after speaker testified to William's great strengths, the manner in which he had saved C. & J Clark and how he had built an entire town around the family business. Before the singing of 'O God, Our Help in Ages Past', John Morland, who was 88, rose to his feet. He was William's brother-in-law and a lifelong friend from their school days. The room fell silent as he prepared his words.

A life such as we have known is one of the best witnesses for resurrection to immortal life that we can have. It is impossible for those who loved him and saw what he did to believe that such a life can pass away into nothingness.

6

We were now in retailing good and proper

HEMLINES WERE RISING, but production was falling. At one point, in December 1926, shortly after William's death, the machine room in Street was so quiet that the company accepted an order from Fox Brothers of Wellington for 5,000 pairs of gaiters, a move described by Kenneth Hudson in *Towards Precision Shoemaking* as 'rather in the spirit of a manufacturer of aeroplanes agreeing to make scooters'.

This must have concentrated minds, because a year later the new chairman, Frank (William's brother), and the board announced a significant change of policy. Whereas John Bright Clark only three years earlier had said that the way forward in the mass market was to drop the Tor name, now he maintained that the Tor branding should be reinstated:

> ... otherwise we should rapidly come to the position where the majority of our shoes went out without our name on them. We should thus lose the goodwill attached to the name of Clarks that we have spent so many years in building up.

He was, however, quick to stress that:

> ... we still attempt to make them with the care and attention to individual differences which we give to our high-priced shoes ... it is more

and more necessary to get out striking and novel designs at fairly frequent intervals throughout the year, if we are to pick up every scrap of trade that may come our way.

Whatever business you were in, picking up trade was a shared national burden. The 1926 General Strike, called by the Trade Union Congress (TUC) in support of miners who were fighting to protect their jobs, wages and working hours, cast a shadow across the whole country. Fortunately, members of the National Union of Boot and Shoe Operatives (NUBSO) were not asked to join the strike and even if they had been there was no certainty they would have fallen into line. The official NUBSO history refers repeatedly to cooperation between management and workers rather than conflict. As Spencer Crookenden recorded in *K Shoes: The First 150 Years, 1842–1992*:

> The leading figures of the employers' side were not remote from the productive process; they were in active control of their own businesses and closely in touch, through their conciliation and arbitration activities on local boards, with the routine technical details of their industry.

The economic downturn that followed the general strike, culminating in the Great Depression sparked off by the Wall Street Crash in 1929, would prove long and deep. Economists today are still divided over who was responsible for what and whether the US government could have done more to avoid the catastrophe. One view, to which many Quakers would have subscribed, was that it represented a systemic failure of free market capitalism.

Regions such as South Wales that were dependent on heavy industry suffered greatly, certainly more than areas that relied on new technologies. The car industry, for example, boomed in the 1930s and Britain's much discussed north/south divide began to loom large. Generally, anything to do with modernisation (construction, electronics, transport) found itself in the fast lane, while traditional industries (textiles, steel, shipping, coal) were left to languish on the economic hard shoulder. Exports of shoes made in Britain had reached 17.5 million pairs in 1913, but fell to 12 million in 1924, dropping to 4.5 million in 1935.

C. & J. Clark responded to the recession with a bullish resolve. 'We do not consider that our position is sound if we are only maintaining past years' sales,' said John Bright Clark in 1927. This was bold at a time when many other manufacturing companies were extremely happy if they were able to do just that. At C. & J. Clark, pride in the product and a reasonably contented workforce always had to be factored into any shift of strategy. William S. Clark had established a strongly patriarchal, paternal tradition, something that would filter down through successive generations and which still largely exists today. The idea of looking after your employees and your employees responding accordingly was not merely an aspiration at C. & J. Clark.

Quality was taken seriously too, but the company had to adapt to the times and innovate. John Walter Bostock, the production 'moderniser' with strong American links who had been hired by the business in 1908, was determined not to compromise in the face of competition from rival shoe-makers, particularly those in East London who were churning out foot-wear at prices and speeds that were unrealistic for a structured company such as C. & J. Clark. In the early 1930s, it took nearly four weeks to get a pair of shoes through the factory in Street, whereas in some London sweatshops it could be done in eight days.

Bostock had visited retailers in London who stocked Clarks shoes, and was not always happy with what he heard. The proprietor of one West End store complained bitterly of a slip in standards of shoes produced in Street, prompting Bostock to give the Factory Council chapter and verse on what he had been told during his travels in the capital.

He [the shop owner] brought out ten pairs of shoes which certainly should never have left the factory. There were two pairs of black crepe-de-chine machine-sewn courts on which the narrow galloon binding had in one or two cases broken away because the stitching had not caught; then there were two pairs with damaged heels – in one the attaching nail could be seen protruding through the heel cover, whilst in the other, one of the top-piece rivets had cracked the heel; there were several pairs of satin turnshoes and one pair of gold kid on which the toes had blistered badly.

Through the council, Bostock reminded everyone how London-based operations were undercutting traditional manufacturers and warned that in Street there had been:

... much petty negligence throughout the factory ... in these days of increasingly keen competition and bad trade, these serious defects in our shoes will very rapidly tell on the amount of business we obtain.

No one doubted Bostock's expertise and influence. And his position in the company concentrated minds over the issue of non-family members occupying, or not occupying, senior positions. When a Clark cousin, Antony Walter Gillett, joined the firm in 1930, John Bright Clark felt it fitting to write an article in the *Monthly News Sheet*, entitled 'Family Business or Not', in which he said that although C. & J. Clark:

... may usually be considered a family business, no one can expect to obtain or to hold, through family interest, a place for which he is not fully competent. In a choice between two equal men, the family interest would undoubtedly have preference. But there can be no favouritism. In the years to come, the most important places at the top of the tree will be open to anyone having the necessary qualifications and with the power, energy and initiative to work up to them.

Bostock was living proof of this new egalitarianism. He brought to C. & J. Clark a shoemaker's craft, a keen, lively and stubborn intelligence, and a knowledge of American techniques. As recorded in *Clarks of Street, 1825–1950*:

He learned Clarks shoemaking as he created it, and he absorbed the old hand craft which he found in Street and turned it to new use. Besides the shoemaking craft, he brought into the Street circle an ardent Toryism, with blue ribbons at election times on his horse and dog-cart, which added variety of colour to the consistent Liberalism of the Clarks.

Never mind his politics, Bostock's emphasis on producing quality footwear was met largely with approval by the workforce. The desire not to be part of the shoemaking herd also went down well in Street. On one occasion, both the president and secretary of the Factory Council visited the annual Shoe and Leather Fair in London and commented scathingly about the inferior quality and cheaper prices of competitors. On their return, some members of the council wanted to know why C. & J. Clark was not formally represented at the trade fair, receiving the answer from the Factory Council secretary that 'we could only get some little hole-in-the-corner place that was scarcely suitable to our position in the shoe trade, so we abandoned the attempt'. A further justification was issued: 'Those who have visited the Fair will easily imagine that a week in the thick atmosphere one finds there must be exceedingly bad for the health.'

But perhaps it would have been good for business. Sales of C. & J. Clark's 'cheaper' Tor-branded shoes were not doing as well as expected in 1927. With unemployment rising, consumers were not only price-conscious but value-conscious. Their buying habits indicated that they regarded C. & J. Clark's unbranded mass-production lines as offering better value than the company's cheaper Tor lines. As a result, in October 1927, it was decided to launch 'Wessex Shoes' as the umbrella brand for those mass-produced lines not carrying the Tor name. Even in the all-important children's trade, travellers were reporting back to Street that a cheaper line was urgently needed. An upturn in sales was the much-needed result, but this was offset by rising costs. For example, between July 1927 and January 1928, the price of sole leather increased by 50 per cent.

Women, meanwhile, were beginning to enjoy themselves like never before.

They could vote and smoke in public, and dancing became something of a craze both in America and Britain, opening up a new fashion front. This led to demand for what was called a 'T-bar pump' with a sturdy, medium heel – the 'T' over the instep often made in a contrasting colour or fabric. This was a party shoe. And partying meant dancing. The Austrian artist Mela Koehler designed a showcard for C. & J. Clark's range of dancing shoes. It portrayed three young girls sitting out a dance, dressed impeccably, fanning themselves. They were all wearing the same dancing shoes, with pretty ankle straps made of wispy ribbon.

Howard Carter's discovery of Tutankhamun's tomb in 1922 provided yet more inspiration for shoe designers. The French shoemaker François Pinet created an intricate Egyptian-style brocade court shoe with jewelled heel, while gold shoes inspired by Tutankhamun's casket gained favour with more adventurous women.

The Art Deco movement, which took its name from the 1925 Exposition Internationale des Arts Décoratifs Industriels et Modernes, held in Paris, rejected the elaborate, the fussy and the dour and celebrated a crisp and colourful modern world. A 1928 advertisement for Varese showed a smiling young woman with a kiss curl on her forehead, holding up a sleek, shiny court-style shoe with ankle strap.

The birth of celebrity, delivered by the cinematic 'talkies', sprinkled shoes with extra Hollywood sparkle, and one all-encompassing fashion trend was the advance of the rounded toe in contrast to the pointed toe. In addition, two-tone shoes made of leather and fabric were worn and endorsed by, among others, Greta Garbo, Norma Shearer and Marlene Dietrich. Celebrity endorsements were to become commonplace at Clarks.

Frank Clark had taken over as chairman of C. & J. Clark Ltd following his brother William's death, with John Bright Clark and Roger Clark as joint vice chairmen and sharing the role of managing director. John Bright had been a long-time member of the Boot & Shoe Manufacturers'

Federation and became its president in 1929, just as negotiations with the National Union of Boot and Shoe Operatives were reaching a delicate stage over planned wage reductions and the introduction of the 46-hour week.

A keen fisherman with a great love of horses, dogs and for enlarging the scope of people's thinking, he was good at finding the balance between tact and getting his point across. As described in *Clarks of Street, 1825–1950*:

> His anxiety for justice and his sympathy with opposing points of view gave him a very special influence for conciliation ....These were critical days and things were to become worse, with unemployment rife, shipping lying idle round our coasts, the balancing of the national budget an anxious problem. At such a time, John Bright Clark's qualities of mind and heart were of special value.

He could be steely, too. In 1933, C. & J. Clark decided not to close the factory on Good Friday. This sparked a letter of complaint from the local rector, the Reverend Buckingham, and two of his clergy colleagues, who argued that such a move 'is calculated to do irreparable harm to the cause of Christ, not only here but further afield as well'.

John Bright Clark replied:

> We always make it clear that no obstacle shall be placed in the way of any persons in our employment who wish to leave work to attend religious service, and our feeling was that this met the views of those who wished to observe the day in a religious manner quite as well as the making of it a general holiday. My recollection of being in Catholic countries on Good Friday is that business went on as usual simultaneously with the churches being full.
>
> We are placed in an extremely difficult position at the present time. The recent influenza epidemic disorganised our works and threw us considerably more than a week behind on our estimated output. Orders have been coming in well lately and the present prospect is that, unless a great effort is made, we shall be unable to deliver the goods that are

John Bright Clark in the 1930s.

wanted between Easter and Whitsuntide, and which will not be taken afterwards. This means loss of wages to our workpeople, not only in respect of the goods that will not be made and delivered this spring, but as damaging our prospects for another season. This might not matter so much in normal times, but today, when employment is so precarious, loss of business is a very serious matter, not only for ourselves but for all those who are depending upon us for their livelihood.

I would only say in conclusion that I should be very sorry if anything occurred to mar the pleasant spirit of religious harmony that has been obtained throughout Street lately, but at the same time, we are really in a serious dilemma.

On 6 April 1933, not long after that contentious Easter, John Bright Clark died at the age of 66 while sitting in his brother Roger's office, known as Number One office. Then, fourteen hours later, Tom Clothier, the architect son-in-law of William S. Clark, died from a fatal illness, prompting

John Bright Clark in Number One office at the Clarks headquarters in Street, 1931.

Roger to write in his journal that both men had been 'pillars' in his life. Roger was glum:

> And so the days go by and here is the end of April and tomorrow I shall say it was last month that John and Tom left us – yesterday, last month – and soon it will be last Spring and then last year and oh! what a burden.

Two years on, in 1935, Roger again found himself in mourning, this time for his grandson Giles, the second child of Bancroft, his eldest son. Bancroft had married Cato (Catarina) Smuts in December 1928. She was the daughter of Field Marshal Jan Smuts, whose statue by the sculptor Sir Jacob Epstein stands on a plinth in Parliament Square in London. Giles, their second of seven children, was only two when he died. Then in July, soon after Giles's death, Roger's sister, Esther, also died. Roger wrote:

> The bottom is knocked out of our life here ... I have lived close to her for

Hindhayes Infants School in Street, built in 1928 by Roger and Sarah Clark
in memory of their son Hadwen, who died aged sixteen in 1924.

60 years – 62 – and always consulted and talked over everything and
enjoyed fun together. I feel terribly lonely.

He did not have long to dwell on his misfortune. On 21 November
1935, Roger became chairman of C. & J. Clark on the death of his 85-year-
old uncle Frank. Two months later, Peter T. Clothier, son of Tom Clothier
and Esther Clark (William's eldest daughter), was appointed a director. J.
Anthony (always known as Tony) Clark, who was John Bright Clark's son,
was made a director in April 1936.

In 1935, Clarks took a major stride towards becoming a high-street retailer
when it acquired a business that had been an agent of C. & J. Clark, called
Lane & Robinson, on Whiteladies Road, Bristol. It was agreed to keep the
proprietors on to run the store, mainly because Wilfrid Hinde had got to
know them well. Additionally, in the spring of that year, Hugh Clark, who
was now living in London but was still in charge of sales, negotiated a
lease on Mitre House, at 177 Regent Street, to where the London office and
showroom moved from its premises in Shaftesbury Avenue.

Other shoe manufacturers were moving into retail. K Shoes, Lotus and Norvic were all buying up shops, which meant C. & J. Clark was in danger of losing vital sales outlets. So in December 1935, at the instigation of Hugh Clark, the firm paid £800 to buy Walwyns, a shop in Moseley, a suburb of Birmingham, after it had gone into voluntary liquidation. Reggie Hart, who had joined C. & J. Clark a year earlier, and who would spend the next 30 years with the company, was put in charge of this operation. In addition to the shops in Bristol and Moseley, a third outlet called John Southworth was acquired in Preston, Lancashire, when Frank Jamieson, who sold Clarks footwear in his store, wanted to launch his son in business and sought help from C. & J. Clark.

There were bigger retail fish in the sea at that time and C. & J. Clark was soon circling. In 1937, Abbotts Phitt-Easy Ltd, which owned a chain of shops trading as Abbotts, found itself in trouble after opening too many outlets too quickly. The company had 60 shops, mostly in London, but some were in other towns and even a few overseas, notably in France. Abbotts approached Somervell Brothers, the Kendal-based firm that made K Shoes. The proposition was that Somervell would take over the management of Abbotts and keep it afloat financially while new leases were drawn up and stock sorted out. The shops in Paris would be sold and Somervell given the right to buy a controlling interest in Abbotts if the new arrangement worked successfully.

But Somervell did not want 60 shops and made contact with C. & J. Clark. Vigorous negotiations ensued, culminating in an agreement in June 1937 to split the stores between the two companies on the understanding that C. & J. Clark would not trade under the Abbotts name. Hugh Clark suggested setting up a new company called Lords, which he thought was resonant of England and of quality. The board liked the idea, but thought the name pretentious, and so it was agreed to call it Peter Lord Ltd – with the shops trading under the name Peter Lord – and with Reggie Hart as the new company's first managing director.

Hart had been educated at Bradford Grammar School and gained a classics scholarship to St John's College, Oxford, where he was awarded a Blue in rugby football. On leaving university, he joined a rubber company and targeted C. & J. Clark as a potential buyer of black rubber soles – though it's unclear if he ever made a sale. He then worked as a department sales manager in menswear for Lewis's in Manchester – not to be confused with John Lewis, an entirely different company – before C. & J. Clark recruited him as assistant to the head of sales, Hugh Clark. Hart became an integral part of C. & J. Clark's early days in retail.

Many years later, in the *Clarks Courier*, a newspaper started by the company in 1957, Bancroft Clark wrote:

> He chose the sites, he designed the Peter Lord retail image, he saw to it that Clarks' shoemaking got the benefit of retail advice. R.C.H [Hart] created our retailing system and transmitted back into manufacturing, the knowledge thereby gained. He was an architect and builder of the company's growth in the UK.

Most of the eight Peter Lord shops were in provincial towns, but the head office was at 98 Kensington High Street, in West London. Not trading under the Clarks name was eminently sensible because the company's shoe range was not large enough adequately to stock a whole shop. It also enabled Clarks to continue selling to existing third-party outlets without antagonising their owners. As Bancroft Clark put it:

> The policy direction to Peter Lord was that they would be leading retailers specialising in Clarks shoes, but they were not required to buy any particular Clarks shoes or any prescribed proportion of Clarks shoes, and were to get supplies elsewhere on the market as best seemed to them.

The proportion of sales of Clarks shoes in Peter Lord shops was around 40 per cent at first, rising to 80 per cent in the 1960s. Those sales amounted to £30,000 a year in 1937, reaching a high of £3.5 million in 1965.

'We were now in retailing good and proper with eleven shops,' wrote Bancroft. He continued:

Bancroft Clark with Bert Bridge from the Sole Room in 1943.

The turnover of Clarks shoes disposed of through those eleven shops was about 10 per cent of the total turnover in Clarks shoes in the UK. We laid down the policy that we would keep our own retailing at this 10 per cent proportion to the rest of our UK shoe trade. The object was to enable us to get an eye on the public demand, to learn about retailers' problems, to learn about point of sale presentation to the public.

Members of the board of C. & J. Clark travelled widely in the 1920s and 1930s – to North America, South Africa, Italy, France, Switzerland, Denmark, Czechoslovakia – picking up fresh ideas about machinery, factory organisation, marketing. Senior executives made no fewer than 32 overseas trips between 1925 and 1939, returning several times to some countries, not least America and Denmark. They were exceptionally impressed by Bally, a close rival in Switzerland, where the factory in

Schoenenwerd was spotlessly clean, its canteen served inexpensive, wholesome meals and machines in the making room were driven by individual motors that required no overhead belts. It was noted that shoes could complete their passage through the Bally factory at great speed, and even standards of personal hygiene were admired. 'We looked at the workpeople's fingers and found them as clean as any clerk's hands' reported members of the board.

And when two directors returned from a tour of America in 1936 they concluded that:

> ... women of all classes are better dressed than in England ... they are more smartly turned out, and this does not only apply to paint and lipstick, but also to clothes and shoes.

Bancroft Clark made a robust defence of the board's enthusiasm for foreign travel. In November 1928 – the year he became a director – he said:

> Why send people to America? The trip will cost the firm at least £300 – enough to pay two days workers' wages for a year. And what will there be to show for it? We go primarily to see shoe factories, to see new machines, new methods ... such things we hope to learn and bring back home to imitate or adapt for our purposes ... so send them [managers] away, tell them to look at other people's ways and learn to improve their own, give them the opportunity to broaden their minds.

Members of the board travelled closer to home as well. A visit to the Norwich factory of Sexton, Son & Everard in 1935 offered the chance to inspect an innovative, albeit complicated, conveyor system in the making and finishing departments. As Kenneth Hudson wrote in *Towards Precision Shoemaking*:

> This conveyor was laid out in short units, each conveying a sequence of operations, and between the different units there were storage fixtures which acted as safely valves and prevented congestion on the conveyor

John Fox (at left), an 82-year-old shoemaker, was presented with a £5
gift from Clarks in December 1937 in appreciation of his long service.
He had been an outworker for 73 years, since the age of nine. Frank
Clark (at right) made the presentation in Number One office.

itself. These same fixtures were used for drying finished work, so that
the time the trays spent on them was not wasted.

C. & J. Clark's willingness to embrace new technology had been a hallmark of its formative days and remained just as strong 100 years later.
The emergence of rubber soles was becoming more widespread and it was
C. & J. Clark which developed something called 'pussyfoot soling', which
gave shoes more springy, spongy soles than was possible with ordinary
hardened rubber. Such was the popularity of rubber soles and heels that
by 1941 the company's rubber department had doubled in size.

The hugely profitable 'Joyance Sandal' had been introduced by C. & J.
Clark in 1933. It had a crepe rubber sole – which 'Won't slip on polished
floors' as a showcard said – and a Hawthorne red grain leather upper,

and it was relatively cheap to produce because it was Veldt sewn or 'stitch down', as this was known. A year later, C. & J. Clark pushed into production the men's 'Jersey Sandal' in brown, which was also Veldt sewn, but had leather soles. 'Give your feet a holiday' said the showcard, which portrayed a man leaning against a wooden fence, stick in hand, pipe in mouth and accompanied by a loyal dog staring lovingly up at him. 'Men's sandals for country rambles, summer golf – the seaside, yachting, river wear ...' said the copy.

By 1937, signs of recovery were wafting through the economy – and for the first time in many years C. & J. Clark's employees were asked to work overtime. There was good news, too, at C. & J. Clark's sister company, the Avalon Leather Board Company at Bowlingreen Mill, which made stiffeners for shoemaking. A dramatic restructuring, combined with the introduction of a new stiffener and insole board, had resulted in a celebrated turnaround. Ever since its founding by William S. Clark in 1877, the Avalon Leather Board Company had been run independently from C. & J. Clark, but by 1921 turnover had fallen to £26,671, making it impossible to justify employing its own sales force and so it relied instead on outside agents. Roger Clark took over as chairman of the Avalon Leather Board Company on his father's death in 1925, but day-to-day management was in the hands of Joseph (Joe) Ward, a Congregationalist, dedicated teetotaller and supposedly a confirmed bachelor until he astonished everyone by announcing at the end of the First World War that he was marrying a fellow member of his church. He was 55 on his wedding day.

By the time Ward died in 1931, the Avalon Leather Board Company had a workforce of some 77, including ten women and six administrative staff. At a board meeting on 28 March 1931, the directors put their appreciation of Ward on record:

> The Mill has always been his [Ward's] first interest and has benefited during all these years from his faithful and devoted service and his very considerable ability.

The *Central Somerset Gazette* noted his 'wonderful tact and discretion in preventing friction – his very presence in a group tended to ensure harmony and good fellowship'. Promoted to production manager to take over the running of the factory was the 23-year-old Bryan Morland, grandson of John Morland, who had married James Clark's daughter, Mary, and who was a partner in the rug-making company, Clark, Son & Morland.

The Avalon Leather Board Company was in profit – but only just. Shoe-makers increasingly were buying cheaper stiffeners from the continent and because ladies' shoes were now made of softer leather, they required softer stiffeners. If the Avalon Leather Board Company was to survive, it needed help. Fortunately, Bancroft had, like his father, Roger, a foot in both camps and saw the need to establish closer formal ties between the Avalon Leather Board Company and C. & J. Clark Ltd.

'We scarcely get orders enough to work the Mill half time,' wrote Roger Clark in September 1932. But Roger and Bancroft were determined to keep the business going. At one point, Roger praised Morland for the 'energy and interest you are throwing into your work' and referred back to the dark days of 1863 when William S. Clark saved the shoe company from bankruptcy. 'He [William] pulled through all right and we confidently expect you will be equally successful in your job.'

The Avalon Leather Board Company did pull through, but not without the help of £5,000 from C. & J. Clark to invest in new equipment. In addi-tion, the shoemaking business placed a regular order of some 12,000 pairs of stiffeners a week, with the proviso that they be made and delivered within seven days. Even so, Morland grew increasingly despondent about the future of the Avalon Leather Board Company and finally tendered his resignation in November 1935 after only four years in the post as produc-tion manager.

Stephen Clark, Bancroft's younger brother by eleven years, took over, aged 21, and set out to make a stiffener and insole board that met C. & J. Clark's exact requirements under a new trade name of Springbok. It took time, but Springbok was a significant breakthrough in its use of a combi-nation of rope and paper, with additional chrome leather shavings mixed with latex and animal and vegetable oil. It was a big success. The Avalon

This family group, the descendants of William Stephens and Helen Priestman Bright Clark living in Street, was photographed at Whitenights, Roger and Sarah Clark's home outside Street, on 24 April 1937, shortly before Stephen Clark went to work in the USA. Standing, left to right: Tony Clark, Roger Clark, Peter Clothier, Stephen Clark, Cato Clark, Nathan Clark, Eleanor Clark, Bancroft Clark, Jan Clark, Priscilla Clark. Front row, seated, left to right: Mary Clark, Caroline Clark, Sarah Clark, Goldie the cat, Cyrus Clark, Violet Clothier, Anthony Clothier, Daniel Clark, Eileen Clark, Lance Clark.

Leather Board Company made a net profit approaching £1,500 in the year ending 31 March 1938, rising to more than £20,000 in the year ending 31 March 1943.

Stephen had joined the Avalon Leather Board Company after coming down from Cambridge University, but in May 1937 – after a short period driving an ambulance during the Spanish Civil War – he left to work at Joseph Bancroft & Son in the USA, which was owned by his mother's family. He was recalled to Street in 1941 and given back his old job, by which time the Avalon Leather Board Company had become a subsidiary of C. & J. Clark Ltd, thus giving the parent company full control of it.

Stephen was quick to credit Bancroft for the Avalon Leather Board Company's's resurgence. In 1947, he wrote:

> It would be correct to say that Avalon as it is, is his [Bancroft's] creation. No, it would be better to say that he is the goose that laid the egg that the rest of us have hatched.

In his history of Bowlingreen Mill – the headquarters of the Avalon Leather Board Company – Michael McGarvie also singled out Bancroft for his contribution:

> He was until after the Second World War a decisive influence, stimulating the management, putting forward his own ideas, supporting those of others, throwing down opposition, chivvying the slow and blasting the inefficient. By pursuing a policy of 'the market needs this, let's try to make it', he became one of the architects of Avalon's revival.

The single word Clarks (with no apostrophe) began to be used by the company in the 1920s and was registered as a trademark – something to which a firm called Clarks of Kilmarnock, in Scotland, initially took exception. Slowly, Clarks took over as the brand name from Tor. The suggestion to depict the word Clarks in handwritten style came from Bostock, but it was Bancroft who came up with the overall design of the logo, even though he was not clear when exactly it was created.

As Bancroft said in a note written in 1981 to Judith Dempster, curator of the Clarks museum:

> In the early or middle 1930s there was an International Exhibition in Paris to which I went ... Apart from seeing the Exhibition I was in my hotel bedroom drawing out trial runs of the word Clarks. This used the 'C' as written by Hugh Clark and the rest of the word as I thought I

should like to write it myself. It was not, of course, a signature but a work of art!

Hugh Clark was especially involved with the company's first national advertising campaign in 1933, in which Clarks sandals took centre stage. Until then, the company's main method of publicising its wares had been through catalogues to the trade and its showcards. One of the first high-profile artists commissioned by the company to develop the brand was the American-born and highly regarded Edward McKnight Kauffer, whose work is much sought after today. After studying at the Mark Hopkins Institute of Art in San Francisco, Kauffer was sponsored to further his training in Paris, to where he moved as a young man, enrolling at the Académie Moderne. He relocated to London in 1915, where he had a chance meeting with Frank Pick, head of publicity for London Underground Electric Railways.

This led to Kauffer producing more than 140 posters for the London Underground. Known for his Cubism and Vorticism, Kauffer's output was prolific. For C. & J. Clark, he designed five showcards in the 1920s. One of them, for children's sandals, had a surrealist edge to it, with an open door, leading to green fields and blue skies. The caption read: 'EVERYWHEN for indoor and outdoor wear'.

The 1933 sandals advertisement was restrained, simply showing the shoe, accompanied by the strap-line: 'Sandals for summer' followed by a brief, somewhat leaden description of the benefits of owning a pair. It appeared first in the *Radio Times*, followed by *Health for All* and *Sunday Pictorial*, which had a circulation of 1.7 million. A year later, the board agreed to spend a further £350 to advertise in *Britannia*, *Sketch*, and *Sporting and Dramatic*. Then, in 1935, Bancroft persuaded the board to increase production of children's shoes to allow for a projected 50 per cent increase in sales, with an agreement to spend 2 per cent of turnover on advertising.

A year later saw the West End production of Charles B. Cochran's revue, *Follow the Sun*, featuring the chorus line known as 'Mr Cochran's Young Ladies', comprising 24 glamorous, happy and – for those

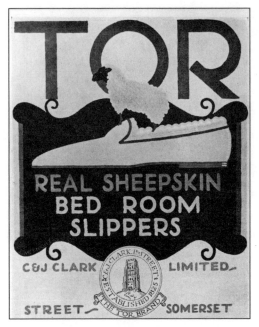

One of Edward McKnight Kauffer's iconic 1920s showcards, for Tor sheepskin slippers.

days – scantily-clad women, all wearing C. & J. Clark's 'Colorado' sandals, intimating to consumers (and theatre-goers) that Clarks was a brand of the moment.

Cecil Notley was brought in to work on advertising and publicity in 1937, the year advertisements were placed in *Vogue* for the first time. Three insertions also ran in the *Daily Express* with the strapline: 'Selling the name of Clarks'. The board was now fully committed to advertising and, despite rationing and a shortage of some raw materials during the Second World War, it agreed to 'keep our name before the public as one of the leading firms in the shoe trade'.

Notley, supported strongly by Hugh Clark, whose official title was sales director, embraced this plan with a flourish, pushing for celebrity associations with Clarks whenever he could. Some 40 actresses were commandeered to wear Clarks and, more important, be seen to be wearing Clarks.

'In the lead of films and fashion – charming Ann Todd wearing Clarks shoes' said one advertisement, showing the actress perched decoratively on

One of C. B. Cochran's glamorous 'Young Ladies' (Kitty Glen, later Mrs John Powell) in 1936 – wearing Clarks sandals, naturally.

a window seat, her long, bare legs dangling before her. Margaret Lockwood and Anna Neagle launched ranges of Gatwick Boots, Mendip, Norwegian Lace and several wooden-sole shoes. The advertisement featuring Neagle showed her dressed in her role in Jane Austen's *Emma*, sporting a pair of replica 1845 shoes 'as worn by the fashionable ladies of the period ... fashions have changed but still today Clarks shoes are the choice of well-dressed women'. Dolores Gray was photographed wearing a pair of Clippers as she stood on the step of a steam-train engine looking fondly into the eyes of the driver. And Bebe Daniels was pictured wearing a special pair of wood-soled sandals on the set of the 1944 musical *Panama Hattie*. The photograph of Daniels was taken at the Piccadilly Theatre by John Hinde, son of the Clarks director, Wilfrid Hinde, and at first caused some consternation when the actress was shown drinking a glass of red wine. Teetotaller Roger Clark disapproved. In response, Hugh Clark suggested 'changing the colour of the liquid to orange', but noted that 'even Mr

The Western Temperance League holding its centenary
lunch in the Crispin Hall, Street, in 1935.

Roger Clark knows that orange juice is sometimes mixed with gin!' A
compromise was reached when Daniels was shown enjoying an ice cream
soda with two straws sticking out of it.

The whole cast of *Panama Hattie* took to wearing Clarks, with the
company keen to stress that a three-hour show of that kind required the
very best footwear. Daniels's shoes in the advertisement were red and
appeared in *Vogue*, but, unfortunately, the show itself was taken off after
300 performances because of bomb damage to the theatre. Happily, it then
went on tour, in effect showing the shoes to audiences all over the country.
Advertising expenditure amounted to £13,487 in 1939, increasing to
£30,581 by 1946 and £53,579 in 1948, some £1.5 million in today's
money.

C. & J. Clark had a good war. Regulations on shoe manufacturing during the Second World War were extensive and included leather and footwear rationing and price controls, but the company would emerge largely unscathed. The wartime coalition government introduced a system of 'utility footwear' whereby 50 per cent of a manufacturer's civilian shoes had to be low-price and would be exempt from purchase tax in order that people on low incomes could still afford to be properly shod.

The rationing of upper leather saw the company move swiftly to find an alternative. In 1939, the board announced:

> We shall reconsider all existing designs with a view to cutting down the amount of leather used. Celluloid will be substituted for all leather heel covers. Leather piping and trimmings will be left off all shoes and, generally speaking, we shall withdraw or redesign all shoes which use more than 1¾ feet per pair.

C. & J. Clark was designated by the Board of Trade a 'nucleus firm', making it less likely that its workforce would be called up. It also meant the company had government contracts, in particular providing footwear to the Auxiliary Territorial Service and the RAF, including, in the case of the latter, flying boots. Another sideline was the rebuilding of worn American army boots, undertaken on behalf of the Ministry of Supply. Some 2,000 American lasts were sent over to Street for this purpose and between 1943 and the end of 1944, 180,000 pairs were taken apart and welted with rubber soles and heels. American servicemen reportedly said the reassembled models were more comfortable than the originals. C. & J. Clark also made thousands of 'Mae West' lifejackets as part of the war effort.

In August 1940, C. & J. Clark signed a contract with the Bristol Aeroplane Company to make parts for Hercules engines and for Lancasters, Stirlings, Wellingtons, Halifaxes and other planes. During the summer of 1941, the factory's Big Room took on a new look when the Admiralty arranged for Whiteheads, a machine-tool firm in Weymouth, to move in and begin making torpedo parts, a development that might have been hard to accept for those with acute Quaker sensibilities.

During the war, in keeping with the Peace Testimony issued by Quaker founder George Fox in 1661 (which committed the Society of Friends to pacifism and non-violence), many Quakers became conscientious objectors and pushed for a negotiated settlement. Others gave reluctant support to the war effort. Among the latter group was Roger Clark, who appeared to have little time for the appeasement argument. On 30 September 1938, he wrote in his diary:

As I supposed, [Neville] Chamberlain and [Edouard] Daladier [the French prime minister at the start of the war] have given everything – practically – away in face of the intimidation of Hitler, aided by Mussolini; I expect Spain also has been handed over to the latter. Chamberlain has shown himself to be a most incompetent negotiator; he seems to have got nothing whatever in return for what he has given away with both hands. Of course one must be thankful not to have war, but I can't join in praise of Chamberlain for buying off at the Czechs' expense.

No pressure was exerted on C. & J. Clark's workforce to sign up or not sign up. A total of 310 men and 61 women did volunteer, of whom twelve lost their lives.

The war saw the arrival in Street of child evacuees from London, including two boys and two girls from a family in Romford, Essex, who were taken in by Roger and Sarah Clark. One of the boys, Edgar Smith, recalls:

My mother took us down by train. We went to Bristol Temple Meads station and Mrs Clark met us there in the family's Lancaster ... On arrival in the house, we had tea from a silver tea pot in the drawing room served by a maid in frilly cap and apron. It made quite an impression on us. We always ate with the family, even when there were guests, which usually were other Quakers. Mr Roger Clark was a remote figure to us. He always read the Bible at breakfast.

The Street Women's Auxiliary Fire Service during the Second World War, with Karl Hinde, a grandson of James Clark and chief engineer at Clarks from 1920 to 1952, standing at the middle of the back row.

Edgar remembers the house being busy and that he and his siblings were encouraged to develop hobbies:

> They bought a violin for my brother Ray and gave him a beehive. I got interested in birds and this has stayed with me all my life. I visited Mrs Clark with my sister Pauline when I was about 17. Later, as I travelled on business, I called in to see her. She was very old then. I remarked how the garden wasn't as I remembered it and she said: 'Never look back, Edgar. Never look back.'

Shoemaking in Street was reallocated to other buildings during the war with Germany, an inconvenience at the time, but something that proved to be an important turning point, simplifying and improving the whole process by breaking production down into smaller controlled areas. This was the precursor to a totally new way of working: individual factories presided over by individual managers, producing individual parts of a variety of different shoes. Bancroft Clark led this particular revolution and would pursue it with great energy once the war ended. He announced in 1941:

> It seems likely that future shoemaking policy will be to set up indepen-
> dent manufacturing units, certainly from lasting to boxing and possibly
> from closing to boxing, each doing 5,000–8,000 pairs per week of
> homogenous type of work. The man in charge of each would be more
> independent, have greater control of the shoes that he makes and have
> an easier organisation problem. Other advantages would be quicker
> output, and faults would be remedied more easily.

Full-scale decentralisation was Bancroft's goal, even though it was not until 1941 that the last outworker dropped off his hand-sewn work to the factory foreman, something William S. Clark had wanted to happen 100 years earlier.

During the war, the first issue of the company's trade publication, *News from Clarks of Street*, rolled off the presses. It was aimed at retailers, forecasting fashions and drawing attention to special sales promotions. In the November 1941 edition, Hugh Clark came up with a rallying cry:

> We have no sales problems, only supply problems. People are so anxious
> to get shoes that they might be tempted to become lax about quality. I
> think it is up to us to be careful about this. We at Clarks are very jealous
> of our century-old reputation for sound footwear and we are deter-
> mined to do our utmost to keep that flag flying. If you find us slipping
> up in any degree, do not hesitate to tell us at once, in spite of the fact
> that you could probably sell our shoes even if quality was not up to
> standard.

From 1942, the Board of Trade encouraged shoemakers to produce wooden-soled footwear to combat the shortage of leather. Bostock and

Sales director Hugh Clark (at left) with George Pursey, his
assistant sales manager, in November 1943.

his senior lieutenants rose to the challenge, inventing a hinged wooden
sole for use on ladies' walking shoes called Limbers. This proved to be far
more comfortable than it sounds once the company decided to use beech
wood and developed a method for drying out the timber, using a special
kiln recommended by the Timber Research Association. Wooden soles
gave good support to weak arches and, although the Board of Trade had
initially been wary about granting C. & J. Clark a licence for them, such
was their success that the technique was circulated officially throughout
the British shoe industry.

Between March 1943 and June 1945, C. & J. Clark produced 146,000
pairs of wooden-sole shoes, some 12 per cent of their total output for
women. But because the cost of wooden soles was almost 25 per cent
greater than leather, they were phased out once the war ended and leather
became more freely available.

Sales of children's sandals held up remarkably well during the war.
They were deemed as suitable shoes for children sent off to the countryside

The new Peter Lord shop in Bristol, photographed in 1946.

away from congested urban areas at risk from German bombings. And women were encouraged to buy sturdy Clarks shoes, spurred on by a 1941 showcard that played on the government's 'Walk when you can' poster. 'Ease the burden which war puts on transport – but do it comfortably in Clarks shoes.'

Utility shoes and wartime restrictions did not mean that Clarks gave up on the pursuit of new designs, or new designers. Far from it. In 1936, Hugh Clark had commissioned André Perugia, the French shoe designer who had opened his own shop in Paris at the age of sixteen, to come up with six creations at 100 francs apiece. And Bancroft made contact with Mabel Winkel, whom he described as the 'ablest shoe stylist in America'. Somervell had hired Winkel in the mid-1930s and she also worked with Lotus. She seemed poised to sign a contract, but wanted $7,500 a year for her services, which scared Bancroft off. He was, however, committed to post-war creativity, noting how style was no longer:

... merely a matter of upper colour and decoration ... style is an expression of the desires and wishes of the buying public ... style will move faster both in the sense of change ... and in spreading rapidly throughout the country.

Street escaped the bomb damage that devastated some parts of the West Country, but in Bristol, the Peter Lord shop in Queen's Road was virtually demolished during a heavy raid on 24 November 1940. The following morning, Hugh Clark drove to Bristol and negotiated a lease for new premises almost opposite the old ones and it was business pretty much as usual. Similarly, the London office was hit and had to be moved temporarily to Watford before eventually returning to Mitre House.

Bancroft Clark succeeded his father as chairman on 1 January 1942, although Roger remained on the board until 1947. Retirement clearly did not sit comfortably with Roger.

I don't pretend to like it, but it is obviously the only thing to do at my age ... I have said I wished to receive notices and agendas and to attend meetings as hitherto and of course they agreed to this. I may continue to make the minutes a while longer.

Indeed, Roger continued to write the minutes of directors' meetings at the Avalon Leather Board Company until 1959, long after his retirement as a board member of C. & J. Clark. His official retirement brought the directors together in Bancroft's office at 2 pm on 1 July 1947. He wrote in his diary:

I have thought some time of retiring – my deafness so much now that I don't really understand – and as Hugh [Clark], just 70, is retiring from the Board (I think he should have been asked to stay to 75) Bancroft suggested I should give up too. Bancroft said much of what Hugh has done for the business in many ways and the others spoke warmly – his energy and judgement as to styles – selling – and everyone spoke of his human kindness and friendship. I suddenly broke down in what I tried to say and was speechless for a moment – and tears ...

7

Measuring feet, maximising profit

IN THE YEARS that followed the Second World War, Britain was to change beyond recognition – but not immediately. As the country celebrated the end of warfare and the beginnings of wide-reaching reform under a victorious Labour government, the cultural and economic landscape in 1945 was far from fertile. Making do was the edict of the day.

As David Kynaston described in *Austerity Britain, 1945–51*, there were:

... no supermarkets, no motorways, no teabags, no sliced bread, no frozen food, no flavoured crisps, no lager, no microwaves, no dishwashers, no Formica ... Central heating rare, coke boilers, water geysers, the coal fire, the hearth, the home, chilblains common ... White faces everywhere. Back-to-backs, narrow cobbled streets, Victorian terraces, no high-rises. Arterial roads, suburban semis, the march of the pylon. Austin Sevens, Ford Eights, no seat belts, Triumph motorcycles with sidecars. A Bakelite wireless in the home, *Housewives Choice* or *Workers Playtime* or *ITMA* on the air, televisions almost unknown ... Milk of Magnesia, Vick Vapour Rub, Friars Balsam, Fynnon Salts, Eno's, Germolene. Suits and hats, dresses and hats, cloth caps and mufflers, no leisurewear, no teenagers. Heavy coins, heavy shoes, heavy suitcases, heavy tweed coats, heavy leather footballs, no unbearable lightness of being. Meat rationed, tea rationed, cheese rationed, jam rationed, eggs rationed, sweets rationed, soap rationed, clothes rationed.

Within a year of VE Day, disgruntlement was seeping into the system. The *Sunday Pictorial*, sister paper of the left-leaning *Daily Mirror* – and one of several publications in which Clarks shoes were advertised – launched a '100 Families to Speak for Britain' campaign, in which readers were invited to get their grievances off their chests and on to the national agenda. One woman, Eileen Lewis, from Croxley Green in Hertfordshire, told the newspaper: 'I can't get shoes for my kiddies. A couple of weeks ago I spent all day trying to buy two pairs of shoes. I must have called at twenty shops'.

Mrs Lewis's frustration would have found sympathy in Street, where a contributor to the first issue of *Clarks Comments*, a new in-house publication for staff, retailers and suppliers, railed against ongoing wartime restrictions. The unnamed contributor was particularly exercised by the:

> ... absurd regulation which prevents a shoe manufacturer from saving materials and making open ventilated sandals. In America, they have been wiser than we in this respect, and have allowed the manufacture of ventilated shoes; indeed, half the shoes women wear today are toeless and heel-less ... Women's shoe styles in America are now blossoming out again. During the five years of relative separation, they have made considerable changes. Their lasts are broader in the tread, shorter in the forepart length and bigger in the joint measure.

Shoemakers had often looked enviously at their counterparts across the Atlantic both in the context of styling and technical breakthroughs. In the 1940s, Americans had developed the 'slip-lasted' shoe method, often referred to as the California Last construction. This required no stiff insole board. With a slip-lasted shoe, the upper materials were stitched to a fabric sock. The last was then forced into the shoe, the platform cover neatly wrapped over a lightweight flexible board and the sole attached in the traditional way. This process created more flexible and therefore more comfortable shoes, though they coped less well in wet conditions.

In Britain, people tended to walk more than they did in America, where, by 1946, the motorcar was a common feature of post-war life. But even so – and much to the chagrin of Bancroft Clark – Americans were presented with a far wider choice of what to wear on their feet and were buying twice as many shoes per head as the British.

To find out why, Bancroft dispatched Tony Clark to America in April 1946, along with Leslie Graves, a factory manager with proven production and design skills, and two other heads of department, one in charge of last and wooden heel-making, the other responsible for pattern cutting. They visited New York, Boston, St Louis, Cincinnati and Buffalo, where they inspected the maple trees from which the Clarks last-making blocks were cut. The trip resulted in a stark observation: 'The chief impression, which we brought back about shoemaking was the great superiority of American machinery over ours,' wrote Tony Clark in *Clarks Comments*. He continued:

> Here, we are suffering badly after six years of war through having to operate worn-out and obsolete machinery which we cannot even get repaired satisfactorily, let alone replaced by new and improved types ... The type of machine they are using [in America] is in many ways more efficient and up-to-date than ours. We saw in every department machines which we need badly and which, if we had them, would lead to an immediate improvement in the quality of our shoes and also to increased output.

Bancroft had travelled to America himself immediately after the war and was convinced that despite continued rationing and other impediments to the growth of the UK economy, the shoe trade was ripe for expansion. He predicted that if employment picked up and foreign trade treaties were reformed, shoe manufacturing would be set fair. Crucially, he recognised that if buying power became stronger it would be women doing the spending:

> Women will want to feel neat, trim, smart and lovely ... Their outward

appearance will be an expansion of and a cause of their inner well-being ... Women will want more clothes and that includes shoes. With a shorter working week they will have time to think about nice clothes and [have] more time to wear them ... Shoe style is not merely upper colour and decoration. One of the most important elements in women's style will be fit. A shoe that does not fit and does not keep its fit will slop, lengthen, gape, bag, wrinkle. Whatever eye appeal it may have in the window, it will not be style on the foot. What women will want to buy, what they will be educated to buy, will be style on the foot.

Bancroft was convinced of the urgent need to widen Clarks' production capabilities, something that had been tried and tested several years earlier in 1938 when the company entered into a formal and successful arrangement with John Halliday & Son to make shoes in Ireland. Halliday was a former Leeds manufacturing firm founded in 1868, specialising in heavy agricultural boots. In 1928, it closed down in the north of England and opened up in Ireland after buying an old cholera hospital in Dundalk, County Louth. But, hindered by the decline of Irish farming and the new-found popularity of the Wellington boot, it struggled. Arthur Halliday, the company's managing director, needed to diversify and was approached by four different companies: Padmore & Barnes, Lotus, Somervell, which made K Shoes, and C. & J. Clark. Halliday was educated at the Quaker Bootham School in York and it must have been clear almost immediately that he would slip seamlessly into the Clarks culture – and so it proved. Once the deal had been signed, Bancroft wrote that Arthur Halliday was 'our strongest card ... [who] likes to have our support against the Wild Irish who are his workers, staff and directors'.

A five-year contract was drawn up between C. & J. Clark and John Halliday & Son, and a new subsidiary, Clarks Ireland Ltd, was formed. Initially, the Irish operation made only women's shoes, but within a year it had moved into children's footwear. The contract was extended in 1943 and by 1948 Halliday's was producing 500,000 pairs of Clarks shoes a year.

Such was the importance of the Irish market that Arthur Halliday

Bancroft Clark, chairman from 1942 to 1967.

joined the board of C. & J. Clark Ltd on 1 January 1947, shortly after John Walter Bostock retired and a few months before Wilfrid Hinde stood down, both big characters who had enjoyed starring roles in the company in the first half of the twentieth century. Meanwhile, H. Brooking Clark, son of Hugh Clark, joined the company after leaving Oxford university and serving as an officer in the Scots Guards in North Africa. Brooking would be invited on to the board in 1952 and later became company secretary before leaving C. & J. Clark in 1965.

During the war, owing to a lack of space in Street, Clarks had opened a closing room in St John Street, Bridgwater, to machine-finish the uppers of shoes for the armed forces and then, after the war, to make demobilisation footwear. This led to the launch of a full-scale factory in Bridgwater in June 1945 when Clarks exchanged contracts on a former dairy, where the emphasis was on developing the slip-lasting process that had proved so successful in America. In time, the factory was enlarged with the construction of a new building in the dairy yard that had become a recreational area for employees. The women workers lost their netball pitch but Clarks gained a valuable making room, where local unskilled labour was trained by teams sent from Street to Bridgwater each morning.

A second factory was opened in Shepton Mallet, built on the site of Summerleaze park, where American forces had been based during the war. On taking possession of it in June 1946, Clarks acquired eight double Romney huts, which had been used as aircraft hangars and then warehouses. A mere seven days after being granted a licence by the Ministry of Works, the huts were converted and production of 'Infants Playe-ups Sandals' (known shortly afterwards as 'Play-ups') began.

Bancroft Clark had long been a believer in decentralisation and pursued it like a man on a mission. Several years earlier, following a visit to Bally in Switzerland, he had reported seeing:

> ... factories scattered about in different villages so that they do not get either too many people living close together, or too large a proportion of their workpeople coming long distances.

In 1945, he outlined his overall strategy, talking about how the new additional factories would 'take the lid off people' with 'each main unit ... separately managed by a manager of potential directorial status'.

The Shepton Mallet factory was managed by A. William (Bill) Graves, the younger brother of the production expert Leslie Graves, who had been responsible for the factory in Bridgwater. Shepton Mallet employed ten women and eight men and in its first week produced 200 infants' Play-ups – all of which turned out to be sub-standard. There was no disguising this from Bancroft when he visited at the end of that week. The chairman expressed his displeasure, after which Graves made sure that any deficiencies in the system were ironed out, and by the end of 1946 the factory was making 1,000 pairs a week. A year later, Number Two Factory, as it was called, opened on the Shepton Mallet site, followed closely by Number Three Factory. In 1953, the UK Shoe Research Association declared the Shepton Mallet factories the most efficient in the country, and Graves went on to open a further eight factories in the West Country.

In Bridgwater, a new building at Redgate Farm, to be known as the Redgate factory, opened in January 1947, covering 20,000 sq ft and costing £20,500. Here, within twelve months, a highly efficient mass-production capability boosted output to 4,650 pairs a week, mainly of women's casual shoes, particularly 'Clippers', which were advertised as 'Clippers in gay colours for playtime'.

It had been a swashbuckling start to peacetime trading. Sales in 1946 were up 28 per cent on 1945, with profits rising by 23 per cent, a result that may not have come as a surprise given that Clarks was one of only a few companies which managed to maintain their output during the war. The firm produced 70 per cent more shoes in 1946 than it did in 1935 and for the first time it was making the same proportion of women's and children's footwear. This growth would continue at an even faster rate. Clarks made 1.25 million pairs in 1946, rising to an astonishing 2 million in 1948, and in terms of personnel, by the end of the year there were close to 2,000 men and women working across all the Clarks factories.

Bancroft was not sitting in his chairman's chair with any sense of complacency, however. In the 1946 annual Directors Report and Accounts – which was read only by senior members of the company – he was quick to point out that government subsidies to tanners for help with the cost of hides and skins had created an 'artificial position' and therefore he was revising down his forecasts for the coming year. He also took the opportunity to make some critical observations about the work-force: 'a certain laxness in time-keeping ... [and] difficulty in getting new employees to reach the speed of output required in a competitive shoe industry.' Things had not improved greatly a year later: 'Our only grumble with our employees is a certain slackness about time-keeping' he told the directors. 'Our industry works a 45-hour week, but the actual hours worked in Street are well short of that.' Perhaps, but there was nothing slack about the figures. Turnover in 1947 reached £1,681,270, compared with £1,288,468 the previous year.

Time-keeping was not the chairman's only gripe. Shortly after New Year 1948, he told the Factory Council that shops were still returning too many faulty shoes and that output had to increase still further. The

Americans, he said, were producing 'about half as much again per head per week as you do here. Our machines are the same, the conditions are the same; the only difference is the tempo of the work.'

Production did increase following the purchase of the manor house next to the Shepton Mallet factory, which came with twelve additional acres of land earmarked as the site of a new factory expressly for children's shoes. And extra units were built in Bridgwater, which meant that by 1948 nearly a quarter of all Clarks shoes were made outside Street.

Bancroft developed the concept at Clarks that each manager had to draw up his own budget annually. These were added together to form the main budget, which the board reviewed and modified as appropriate. The revised figures were then handed back to the managers. Monthly accounts had to be produced with all items matched against their respective budgets. These accounts were published internally for the benefit of senior managers and directors in a 'blue' book, a process which still continues today.

A greater emphasis was put on time and motion studies, developing new manufacturing techniques and generally monitoring efficiency in minute detail, all of which had the unanimous support of Peter Clothier and Tony Clark, who were Bancroft's right-hand men during the years of factory expansion. One member of the Clark family has described these three as 'the Holy Trinity'. They were certainly close. Bancroft was the oldest – by six years from Tony and eight from Peter. Tony and Peter had spent a lot of time together as small children because Tony's mother, Caroline Pease, died from an embolism twelve days after giving birth to her only child. Esther Clothier became something of a surrogate mother to Tony and it was through the Clothiers that Tony developed a great love for Bantham in South Devon. After the war, Peter Clothier and Tony Clark both bought houses there and in later years other members of the Clark family did likewise. There is still a strong family tradition of going to Bantham for short breaks and holidays.

Peter had been made managing director of the Avalon Leather Board Company in 1936 and became a director of C. & J. Clark three years later. His great expertise was machinery, whereas Tony Clark had a reputation for being, in the modern parlance, a 'people person'. Tony was a liberal

Tony Clark, described as one of the 'Holy Trinity'; the other
two were Bancroft Clark and Peter Clothier.

Quaker. He drank alcohol and hunted to hounds (as did his father, John
Bright Clark). Bancroft was seen as the intellect, Peter as the technocrat
and Tony as the life-enhancer.

All three were adamant that establishing new centres of production
under the control of competing managers was the way forward, and so
rapid was this expansion that by 1960 there were, in addition to Bridgwater, Shepton Mallet and Street (which in itself had been greatly enlarged,
especially with the opening of The Grove in 1950), eleven factories in
the southwest – in Midsomer Norton (1952), Radstock (1953), Glastonbury (1954), Minehead (1954), Warminster (1956), Plymouth (1957),
Weston-super-Mare (1958), Ilminster (1959), Yeovil (1960), Castle Cary
(1960) and Bath (1961). Yet more would be opened during the 1960s in
Exmouth, Barnstaple, Rothwell and New Tredegar (in south Wales). The
Rothwell factory near Kettering in Northamptonshire, was bought in
1966 expressly to make men's shoes.

The first truly devolved factory was Mayflower in Plymouth, which opened in October 1957. It was financed with help from Plymouth Corporation, which then rented it back to the company on a long lease. The Lord Mayor of Plymouth, Alderman Leslie F. Paul, cut the ceremonial ribbon, watched by Peter Clothier, who had ultimate responsibility for the factory. Plymouth concentrated on fashionable women's shoes in the Wessex range. It was instructed to implement tight fiscal control over every aspect of its business, but had its own accounts department and work study team, which answered to local management rather than to Street. It also developed its own system of training unskilled labour and was seen as a pioneer of new technology. Every new employee received individual training and he or she was encouraged to suggest ways to speed up or simplify the work. If any of their ideas were adapted, they were rewarded. This scheme was another means of increasing production speeds, encouraging workers to resolve any issues around them and work together as one unit.

The imperative for efficiency was greater than ever as shoe imports from Western Europe surged: some 3.3 million pairs were imported in 1956, three times as many as in 1953, with Italy posing the greatest threat at the higher end of the market. Furthermore, the price of sole leather had continued to rise and this had to be passed on to retailers, who were beginning to baulk at what they were being asked to pay for stock.

Clarks, like other UK shoe manufacturers, was keen to use alternative resin-rubber soling material, but the government was allowing only small quantities of the ingredients needed to produce this to be imported from America and Canada. Factories such as the one in Plymouth had to find other ways not just to compete but to outperform their continental rivals. Speed of production was crucial. Peter Clothier determined that the conveyors in Plymouth were only to carry shoes being worked on at the time and not those awaiting attention. Maintenance of machinery was given a high priority on the principle that money spent on preventing breakdown was a saving on acquiring new equipment. There was also a radical rethink on the use of lasts. When the Mayflower factory opened, each last was used on average twice a week, in keeping with conventional shoemaking practice, but within months, individual lasts were being used on average 23 times a day – and a pair of shoes passed through the Mayflower factory in a mere three days.

Plymouth also developed a method whereby shoes were softened to make them easier to shape and work with in the final stages of assembly. This was called 'rapid-mulling' and involved the use of steam, as prescribed by scientists working at the Clarks laboratory in Street. According to *Clarks of Street, 1825–1950*:

> They were exciting times for all concerned. Managers had to create, in their area, all aspects of factory activity, from the production of finished shoes to the organisation of workers councils. On their efficiency would depend the success of the firm in beating its rivals. In the early days, on the sturdy principle that they had to pay their own way, there had to be a good deal of improving, and anyone at any level who saw a real way to saving money or time was rewarded according to the amount saved.

Before the war, Clarks had developed the process of making what was called 'Pussyfoot' sheets from scrap crepe that proved suitable – and hard-wearing – for shoe soling, but this was suspended except for certain government requirements. Then, immediately after the war, Clarks pioneered a new soling material called Solite, which wore significantly longer than leather and was regarded as more comfortable than Pussyfoot. Showcards for Clarks shoes made with Solite claimed they provided three times the wear and mothers were reminded that 'active feet can run through a mint of shoe leather'.

Solite was developed out of a material initially discovered in the United States under the trade name Meolite. Its formulation was a closely guarded secret and was not easy to obtain in the UK. However, Clarks acquired samples and an in-house chemist, James Hill, analysed the material and found it was a styrene/butadiene co-polymer. By adding more styrene the end product was hardened whereas more butadiene softened the material. It could therefore be adapted to suit different types of footwear.

Clarks developed its own formula, and production began in the Rubber Department in Street in 1949. It was then manufactured in bulk at the

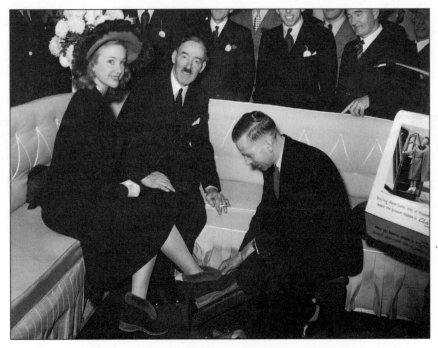

The actress Moira Lister being fitted with Clarks Skyborne
bootees at the Quality Footwear Exhibition, Seymour Hall,
London, in November 1947. Hugh Clark is at her left.

Larkhill Rubber Company in Yeovil from around 1966 and sold to the
external trade in addition to its own domestic use. The Plymouth factory
used Solite extensively well into the 1970s, producing some 50,000 pairs
of Women's Court shoes a week.

One of the other major technological breakthroughs during this
period was the introduction of the Construction Electric Mediano Auto-
matico (CEMA) machine, which resulted from C. & J. Clark collaborating
with the Grimoldi company in Spain, whose founder, Gonzalo Mediano
de Capdevilla, was a circus performer and trick cyclist from Barcelona.
CEMA allowed for the moulding of rubber soles directly on to the lasted
leather upper, a revolutionary breakthrough because it did away entirely
with labour-intensive methods of both machine-sewing and welting. It
greatly improved the bond of sole to upper and was particularly suitable

for children's shoes and heavyweight men's footwear, especially boots. CEMA produced shoes with far greater traction and soles that were waterproof. They also retained their shape and were regarded as supremely comfortable.

Mediano de Capdevilla's first contact with C. & J. Clark had been in 1949 when Nathan Clark, one of Roger Clark's sons and the inventor of the Desert Boot – who was then working with Arthur Halliday in Ireland – asked Bancroft permission to send Jack Clarke, the company engineer, to Barcelona to investigate this new discovery. Clarke was accompanied by Bob Cottier, Nathan's assistant, who spoke good Spanish. Within weeks, an agreement was reached and by Christmas a CEMA machine was set up in Street, and Mediano de Capdevilla sent over two men, one a rubber technician, the other a mould maker, to demonstrate its powers. The two Spaniards stayed three months, during which time various modifications were made to their machine. If C. & J. Clark was to benefit fully from CEMA, it needed to be used on lines with long production runs (to keep mould costs low) and the curing time of the rubber needed to be as short as possible. The original Spanish machines had cure times of fifteen minutes, but the company's own engineers managed to reduce this to as little as 3.5 minutes, depending on the style of shoe. In July 1950, C. & J. Clark placed an order for seven such machines from a firm of engineers in Chard and the company gave an undertaking to Mediano de Capdevilla that it would produce 2,500 pairs per week of children's shoes in the Shepton Mallet factory – and that he would receive a royalty of one per cent on every CEMA-moulded shoe sold.

CEMA-moulded footwear was popular with the public and by December 1957 the two millionth pair of shoes made using this method had rolled off the assembly line. CEMA was a bright light in shoe production, and was only eclipsed in 1962 when Clarks began experimenting with injection moulded polyvinyl-chloride or PVC that required no curing time at all – although CEMA was still used on boots. Later, polyurethane (PU) proved even lighter and more hard-wearing than PVC.

Bancroft was jubilant about CEMA:

We believe we are the first in this country to make shoes this way and we think we are the only people making them with the precision necessary for our type and grade of product. We have faith that the project will be successful and hope that time will prove us right.

Bancroft recognised that the post-war 'baby boom' was good for business, possibly very good indeed. But winning the trust of the next generation of mothers was imperative if that business was to come Clarks' way. Housewives needed to be convinced that their children would be wearing not just properly fitting shoes but shoes that would care for their feet. In the 1930s, many shops deployed the Pedescope to measure a child's foot. This bulky contraption required the customer to stand on a step and look down at his or her feet through a pane of glass. It would remain a common feature in shoe shops until the early 1960s – but it came with a health warning: 'Repeated exposure to X-rays may be harmful. It is unwise for customers to have more than twelve shoe-fitting exposures a year.' On the other hand, you could have as many shoe-fitting exposures as was humanly possible if it involved the Clarks Footgauge.

This simple method of measuring feet accurately and quickly had been developed principally by John Walter Bostock during the late 1930s and early 1940s. American shoe manufacturers were well practised in offering their customers a variety of shoe sizes, though Clarks was not far behind them, especially with its anatomical range of Hygienic shoes that came in three separate widths and the women's Wessex lines, which were offered in five width fittings and twelve sizes. After the Second World War, soldiers complained that their feet had suffered as a result of poorly fitting boots, prompting calls from the Boot and Shoe Industry Working Party Report for multi-fitting footwear in a variety of widths at affordable prices. It wanted 'some enterprising medium price manufacturer (and/or distributor) to extend the multiple fitting trade downwards to the mass volume middle ranges of trade'.

Clarks and Somervell were at the forefront of this particular revolution, joined by the likes of Abbotts, Church's, Feature Shoes, Lilley & Skinner, Lotus, Novic, Sexton and Timpson. In a 1947 document laboriously entitled 'Retail Margins on Multiple Fitting Shoes', a representative from Somervell told the board of the Trade and Federated Associations of Boot and Shoe Manufacturers that:

> ... there is no difficulty about measuring a foot with reasonable accuracy, and there is no difficulty in carrying a stock that will fit the bulk of feet, but measuring feet takes time and fitting feet slows down stock turn ... You are only likely to get a reasonable standard of shoe fitting where people are prepared to pay for that standard of shoe-fitting and where the retailer finds it profitable to provide it.

Clarks begged to differ – and had done its homework. During the war, Bostock had arranged for every child in Street and every woman in the factory to have their feet properly measured. Then, in 1946, special fitting courses were held at the factory for Peter Lord salespeople and for those who worked in independent shoe shops that sold Clarks. These courses, which were normally held in rooms at The Bear Hotel opposite the factory, were expensive and time-consuming, but made sure Clarks was known as the company that looked after children's feet (although the 'Finder Board' used by K Shoes and Howlett & White's plastic gauge were widely available and would have claimed to do the job just as well).

Those who came to Street for one of these courses went away with a full set of instructions on a flyer entitled *How To Use Clarks Footgauge*, although something of a technical mind-set was required to decipher the full capabilities of this device. The manual started off simply enough: 'Use on sloping table of fitting stool.' But after that the going got heavier:

> The gauge is marked with a scored line exactly nine inches from the inside of [the] heel pillar. Now place the size-scale plate so that when the toe-gauge slide is on this nine-inch line the pointer is exactly level with the 60 size mark. Having done this all other sizes will be

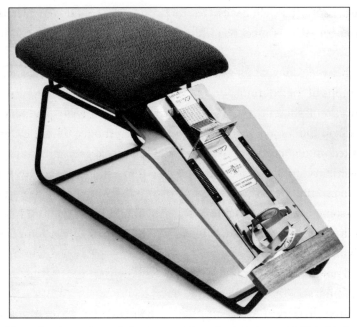

Measuring the customer's foot accurately and quickly is crucial. This Clarks
fitting stool with integrated footgauge of May 1957 did the job perfectly.

accurately measured. See that the foot to be measured is at right angles
to the leg ... keep the toes flat with your thumb while adjusting the
toe-gauge slide.

And on it went:

To measure the girth (or joint measure) move the tape carrier so that
the tape comes immediately central with the great toe joint. The tape
carrier should be pushed back at the outer side of the foot to the full
extent of its swivel movement. This will cause the tape to run diagonally
across the foot and will give a correct average position for measuring.

Eventually, the big moment arrives:

Take the reading on the tape and find the corresponding number from the printed scale in line with the size pointer. The column in which this number (or the number nearest to it) is found shows the correct fitting.

'In between' measures were a different matter and needed their own paragraphs of instructions.

Clarks took shoe-fitting so seriously that it continued to conduct its own research on the subject throughout the 1950s. At one point, the company embarked on a survey – an early exercise in market research – of 1,250 schoolchildren in Somerset and managed to persuade the county council and two prominent orthopaedic surgeons to back it. The survey revealed that in some towns, such as Taunton and Yeovil, as many as 44 per cent of children weren't present when having shoes bought for them. This was horrifying. To Clarks, the very idea of buying a pair of children's shoes that did not fit properly was deplorable. And the younger the customer the better. Children would be parents one day.

In-shop advertisements for Clarks 'First Shoes' spoke directly to responsible mothers:

Isn't it exciting that your child is, at last, walking? And isn't it so important that his or her First Shoe allows the soft, delicate bones to grow in a strong, healthy way? Clarks share your concern. That's why all Clarks First Shoes come in a range of styles, in up to four width fittings and in whole and half sizes. Why we build at least three months growing room into all our shoes. And why the trained fitter in this shop will measure both tiny feet for width and length using a Clarks footgauge for guidance; you really can't put your child's feet in more caring, capable hands.

Where Clarks gained an advantage over its competitors was insisting that retailers carried shoes in all width fittings, and backing this up with a warehouse system that would speedily replenish stock rather than burdening retailers with an excessive number of unsold shoes that they had to store for several weeks.

Then, in the early 1960s, Clarks rolled out its successful 'no fit, no sale'

Shop interior in Cheltenham in the mid-1950s, showing the children's fitting area.

campaign, which cemented the notion that the company prized comfort before profit. Bancroft would say many years later that the footgauge was the idea on which 'the vast expansion in our children's business was founded'.

The teenage market had not been forgotten either. Indeed, in 1950, Clarks was the first British shoe manufacturer to produce a special range for young people, after Bill Graves made several investigative trips to America, where the idea of teenagers seeking greater independence from their parents was far more developed than in Britain. This forward thinking sat comfortably beside Clarks' so-called 'Style Centre' in Street, where all kinds of fashion items from America and continental Europe were studied in detail – buckles, belts, fabrics, pullovers – to see how they might influence the design of shoes.

There was forward thinking, too, in promoting the Clarks brand.

The British film star Margaret Lockwood and her daughter
Toots arriving at Clarks in Street on 23 August 1946.

Advertising and celebrity endorsements had continued apace at C. & J.
Clark as soon as wartime hostilities were over. Advertisements were placed
on trains on the London Underground and in daily and Sunday newspapers, and famous names were invited to tour the factory – with their visits
publicised far and wide. One such exercise in 'under the line advertising'
took place in 1946 when Margaret Lockwood, probably the country's most
popular actress at the time, came to Street with her daughter – and the
Bristol Evening World was invited along. It was, according to the gushing
copy, 'one of those happy occasions when the spirit of good humour is
abroad and everything proceeds with cheerful spontaneity'. Lockwood
– who had starred in Alfred Hitchcock's *The Lady Vanishes* in 1938 and
more recently in the splendidly racy and controversial Gainsborough
Studios melodrama *The Wicked Lady* in 1945 – was photographed arriving
to a gathering throng, signing the visitors' book, chatting to women in
the Closing Room, watching as her daughter's feet were measured and

Margaret Lockwood with women factory workers
during her 1946 visit to the Clarks factory.

generally looking suitably impressed. 'Miss Lockwood enjoys wearing Clarks shoes in private life and says that she frequently receives complimentary comments on her footwear', the article concluded.

Royal connections were fostered. The then Princess Elizabeth and Princess Margaret were seen to be wearing Clarks shoes on their South African tour of 1947 and, by chance, the Queen, accompanied by Princess Elizabeth, Princess Margaret and the Duke of Edinburgh, visited the Clarks stand at the 1949 British Industries Fair at Olympia. A year earlier, Clarks had staged the first invitation-only private mannequin show ever to be held in Denmark, displaying 30 models of shoe. It took place at the Hotel Angleterre and was attended by some 130 buyers from Scandinavia and Holland.

Hugh Clark – in charge of home sales from the late 1920s until 1952 – took a keen interest in advertising and publicity. In April 1946, he explained:

Princess Margaret (at left) and Princess Elizabeth both wearing Clarks shoes during an official tour of South Africa in March 1947. Princess Elizabeth is wearing Montana sandals.

We have, as manufacturers, to educate the public on such things as the fitting of children's shoes, we have to give information about trends in fashion, we have to present a case to the public and try to make people understand what kind of a firm is making their shoes. All these things, and many more, are part of the useful job that advertising must do.

Soliciting feedback from the public was encouraged, if only to pass on any favourable comments to the workforce as morale boosters. On one occasion, in response to the platform-soled, open-backed Roxanne shoe, a former Wren from Maidstone was moved to write a poem and send it to Street. It began:

I was reading the paper, and saw Roxanne.
And straight away out in the street, I ran

Thinking how lovely, how grand, how divine,
If I am lucky a pair will be mine.

Wilfrid Hinde's role as export director had been taken over in 1946 by Nathan Clark, son of Roger Clark, and his department became known as the Overseas Division. Nathan, who had spent six years in Burma and India, appointed a fellow Royal Army Service Corps officer, Jack Rose-Smith, as sales manager, based in Street. Known as something of a free spirit within the Clark clan, Nathan occupied himself mainly with foreign licensing agreements to make shoes, while Rose-Smith took responsibility for direct export sales.

It was while Nathan was an officer in the Royal Army Service Corps in 1941 that he first chanced upon the idea of the Desert Boot. He had been posted to Burma and ordered to help establish a supply route from Rangoon to the Chinese forces at Chongqing. The road was never built after the Japanese bombed Pearl Harbor, triggering a new phase in the Second World War, but Nathan had made a note of what soldiers were wearing on their feet and, minded that Bancroft had asked him to be on the lookout for new designs originating from that part of the world, he duly reported back. As it happened, he had not one but two novel ideas: the Desert Boot and the Chupplee. The latter – which was withdrawn from sale in the 1970s – was an open-toe sandal based on what men wore in Northwest India, with plenty of soft leather covering the contours of the foot. It was certainly not a flip-flop.

Nathan never drew a salary from Clarks and he left the company in 1951 to pursue his own interests. But in 1979 he explained that his inspiration for the Desert Boot came from

... crepe-soled rough suede boots which officers in the Eighth Army were in the habit of getting made in the Bazaar in Cairo. Some of these officers came to Burma, and this is where I saw them. It is said that

MAJOR N. M. CLARK
LLOYDS BANK
LAHORE
INDIA

A Christmas card with a photograph of himself sent home by Nathan
Clark while based in India during the Second World War.

the original idea was from officers of the South African Division in the
desert and that the origin of theirs goes back to the Dutch Voertrekkers
footwear made of rough, tanned leather called Veldt Schoen. This name
is familiar to us in shoe manufacturing as the old name for the sandal
veldt, or stitch-down process.

Nathan sent sketches and rough patterns to Bancroft, but nothing
happened until he returned to Street. Once back, he approached an experienced pattern cutter called Bill Tuxill, but, as Nathan put it:

... every time I went to see how my two shoes were getting on, I would
see the sketches on his back shelf, and he would say with some embarrassment: 'Yes, Mr Nathan, I will get on with them next thing.'

Eventually Nathan began cutting them himself, but when he produced
trial samples they were not greeted with much enthusiasm.

A Londoner, Ken Crutchlow, gave the Desert Boot a spectacular publicity boost when he wore a pair to run across California's Death Valley in 1970. Photographs accompanying the story were widely published.

Then, in 1949, while attending the Chicago Shoe Fair, he showed the samples to Oskar Schoefler, fashion editor of *Esquire* magazine, who was so impressed that he ran a whole feature on the shoe, complete with colour photographs. A star was born. It immediately sold well in America and Canada and became the first adult Clarks shoe to be made in Australia. In a 1957 advertisement, Clarks called Desert Boots the 'world's most travelled shoes'.

In Europe, Lancelot (Lance) Clark, son of Tony Clark, helped to popularise the Desert Boot and it reached record sales in 1971. A publicity coup had come a year earlier when Ken Crutchlow, an eccentric Englishman, ran 130 miles across Death Valley in California wearing a bowler hat on his head and Desert Boots on his feet. This was not a master stroke of product placement conjured up by Clarks executives, but the result of a $1,000 bet Crutchlow had with a friend. Pictures of Crutchlow in his Desert Boots appeared in more than 150 newspapers and magazines and were estimated to have been seen by 30 million people.

The Desert Boot has developed a momentum all of its own ever since – and led to some curious associations. Liam Gallagher, lead singer of the now disbanded rock band Oasis, and Clarks might not seem like a perfect fit, but the former rabble-rouser was so taken by the Desert Boot in the 1990s that he hardly wore anything else and then went one step further by collaborating with Clarks to design his own version of the boot as part of his Pretty Green clothing label. Not to be outdone, Bob Dylan and Robbie Williams were seen sporting Desert Boots around the same time and it wasn't long before others jumped on the bandwagon. Sarah Jessica Parker was spotted in the David Z store in New York's Soho buying two pairs, one brown, one black, because she couldn't decide which colour she liked best. And the Jamaican rapper Vybz Kartel wove Desert Boots into one of his songs. Tony Blair, never one to miss a photo opportunity, opted two years into his premiership to wear a pair of Desert Boots in 1999 while promoting his Cool Britannia campaign.

The Desert Boot was nominated in 2009 by The Design Museum in London as one of the '50 Shoes that Changed the World' and by the beginning of 2012, more than 10 million pairs had been sold in over 100 countries. This is not a bad outcome for a shoe that its creator was told would never sell.

By 1945, exports had shrunk to virtually nothing, but two years later Clarks was doing business with Africa, Australasia, the Middle East, America, Canada, the West Indies, India, Ceylon (Sri Lanka), Iceland, the Faroe Islands, Belgium, Luxembourg, Scandinavia and Holland. In Holland, a Jewish refugee called Bob Arons proved sceptics wrong. Wilfrid Hinde had written to Arons telling him that 'owing to a number of changed circumstances we are doubtful ... our footwear can be sold again in Holland in worthwhile quantities'. A year on, in 1946, and

Arons had sold 10,000 pairs in the Netherlands, turning over £43,500.

Nathan, in charge of the Overseas Division, was keen to find production partners abroad, but Bancroft was more cautious. Deals, however, were signed with two firms in Australia, Alma Shoes Ltd and Enterprise Shoe Company. Alma was founded in 1925 by Thomas Harrison, who had emigrated from Stockton-on-Tees in 1910. He died in 1936 and, although his son took over, the company was in trouble. Clarks agreed to take 51 per cent of Alma's equity as part of what Nathan described to Bancroft as a 'manufacturing service agreement'. Enterprise was a neighbouring shoe factory which was also in dire straits. It specialised in men's boots and shoes. These two acquisitions led to the formation of Clarks Australia Ltd in the summer of 1948, structured in a similar way to Clarks Ireland Ltd.

In a minuted conversation, Nathan told Bancroft that 'the time for development in overseas is now, and ... the opportunity which exists for such development allows for no delay'. He wanted to push on in India, where he believed that independence would lead to protective tariffs on imports. Nathan felt a trading door was about to close. In 1948, he persuaded Bancroft to head East and organised meetings with Cooper, Allen & Co. and with the British India Corporation, but such was the political uncertainty in India that no deal was struck. Leaving Nathan in India, Bancroft returned to the UK on board Pan Am's *Empress of the Skies* from Calcutta. During the flight, Bancroft had watched a small child running up and down the aisle wearing a pair of Clarks shoes. After landing in London, the Lockheed Constellation aircraft took off again en route to Shannon, in Ireland, from where it was scheduled to continue its journey to America. But it crashed near Shannon airport, killing all but one passenger. The child wearing Clarks did not survive.

Bancroft's reluctance to rush into overseas production was not a new issue for C. & J. Clark. John Angell Peck, who had been appointed Clarks representative in Australia and New Zealand back in 1899 and who died in 1941, had repeatedly urged the board to open a factory in that part of the world to avoid import tariffs. But it never happened during Peck's lifetime.

Bancroft's official notes on overseas policy show that the board was 'only prepared to experiment with overseas development ... provided it [does not] endanger our home prosperity'. But Nathan continued to press for it, arguing the case for 'putting our eggs in several baskets all over the world', to which Bancroft responded that such a strategy was 'hard to carry out when you were short of eggs ... it was little use finding the eggs if you could not find the hens to sit on them'.

At one point, a deal was in the offing with the Port Elizabeth Boot Company in South Africa, whereby it would make women's and children's shoes, but this collapsed, whereupon Nathan focused his attention on Australia, New Zealand and Canada.

Clarks Australia Ltd began making shoes in Adelaide in 1949, while in New Zealand, where there had been an embargo on shoe imports for twelve years – with the exception of infants' footwear – plans were afoot to make and market shoes through Clarks New Zealand Ltd.

Bancroft was fourteen years older than his brother Nathan. Their relationship was strained. Towards the end of 1949 – by which time Nathan was working at Halliday's in Ireland – Bancroft jotted down his thoughts about the future of the Overseas Division, but there is no evidence that he made them public. In fact, eighteen months later, on 22 July 1951, he scribbled at the top of the first page: 'No one saw this'. Perhaps his musings were cathartic. Certainly they were unsparing in their criticism of his globe-trotting brother:

NMC's [Nathan Middleton Clark] effort is discursive. He flirts with new ideas such as selling last-making machinery and selling his latest patent on a royalty basis. He does this without carrying with him his home base and in his last promotion in the US makes statements [that are] untrue. In fact which were not checked by the responsible people in Street.

Writing in his own hand, Bancroft continued:

NMC suffers from lack of sustained effort. In Australia there has been no progress because of difficulties which have accumulated that side. NMC blames CJC [C. & J. Clark] for not developing new styles which he said in summer '48 were needed ... [but] NMC is no judge of what is right for the home market. He has no knowledge of it – no experience of it – he has the right and duty to bring back information and suggestions which may help to strengthen CJC in the home market but has no standing or position or right to criticise CJC's home market operations.

Bancroft felt Nathan had wasted twelve months in Australia 'shilly shallying' and believed there was no point pursuing overseas production without a planned sales policy to go with it:

Without it the best manufacturing will fail from vacillation. I have told NMC this many times and sent him to Ireland last summer to work it out but he runs away from the problem.

Such was Bancroft's exasperation that he expressed a 'wide doubt' as to whether Nathan had been suitable to run the Overseas Division at all.

His abilities are very great. He is a tremendous salesman and fruitful in ideas. I think it might be possible to run the OD [Overseas Division] if NMC were accepted as salesman and had under him a permanent deputy head of the OD through which all directions would go and who would be answerable for all actions of the others in the division. NMC has refused this and is working away from it.

Bancroft reported to the board at the end of 1949 that, under Nathan, the exports market had 'on balance lost money' and he expected the situation would not change in 1950.

Working at Clarks meant security – in many cases, a job for life. Maurice Burt joined Clarks in 1948 at the age of nineteen. His father was a labourer and he was brought up with his two brothers in Long Sutton, Somerset. On leaving school at fourteen, he joined a local woodwork company and then spent two

Press cutting at Street for the Skyline range in 1949.

years in the Royal Navy. Speaking in the summer of 2011 at his house in Street within walking distance of the factory, he describes his situation:

> When I came out of the Navy, Clarks was recruiting and really it was just a matter of turning up and filling out a form. They were looking for people and you had to be fairly backward not to be offered something. Because of the war and everything I didn't have much of an education. I realised from an early age that I had to use my hands more than my brains if I was going to get on.

Maurice started in the finishing room doing odd jobs, which was something of a rite of passage for new recruits, a period of unofficial apprenticeship during which the supervisors – known as the 'white coats' – would assess work and attitude and place the men and women accordingly. In 1948, Maurice was on the equivalent of £2.50 a week. There were three grades of employee – weekly, fortnightly and monthly – but it took some

Closing work, 1950.

considerable time to become a proper staff member if you joined straight from school. In Maurice's case, his letter informing him that he was a fully signed-up member of staff was dated 12 January 1962, fourteen years after he first cycled over to Street for his interview.

It spelled out the terms and conditions of employment, making clear he would be joining the Staff Pension Scheme – an 'expensive scheme that can only be maintained at its present level in times of good profit earnings' stressed the letter. His pay rose to £15 a week in 1962 and his appointment was subject to one month's notice on either side.

Patricia Andrews, who would become his wife, also worked in the factory, as did her father and as would Maurice's and Patricia's two daughters. In the November 1952 issue of the company's *News Sheet*, there is a picture of Maurice and Patricia on their wedding day, standing outside the Street Methodist Church.

'It was a sociable sort of place. My wife and I did most of our courting in the factory,' says Maurice. He continues:

Our manager was Peter Clothier and there were a few times when he turned a blind eye to what we were up to. We all used to work 8am to 6pm and on Saturday mornings. But to tell the truth, we never really started working much before 8.30am because there was a lot of chat to sort out first. Once you went on staff you pretty much had a job for life and that was the important thing. The feeling on the factory floor was that everything was alright while the family was in charge but when the outsiders started coming in they were desperate to show how brilliant they were – and things changed.

The company's 125th anniversary was celebrated in June 1950. Every member of staff was given a commemorative silver spoon in a little green box and a party was held in the newly opened Grove factory in Street, enlivened by the Sydney Lipton orchestra from London, which specialised in dance hall music. No alcohol was consumed – on the premises at least. Maurice Burt didn't go because he was unattached at the time and felt awkward attending on his own.

Peter Lord Ltd opened its fortieth shop in December 1952 in Tunbridge Wells, and the actress Yvonne Marsh was invited to cut the ribbon. This outlet was seen as a template for modern retail design, with its large glass doors and glass-fronted displays at the entrance, showing off as many lines as possible. The 'Women's Fitting Room', as it was called, was on the ground floor, children's and men's on the first floor. While having their feet measured, children were given a teddy to cuddle and sat on a chair that looked like a big drum. The message to shoppers was that Clarks represented affordable high fashion, and that Peter Lord sales staff were knowledgeable, trustworthy and always on the side of the consumer.

Bancroft described the Peter Lord shops as 'testing consumer reaction to our merchandise and to our methods of sale and promotion', but he also put out a statement to all sections of the trade in 1953, reiterating

The showroom at Mitre House, the Clarks London office in Regent Street, in 1950.

the company's commitment to the independent retailer and stressing that Peter Lord – which three years later would open a shop in Regent Street, its first in the West End of London – accounted for only 10 per cent of Clarks sales. Maintaining a balance between building up its own Peter Lord retail chain, while not antagonising the independent stores that sold Clarks, was a delicate task. He wrote:

> We must always bear in mind the tremendous advantage the independent retailer has over the multiple retailing organisation ... we also believe that as manufacturers we have shoes the public want, and we know that we have a knowledge of advertising and style to enable them to maintain their favour with the public. We ... believe in the independent retailer, those shops which absorb the major part of our distribution; and we feel sure that our policy of relying upon the independent retailer and the departmental store as the main outlet for 90 per cent of our pairage is a good one because it compels us to continue

the healthy fight of competition in matters of style, quality and value offered.

But the world of shoe retail was about to be shaken like never before. Bancroft was not the only one who thought that footwear in Britain was a potential honeypot. Charles Clore was on the prowl, his prey waiting quietly, invitingly, on every high street in every major town and city and in many smaller ones as well.

Clore was the son of Israel Claw, a Russian Jew born in Kovno, Lithuania, who brought his family to London in 1888. Israel's first job was as a cobbler, but it wasn't long before he had started a thriving rag trade business in the East End. His son was born on Boxing Day 1904 and would become one of the most controversial, feared and enthralling entrepreneurs of the twentieth century. Regarded by some people as the man who invented the take-over, his first purchase was the ailing Cricklewood Skating Rink in 1928, followed three years later by the loss-making Prince of Wales theatre on London's Coventry Street.

By 1953, Clore had amassed a fortune. As a frequent visitor to the United States, he had looked carefully at shoe businesses, noting that American women bought on average twice as many pairs of shoes each year as British women. He reasoned that it was only a matter of time before the British would catch up.

On returning from one such visit, Clore's friend Douglas Tovey, an ambitious and gregarious estate agent who worked for a firm called Healey & Baker, alerted him to Sears & Co (the True-Form Boot Company), which owned Freeman, Hardy & Willis and Trueform, comprising some 920 outlets across the country. Clore was interested in the shoes, but he was even more taken by the shops in which the shoes were sold. With Tovey's help, he worked out that the value of the retail properties greatly exceeded the value of the shares in the company – and in February 1953 he pounced, sending his offer direct to shareholders. As David Clutterbuck and Marion Devine wrote in *Clore: The Man and his Millions*:

To the board of Sears, the sudden attack was devastating. Its response was confused and unconvincing. The idea that anyone would make such an approach direct to the shareholders was unbelievable. Worse, it was ungentlemanly.

Accusations of ungentlemanly behaviour had never stopped Clore in the past. He had studied the tactics of American companies when confronted with hostile bids and was fully prepared for the unfolding furore. According to Clutterbuck and Devine:

> What offended so many people in the City was that Charles [Clore] had broken the convention that acquisitions should be by agreement. It was felt to be the equivalent of being asked to dinner and stealing the silver-ware. It was unthinkable, an outrage, yet it was legal and it was done.

Retail was in his blood from an early age, when he used to sell news-papers on street corners, and he had successfully built up Richard Shops, a retail chain that he bought low and sold high in 1949. Sears chairman Dudley Church was reported as saying: 'We never thought anything like this would happen to us', and the Sears family was incandescent with rage at the speed of events. But the deal was done and within twelve months, the sale and leaseback of properties to Legal & General raised £10 million, with Clore telling shareholders at the 1954 annual general meeting that the company still retained more than £3 million worth of freehold factories, warehouses and shops. Clore said:

> The first call on this money will be the requirements of the footwear business to enable it to carry through the programme of improvements and expansion ... it is not in the interests either of the shareholders or of the National Economy for a Company such as ours to retain vast sums locked up in freehold properties ... our capital should be employed primarily in our own business of making and selling boots and shoes.

Buying up smaller shoe companies was another vital part of Clore's strategy. In 1954, Freeman, Hardy & Willis acquired Harry Levison's

Work in the sole room at Street, 1950.

Fortress Shoe Company, which had 39 high street outlets, a deal that resulted in Levison, whom Clore admired as an arbiter of modern fashion, eventually taking over the entire management of Clore's shoe empire. Fortress was renamed Curtess and then Freeman, Hardy & Willis bought Philips Brothers' Character Shoes Ltd for £700,000.

J. Sears became Sears Holdings shortly before the Philips Brothers' acquisition, after which Dolcis was acquired for £6 million, followed by Saxone, Lilley & Skinner and Manfield in 1956. The Dolcis deal alarmed Clarks. Prior to the September board meeting, Bancroft circulated his thoughts to other directors:

> Clore's group has total assets of approximately £20 million and is therefore about four times as large as we are ... there is nobody in the USA now of similar dimensions.

Others shared his concern. Writing in the *Sunday Express* that same month, Edward Westropp, the paper's City Editor, said it was 'just another dreary financial deal, just another company changing hands. What interest could that possibly be to us – the shoppers of Britain?' Then he went on to answer his own question, warning that Clore was robbing consumers of proper choice

> Now is the time to let the shopper know who he is going to. Let it be obligatory to put the name of the real owner or parent company in big letters over the door.

On seeing Westropp's piece, Cecil Notley, Clarks' advertising man, wrote to Bancroft wondering if the chairman might have 'inspired the article', adding that 'it seems to be just what the doctor ordered'.

Along the way, Clore formed the British Shoe Corporation as an umbrella organisation for his footwear operations, electing to establish the headquarters in Leicester rather than using Freeman, Hardy & Willis's main offices in Northampton. By 1962, the British Shoe Corporation controlled 2,000 shops.

This dramatic concentration in shoe retailing was at odds with the ongoing diversity of shoe production. In 1956, there were still some 1,000 firms in the business of making footwear in Britain, of which more than 80 per cent employed fewer than 200 people. Only around 50 shoe manufacturers had a workforce in excess of more than 400. Clarks was the largest single manufacturer in the country.

Clarks was not only a recognised and respected name on the British high street but was close to becoming a pillar of the establishment. Shortly before Queen Elizabeth II's coronation in 1953 (during which she wore shoes designed by Roger Vivier), the company felt compelled to put out its own statement to mark 'an event so momentous that all ordinary happenings lose something of their importance'. Describing the crowning of a

A mid-1950s window display card for Clarks Teenagers shoes. Clarks had targeted the teenage market from 1950 onwards.

young Queen as a 'symbol of hope, of endeavour, of re-dedication to our duty', the statement went on to declare that

> ... if in these crowded islands we no longer have the surpluses of national wealth our forefathers enjoyed, if we have to depend more and more on hard work and the application of unceasing commitment to industrial, commercial, agricultural and educational needs in order to win through, we feel that in our Queen, already proven in the ordeal of tireless public service, we have a shining example, spurring us on to our goal. Invigorated by the spirit of youth and freedom which she manifests we can, and will, achieve a new and happy way of life.

8

Expansion, contraction – and management consultants

THE 1960S BEGAN WITH A SWING. And in Street there were no signs that the music would stop, or the party end. In the first year of that decade, Clarks recorded sales of £18,482,000 and a pre-tax profit of £1,446,000, up 10 per cent on the previous year.

'Our rate of expansion is rapid,' wrote Bancroft Clark in the Annual Report and Accounts for the year ending 31 December 1960. He continued:

> In the four years from 1956 to 1960, total assets have nearly doubled ... such continuity of good trading is unusual. It may be that the public is turning away from consumer durables, the demand for which, I think, began to fall off before the latest credit squeeze. The public may be more interested in dress, including shoes, than it has been since the end of the War ... we had not forecast such good demand.

This was the period when Clarks factories were at the fulcrum of its business and when the broader Clarks community flourished like never before. Demand was so strong that in the autumn of 1960 the factories were running at full capacity – and yet retailers were still complaining of a lack of stock. Clarks was not the only footwear company in celebratory mode. It had been a spectacular year for the whole of the trade in the UK. But it wasn't just UK shoemakers who were doing well. At the same time, imports of cheaper shoes from abroad also reached a post-war record.

Demand for shoes may have been on the increase, but so too were manufacturing costs. In 1960, wages in Clarks factories increased by 3 per cent – with a further 3 per cent rise scheduled for February 1961. At the same time, in 1960, the working week was reduced from 45 to 43¾ hours. Later on, it was to be reduced yet further to 41½ hours. Rather than increase prices – except on some of Clarks' more popular children's lines – Bancroft's answer to raised costs was to pursue new, more economical methods of production:

> If these come off and if we can exploit them, they should enable us to offer better value, make more money and sell shoes at lower prices ... These are techniques which are used by the vast mass production factories of Russia and Czechoslovakia and which have not, hitherto, generally speaking been applied to the smaller factories and shorter runs of the shoe trade in the western world.

As well as providing inspiration for economical production methods, with a huge order for women's footwear, Russia also contributed to the boost in Clarks exports which, overall, exceeded £1 million for the first time. The interest from Russia would lead to Clarks periodically advertising on Soviet State television, particularly during extreme, cold winters when freezing Russians were reminded of the warmth and comfort of Clarks' wool-lined range of 'Igloo' boots. In 1959, Bancroft and his eldest son, Daniel Clark, were among a group of shoe manufacturers from the UK who visited Moscow and Leningrad in the Soviet Union, and Kiev in the Ukraine. They were accompanied on this busy, eleven-day fact-finding mission by a member of the BBC's Overseas Monitoring Service, who acted as interpreter. The consensus was that the Russians were ahead of the west when it came to the vulcanising of microcellular soling – or rubber soles – and other non-leather progressions in the trade, but were way behind in styling, particularly of women's shoes, which, Bancroft noted, in the Soviet Union tended to have thick, rounded toes and chunky heels. The really good news, however, was learning that although the Soviet Union

Clarks shoes on parade at a fashion show in Moscow in 1956.

intended to increase its shoe production by 50 per cent over the next five years, it had no plans to build new factories to achieve this ambitious goal. Almost certainly, the Soviets would have to rely on imports.

There had also been a development in Canada a few months before the Coronation, when Clarks bought the loss-making Blachford Shoe Manufacturing Company Ltd. Founded in 1914 by two brothers, Blachford specialised in high-grade welted women's shoes, making 100,000 pairs a year, and the board was confident that it could be turned around. With the company came a coast-to-coast sales organisation, which Jack Rose-Smith, who had brokered the deal, hoped would double Blachford sales within two years. In fact, despite the efforts of several senior directors who made visits to Ontario – including Bancroft himself – the Canadian operation was a burden. A loss of £8,000 in its first year was understandable, but explaining further losses of £18,000 in 1954 was more difficult. By the end of 1956, Bancroft wasn't bothering to give exact sales figures, bluntly reporting in the Annual Report and Accounts that 'Canada again lost a large sum'. And in 1960, he simply wrote: 'Canada business is bad'.

Meanwhile, sales in markets elsewhere in the world were mixed. Business in Africa was strong and accounted for nearly a quarter of Clarks exports, while the West Indies and to a lesser extent Europe were proving to be encouraging. Trade with America was tough, but it was better in Australia where, in 1959, the company had bought the majority of shares in G. T. Harrison Shoes Ltd, the firm which had begun manufacturing Clarks under licence almost a decade earlier. Then, in the spring of 1960, Clarks acquired Diamond Shoes Ltd, a Melbourne firm specialising in women's shoes. There were now three factories in Australia, with a fourth soon to open in Adelaide.

Production of Clarks Torflex children's shoes in New Zealand began in 1961, and closer to home a new factory was built on the Dundalk site in Ireland. Shortly afterwards, Clarks acquired the Irish manufacturer Padmore & Barnes Ltd, in Kilkenny, a move which meant that worldwide, Clarks now employed more than 10,000 people and made nearly 11 million pairs of shoes a year.

In an effort to bring together all overseas shoes interests, the board had decided, in 1959, to form a new division called Clarks Overseas Shoes Ltd, which was responsible for exports from the UK, manufacturing in Ireland, Australia and Canada; manufacturing under licence in New Zealand and South Africa; and wholesaling in the United States and Rhodesia (now Zimbabwe). Arthur Halliday was made managing director and Jack Rose-Smith a director.

Meanwhile, at head office in Street, Bill Graves, who was not a family member, became a director. He had joined the company in 1933 at the age of fourteen and attended Strode School in Street. After rising swiftly through the ranks, he proved to be a big success as head of production of children's footwear and was still only 41 when appointed to the ten-man board. In 1960, there were four other non-family directors: Arthur Halliday, Jack Davis, Leslie Graves (Bill's older brother) and Reginald C. Hart.

The issue of what roles members of the family should play in the firm would test Clarks in the years to come. Bancroft found it a vexing and at times tiresome discussion, even though in 1960 he made a point of saying that 'the key to a successful future lies with securing good professional management at all levels'. He went on to explain that by 'professional' he meant:

> ... those who have been trained for the execution of their management duties and who give full-time devotion to them ... we seek to bring in outsiders, as well as able members of the shareholding families who are interested and will accept appointment on these conditions.

Bancroft made a special effort to check up on the fifth generation as they approached the start of their working lives. In the autumn of 1959, he went to see Tony Clark's son, Lance, who was reading geography at Oxford university and considering a career in the colonial service. Lance was an exceptional rugby player, who went on to play for Bath.

'Bancroft said I should try six weeks working in Street – and I've been there nearly 60 years,' says Lance, who, when interviewed in 2011, was still working as a consultant at Clarks, reporting directly to the chief executive.

Lance developed a particular interest in how shoes were made. After building a relationship with Peter Sapper, a German with a small moccasin business called Sioux, Lance, while working at Padmore & Barnes in Ireland (part of Clarks Ireland Ltd), was responsible for 'Project M', which came to fruition in 1967 with the launch of the Wallabee. This iconic shoe – a lace-up with crêpe sole, inspired by classic men's moccasins – was at first regarded as too radical for the British market but enjoyed almost immediate success in North America. To advertise the Wallabees, the largest billboard ever seen up to that time on the North American continent (it measured 185ft by 45ft) was erected in Toronto, Canada, next to a highway used by more than 250,000 motorists every day. By 1973, the two Padmore & Barnes factories – in Kilkenny and Clonwell – made little else other than Wallabees, producing some 18,000 pairs a week.

Other members of the fifth generation who played prominent roles

This billboard advertising Clarks Wallabees in Toronto in 1967
was at that time the largest ever seen in North America.

during the 1960s and 1970s were Jan and Richard Clark, the second and third surviving sons of Bancroft and Cato Clark.

'Most members of the family went down the same route on leaving university' says Richard Clark, who graduated from Cambridge university in 1961. He continues:

> We were a manufacturing company based in Street and our education in the business tended to follow similar lines. I spent about six weeks in various independent shoe retailers and then some time at Peter Lord. I also went to a tannery and a factory in France. Then Bill Graves gave me a job as a factory assistant and had me working on projects related to children's shoes. Eventually, I went to Ireland and ran the New Forest factory at Dundalk, which was making women's runabouts called Serenity.

Bancroft persistently worried about finding jobs for family members – or, at least, the right jobs. Shortly before his retirement in 1967, he wrote a document called 'Management Changes', in which he cited the example of Anthony Clothier, eldest son of Peter Clothier (grandson of William S. Clark), who had gained promotion to 'something within Clarks Ltd, before he had mastered and made a success of his present job'. According to the minutes of a board meeting held in 1967, this was a view shared by Tony Clark, but Stephen Clark said in a note to Bancroft that:

> ... the apparent nepotism that you are feeling puritanical about is an advantage to the business. Without it we would not have had the guts to put people as young as Anthony [Clothier] and Jan [Clark] into their present job. We should have filled them by seniority, with someone of 40 and had we done that we should not have been acting in the best interests of the shareholders.

Anthony in fact rose within Clarks to become a main board director from 1977 until 1986. He was later president of the British Footwear Manufacturers Federation on two occasions, and president of the European Shoe Federation from 1979 to 1983.

The Clarks commitment to Street in the 1960s remained consistent with its Quaker heritage. In 1959, the Clark Foundation was set up to fund educational and recreational opportunities for all ages. In 1963, for example, the Strode Theatre opened, funded entirely by the foundation and drawing in audiences from around the West Country for plays, films, pantomimes and revues. One notable landmark was its staging of the premiere of William Douglas Home's *The Secretary Bird*, which went on to enjoy stellar success in London's West End.

Clarks spent £9,000 on an extension to the Street library, after which more than a third of the town signed up to become registered readers. The

James Lidbetter, the Street librarian, stands in the new library extension built in 1959.

foundation also paid a contribution of £35,500 towards a sports hall for Strode College, formerly known as Strode Technical College, and £80,000 towards changing Strode School into a comprehensive, Crispin School. It also paid £47,000 for a new pavilion and to renovate the field of Victoria Athletic Field and Club for use by members of the public and not just Clarks employees. More controversially, Clarks helped facilitate the provision of a relief road around Street to encourage lorries and other heavy vehicles not to clog up the narrow town centre. Some shops and small businesses expressed their reservations, arguing that they would lose business from the by-pass, but the work went ahead anyway and the road remains in place today.

The sense of community, a world within a world, was reinforced in 1957 when the company launched *Clarks Courier*, a newspaper which for some years was published in addition to *Clarks Comments*. Although intended to fill a perceived need for better and more widespread communication, the *Clarks Courier* – which over the years became referred to simply as the *Courier* – was read not merely by Clarks employees. You could pick up a copy for 2*d*. on Street's High Street. The paper was printed fortnightly on presses belonging to the *Bristol Evening World*, and its policy and editorial content were determined by the Clarks public relations department, which in turn liaised with Vernon Smart, the personnel director, particularly over sensitive matters of labour relations.

To dismiss the *Courier* as a management propaganda sheet would do a disservice to those who submitted copy from the far reaches of the Clarks empire, often with judicious wit and an enviable attention to detail. Correspondents were appointed in each factory and there were regular columns, such as the 'Shepton Notebook' and 'Irish Diary'.

A full listing of cinema showings throughout the region was run in every issue, along with classified and display ads and an entertainment guide called 'The Best in the West'. There was a regular full-page feature called 'Taken for Granted – Courier looks at jobs that rarely make the limelight', and the 'Pet Portrait Competition' was well-received by readers.

'The editorial policy of *Courier* is one of neutrality,' wrote David Boyce, one of the paper's senior editors in 1960:

> The paper is neither pro-management nor pro-employee. It sits on the fence and holds a purely watching brief. It is a mouthpiece for both management and employees alike; within its pages can appear advance news of developments within the industry, details of new techniques, department changes and personality profiles. All reported without fear or favour.

Certainly, at the start of the 1960s, there were plenty of changes to report on as Clarks embarked upon another structural reorganisation aimed at addressing the burgeoning and complex businesses both in Britain and abroad.

In 1960, C. & J. Clark became a holding company with four main subsidiaries, of which the biggest was the UK shoemaking and wholesaling operation, known as Clarks Ltd. Bancroft assumed the role of chairman of both C. & J. Clark and Clarks Ltd. The second subsidiary, Clarks Overseas Shoes Ltd, remained as it was, with Arthur Halliday as managing director and Jack Rose-Smith as his number two; C. & J. Clark Retailing Ltd, which at that stage consisted of the Peter Lord shops, was the domain of Reginald Hart, and Avalon Industries Ltd was a new holding company for various subsidiaries relating to Clarks shoe components and engineering interests. Avalon Industries was under the control of Stephen Clark.

Street Estates Ltd, a property and estates management company, was also part of Clarks, although it was not at this stage included in the annual accounts. It had been formed in 1930 to oversee the non-industrial properties in Street, which the company had either built or bought as housing for its workers. By the early 1940s, there were around 100 such Street Estates properties. In 1961, more than 60 per cent of its portfolio was made up of industrial buildings; 20 per cent residential and 20 per cent of unspecified land in and around the town.

The reorganisation at Avalon Industries meant there were related companies dotted about the West Country, trading variously in materials, chemicals, components and machinery used by shoe manufacturers. In 1961 Avalon Industries was made up of: The Avalon Leather Board Company, based in Street, which had been started by William S. Clark in 1877; C. I. C. Engineering Ltd, in Bath, which would merge with Ralphs Unified in 1966; Avalon Shoe Supplies Ltd, the sales company of the Avalon group; The Larkhill Rubber Company Ltd, which made all types of rubber and PVC soles; Strode Components Ltd, with three factories – in Street, Warminster and Castle Cary – making plastic heels, wedges, cut-crepe soles, insoles, lasts and steel shanks; and Avalon Chemicals, which produced adhesives, resins and polyurethane compounds (often known in the trade as PU) from a factory in Shepton Mallet regarded as the most advanced pre-polymer plant in the world.

Not all of these were run by members of the family, but in 1961 Bancroft's son Daniel, aged 30, was put in charge of Strode Components and Ralph Clark, 35, was made manager of the Larkhill Rubber Company, which moved that year from its cramped premises in Street to a newly built £250,000 factory just outside Yeovil. The rubber factory was particularly important because, in addition to Clarks, it also supplied all three of the other big shoe manufacturers in the UK: K Shoes, Lotus and Norvic.

Ralph Clark was the son of Alfred Clark, a science academic and Fellow of the Royal Society who taught at Edinburgh University. On leaving school in Edinburgh, Ralph was offered a scholarship to King's College, Cambridge, where he read history. On graduating from Cambridge university, Ralph had hoped to join the Royal Navy, but was prevented from doing so because he was colour blind. Instead, he was offered a job in personnel at the Colonial Development Corporation. In 1952, he attended a family wedding in Street and fell into conversation with his cousin, Bancroft, who asked him to join the firm.

I had never thought of going into the business, and to begin with I wasn't sure what my job was. I had more or less a free hand and was expected to attach myself to something or other, generally make myself useful. I hung around the rubber factory and saw that it was grossly mismanaged. Eventually, Bancroft asked me if I would take it over and I had to build up the new factory from scratch. I was a complete amateur and I'm not sure I covered myself in glory.

After a disagreement on sales strategy with Stephen Clark, chairman of Avalon Industries, in which Bancroft took Stephen's side, there were, according to Ralph, 'two years of guerrilla warfare' during which:

... Stephen got a bee in his bonnet about setting up a sales company to handle all Avalon's products. I objected strongly to this because it wasn't as if we were selling a finished project. Clearly, Stephen thought my view was useless and then I found myself in an embarrassing corner when Bancroft sided with Stephen and said I had to go along with what was proposed. I said I would, but not willingly, and that made me even more unpopular. Then we started making serious money and I stayed 20 years at the rubber factory.

Not long after, in 1965, Ralph took over as chairman of Avalon Industries when Stephen became Company Secretary of C. & J. Clark, a post he held until his retirement in 1975.

The Larkhill Rubber Company Ltd, like other parts of the business, benefited from Clarks moving into the computer age. The company had acquired two rented IBM 305s early in 1960, which became a source of much interest among other companies. But it had taken Clarks' computer specialist, Roy Wilmot, more than 24 months to persuade the board of the data-processing merits of computers. This was one innovation that Clarks was slow to embrace. In *Towards Precision Shoemaking*, Kenneth Hudson wrote:

> The use of all this data had not always been immediately apparent to the senior members of the management staff for whom it was intended and, in a wise and successful attempt to improve understanding, a Trojan-horse approach was adopted, whereby a young man who loved and respected computers was somehow attached to each relevant and influential department head, to act as a combination of interpreter and computer's friend. Less reverent observers have described these indispensable aides as plumbers' mates.

Meanwhile, on the high streets of Britain, the growing power and influence of Charles Clore's British Shoe Corporation continued to pose a threat to Clarks, but it also presented the company with an opportunity. The threat was evident enough. Clore's shops could opt to stop selling Clarks altogether as the British Shoe Corporation looked to source cheaper shoes from overseas. And although Clarks had its own Peter Lord outlets, these were under no obligation to buy from Clarks for fear of antagonising the independents specialising in or selling Clarks shoes in high numbers. It was a state of affairs that gave rise to tension between the production and retailing arms of the company, a rift that continued for several decades. It was, in fact, a growing sore that only went away many years later, once Clarks finally stopped making shoes altogether.

The opportunity presented by the British Shoe Corporation was for Clarks to strengthen its position in the unbranded shoe market. Freeman, Hardy & Willis, Saxone, Manfield and many of the other shoe companies that made up the British Shoe Corporation were not manufacturers. They

A shopfront in Ellesmere Port, Cheshire, in 1963, prominently promoting Clarks shoes.

were strictly in the retail and marketing business, buying in unbranded shoes and selling them under their own name direct to consumers. Clarks already had some experience as manufacturers of unbranded shoes, having created a subsidiary expressly for this purpose in 1957 called Wansdyke Shoes Ltd, which operated from a factory in Bath. In the 1960 Annual General Report, Bancroft said:

> Our plans are to extend this company [Wansdyke] so as to be able to exploit the Clarks shoe-making techniques in markets where we are unable to do so on a Clarks branded basis.

Wansdyke had been making shoes for high-end customers such as Harrods and low-end ones such as Barratts ('Walk the Barratt Way'), a company that Clore, much to his annoyance, failed to buy in 1964, despite offering in excess of £5 million for a majority shareholding. In the 1960s, the plan was for Wansdyke to concentrate on making cheaper shoes – mainly sandals – supplying principally the British Shoe Corporation and

Marks & Spencer. It was hoped that Wansdyke would make 10,000 pairs a week, but in reality it seldom produced more than 3,000. The contract with Marks & Spencer stuttered and stalled for a few months before it petered out altogether in May 1962 following rows about price increases and the speed of production. At one point, Marks & Spencer complained that:

> ... when we started with Wansdyke we were given to understand that this venture would receive the fullest support and cooperation of Clarke's [sic] organisation, and that the great fund of knowledge available at Clarke's [sic] would be at the disposal of the new company.

The following year, in 1963, Wansdyke temporarily stopped supplying the British Shoe Corporation, but resumed making shoes for Marks & Spencer. It was also continuing to do business with, among others, Barratts, Debenhams, Lennards, Mothercare and Stead and Simpson. The on-off relationship with Clore's British Shoe Corporation intensified when Clarks bought A. & F. Shoes Ltd in 1962 and London Lane Ltd in 1965, both small, London-based firms producing mainly high-fashion footwear. This was part of a drive to attract younger consumers – the so-called 'with it' crowd. Peter Clothier, who was in charge of women's shoe production in the UK, felt strongly about this market. Speaking at the 1960 annual Dinner of the London and Southern Counties Shoe Retailers' Association, Clothier said:

> To sell more shoes, we must turn to the younger generation who are now so often the initiators and first acceptors of fashion trends. It is no use manufacturers and retailers setting themselves up as a committee of vigilantes to decide what young people will buy ... young people today have minds of their own and only when they see irresistible shoes irresistibly displayed in every shoe shop will the impact be irresistible.

But Clothier appeared less sure of himself when it came to dealing with the British Shoe Corporation. In a confidential note to Bancroft, he outlined eight options facing Clarks. Option three was:

If C.J.C.'s [Clarks] intention is not substantially to expand in retailing there would be clear advantage and not too much danger in developing business with BSC [the British Shoe Corporation].

Option four presented an entirely different scenario:

If C.J.C.'s intention is to expand in retailing, there would sooner or later be a clash with BSC, where they say in effect 'if you go ahead in retailing we throw you out'.

Clothier went on to conclude that:

... in this uncertain position, I would doubt if it is worth going far out of our way or risking serious loss of business from existing accounts to build up even a substantial trade with BSC ... may it not be wiser policy in the long run to build business with, and strengthen our links in every way we can with those multiples who are independent of BSC, both because that business is likely to be on a surer footing and because they are easier prospects for us to absorb as time goes on if we so wish.

Acknowledging that the British Shoe Corporation had 'wonderful sites' and plenty of them, Clothier said Clarks needed to find 'more efficient retailers than BSC' who would offer better terms of business. But, in what could be regarded as an anachronism, the terms of business were not always favourable in relation to the Clarks-owned Peter Lord shops, never mind the British Shoe Corporation or the remaining independents. In fact, Peter Lord was at times more independent than the independents.

Bancroft became sufficiently rattled by Clore that on 30 March 1962 he fired off a letter to Keith Joseph, the Minister of State at the Board of Trade, complaining of what he saw as the British Shoe Corporation's 'monopoly'.

Joseph replied by agreeing that Bancroft should meet his parliamentary secretary, Niall Macpherson. A meeting took place on 10 April 1962, attended by Bancroft, Macpherson and three civil servants. The outcome was disappointing. In a note written the day after the meeting, Bancroft recorded:

> I described the present situation where the Clore group controls 50 per cent of the multiple business, 33 per cent of the specialist shoe shop business, and 22 per cent of shoes sold in the UK ... that the effect of their controlling 50 per cent of the multiple business made them dominant in the city centre selling of shoes, and this was a difficult position ... I asked whether the government's view and policy on monopoly had changed and whether it ought to change. The answer was no, that they are not contemplating any change.

A year later, Sears Holdings – the British Shoe Corporation's parent company – announced record profits that were 22 per cent up on the previous year. Clore was typically punchy, telling shareholders that the directors of Sears and of the British Shoe Corporation 'are constantly examining suitable ways of expanding the activities of the group, whether by acquisition or development of existing businesses'. Sears was already a huge and diverse group, embracing everything from shipbuilding (Furness Shipbuilding Company Ltd) and mining (Parmeko Ltd) to laundry and dry cleaning equipment (Brown & Green Ltd) and air conditioning (Mellor Bromley Ltd). It had also bought two prestigious West End jewellers, Mappin & Webb and Garrard & Co. Ltd.

Over the next few years, Clarks and the British Shoe Corporation played a cat-and-mouse game. In March 1966, Tony Clark, managing director of C. & J. Clark, met his British Shoe Corporation counterpart, Harry Levison, at a 'private, social occasion', during which Levison claimed that Clore left him alone to run the business as he saw fit. The two men discussed the small matter of large mark-ups, with Levison insisting that 45 per cent was his 'minimum standard'. Tony later wrote:

He [Levison] says branded manufacturers, including Clarks, are always welcome and should keep in touch with his various buyers, although they will be wasting everyone's time unless they get the 45 per cent mark-up firmly into their heads!

Clarks' enthusiasm for the youth market led to the national release of two cinema commercials for the Wessex line (Clarks' umbrella brand for mass-produced lines), filmed in colour and shown in more than 1,000 cinemas. In the two-minute version, Wessex shoes appeared in conjunction with McCaul Knitwear, while the one-minute film concentrated solely on Clarks, the soundtrack featuring 'Big Beat Boogie' by Bert Weedon. In the February 1960 issue of *Clarks Comments*, Stanley F. Berry, the Clarks advertising manager, explained the rationale:

> There are two fields in which the young dominate: the Cinema, and Popular Music through the medium of gramophone records. The Rank people, after much research, claim that they can now produce a predestined top ranking disc based on well-proved formulae, and that film advertising associated with such music, without words, is likely to be more effective with young people than conventional cinema advertising.

The commercial was shot at Elstree Studios, with a roof-top set designed by the art director Cedric Dawe, and the action – featuring dance sequences performed by members of the Cool for Cats troupe, who had been a big hit on ITV – was choreographed by Dougie Squires. Squires had made his name on *Chelsea at Nine*, a television series starring Billie Holiday, and on the BBC's *On The Bright Side*, made famous by Stanley Baxter.

Even more striking advertisements would follow. In the summer of 1964, two television commercials went on air with a James Bond theme. They were produced by Terence Young, who had worked on *From Russia*

With Love, and the Bond-style music was arranged and conducted by Malcolm Mitchell. The idea of these two commercials – which were shot mainly in Palmers Green in London – was to remind viewers of Clarks' fitting service and what became known as its 'No Time Limit' guarantee.

In a similar populist vein, Clarks provided Honor Blackman with her shiny thigh boots and other footwear that she wore in the role of leather-clad Cathy Gale in ITV's *The Avengers* series, which regularly commanded an audience of 6 million on Saturday nights. And in 1967, Clarks hosted the BBC's *Any Questions* live from its Plymouth factory, when the panel, chaired by Freddie Grisewood – who was nearly 80 at the time and had been on the programme since its inception in 1948 – included Sir Gerald Nabarro, a flamboyant, handlebar-moustached Tory MP, and a future leader of the Labour Party, Michael Foot.

Compared with women's shoes, little money was spent marketing the Clarks men's range – because there wasn't much of a range to market. But in 1962, Clarks bought the established men's shoe manufacturing business of J. T. Butlin & Sons Ltd. This company, based in Rothwell near Kettering in Northamptonshire, specialised in mail order sales and had a sound reputation for the more formal men's shoe market. This was a contentious acquisition because Clarks had always approached men's shoes with a diffident air – making a mere 0.8 per cent of men's shoes in the UK in 1959. But the decision may have been influenced by the fact that John Butlin, the managing director, was married to Honor Impey, a great-granddaughter of James Clark.

In 1941, Clarks had made men's boots as part of its commitment to the war effort and shortly afterwards it experimented by subcontracting work to G. B. Britton & Sons in Bristol, hoping this might lead to a more concerted commitment to men's shoes. But it never quite happened. In the 1940s, the board had concluded that G. B. Britton & Sons did not produce the quality of work that Clarks required – or, at the very least, a standard that could command the sort of prices necessary to justify a bigger invest-ment in the men's market. Prior to the purchase of J. T. Butlin & Son, Bancroft had considered a bid for an alternative Northamptonshire firm, Crockett & Jones, which also made men's shoes, but this came to nothing.

Traditionally, it had been left to the factories in Ireland to manufacture most of Clarks' shoes for men, particularly the successful 'Flotilla' range, which was first introduced in 1954 and then gained its own separate cata-logue in 1958. By 1962, Flotillas supplied everything a man could need by way of footwear: 'Brogues'; 'Suedes'; 'Casuals'; 'Contemporaries'; and 'Sandals'. Appropriately, the sales slogan for Flotillas was: 'The City to the Sea'. Not until 1970 was the Clarks Flotilla range superseded by Craftmas-ters, City and Club shoes.

A touch of design class was introduced to Clarks' range in 1963 with the appointment of Hardy Amies as consultant designer, a man whose other clients included the Queen and the Queen Mother. Amies, a Londoner born in Maida Vale, was 49 when he began working for Clarks and seemed in no doubt about his expertise. Speaking at an event organised by the Royal Society of the Arts, Sir Hardy, as he later was to become, said:

> A dress designer is not just a frivolous person catering to the whims of rich women, but someone who, properly used, can play a part in the industrial life of this country.

His credits included a variation on the Chelsea Boot, elastic-sided shoes and slip-ons, and it was he who coined the phrase 'the laceless look'. Amies was invited to share his vision with readers of the *Courier* in October 1964, advancing the cause of raised heels. 'There are few men who would scorn at being an inch taller,' he said, before stressing that 'the shininess of well-polished leather is the best possible contrast to the mattness of a wool suit, still the basis for modern men's dressing.' He ended up deploring young people's 'disregard of grooming ... an attitude of mind backed up by a shortage of domestics'.

Young people who met with Amies' disapproval were not the natural customers of Peter Lord. They would be catered for later when Clarks

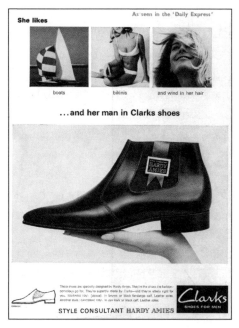

A 1965 press advertisement produced during
Hardy Amies' stint as a consultant for Clarks.

bought Ravel, which targeted fashion-conscious young men and women with cash to spend on contemporary footwear. Peter Lord, regarded as the purveyors of sensible shoes, continued to grow. After opening for the first time in London's Oxford Street in 1960, with a staff of 24, the chain's 70 outlets were selling nearly one million pairs of shoes a year. The Oxford Street branch was competing with no fewer than 30 shoe shops on that street alone, but it did so with aplomb, its huge glass windows catching the eye of passers-by, and that same original site, within a few minutes' walk of Oxford Circus Underground station, is still occupied by Clarks today.

In 1962, the British Shoe Corporation controlled around 2,000 of the UK's estimated 14,000 shoe shops. British Bata, the biggest independent, had, by comparison, fewer than 300 outlets. But size was not everything. Clore's British Shoe Corporation had its critics, not least because Clore himself had his critics – in growing numbers. Felicity Green, women's editor of the *Daily Mirror*, wrote scathingly in the spring of 1963 about his cavalier style in what amounted to an open letter:

> When you moved into the shoe business you obviously organised things in your usual efficient manner. No doubt your trusty accountants moved in first and, when they had things on a sound financial basis you proceeded to sell shoes scientifically as you might sell fish or saucepans.

The *Sunday Times* Contango column ran a piece headlined 'The village shoemakers match up to Mr Clore', which referred disparagingly to the 'Clore colossus' that had 'squeezed out the smaller multiple chains'. It continued:

> The Clarks – like the Frys and the Rowntrees and the Cadburys – are Quakers. And they believe in living in the heart of the place that their enterprise has created. Bancroft Clark's house is in the middle of the village, where the buses stop, and the teenagers' motor-cycles change gear. Nobody notices particularly when he drops into the social club or strolls down to the Post Office.

This idealistic account of life in Street ended with a quote from Bancroft:

> The women's magazines know nothing about style. It's the little girls in short skirts showing their knees who change style. And we can't let Mr Clore always see the changes first.

The *Financial Times* had warned a year earlier that it was in 'manufacturing rather than in retailing that the biggest opportunities are to be found ... retailers appear to have exhausted their opportunities for the time being'. Certainly, 1962 was a difficult year for all UK shoe retailers, but, despite the *Financial Times*'s foreboding, 1963 saw Peter Lord making a welcome recovery, with sales of £3 million. And the *Financial Times* would also be proved wrong about manufacturing as more and more footwear companies began to source shoes from overseas rather than making them in Britain.

Sourcing shoes from outside the UK – also referred to as resourcing – would haunt Clarks for many years to come. It's easy to conclude that the company should have moved towards sourcing with greater speed, but buying-in footwear was utterly at odds with Clarks raison d'être as a shoemaker. The company's whole culture and history were based on making shoes. Manufacturing shoes was not so much what Clarks did best, but what it *did*.

Even so, in 1960, Hugh Woods, who worked for Clarks Overseas Shoes Ltd, went to Italy and began sourcing ready-made shoes that retailed in Canada and North America under the Clarks name. Woods was acting with Bancroft's full approval, but it did not go down well in some of Clarks West Country factories. In an interview in 2005 with Dr Tim Crumplin, Clarks archivist, Woods said that the

> factory managers were incensed because nobody had ever bought foreign shoes and branded them Clarks. I was known as the Clarks Wop.

One of those who took up a post as sales assistant in Peter Lord's Oxford Street branch in late 1966 was Roger Pedder, who, 30 years later, would become chairman of C. & J. Clark Ltd. Pedder read economics at the University of Liverpool, where one of his tutors was Dr Roland Smith, a future chairman of House of Fraser and a man who had close links with the then powerful Boot & Shoe Association. Smith knew people in high places at Clarks and helped Pedder get an interview in 1963 for a place on the graduate trainee scheme. Pedder was successful.

Clarks took on five graduate trainees each year, all of whom would spend their first week learning to make a pair of shoes from scratch. Bancroft was in the habit of picking one of these trainees as his personal assistant. Towards the end of 1963, he chose Pedder.

'I used to pay the cook, the cleaners, the gardeners, arrange the family holidays, you name it,' says Pedder. He adds:

Bancroft had an absolute dedication to the company in all its aspects. He was very much of his time, the master, but he was also inclusive and commanded a great deal of respect. He saw the business in the context of the international economy and he had a high ethical sense for what was right. He was straight talking but careful in his dealings with people, especially members of the family. But there was never any doubt who was boss.

One of Pedder's early tasks was to drive down to Portsmouth in a van to pick up a trunk belonging to Sibella Clark, Bancroft's daughter, who had returned to England after graduating in history and fine art from Swathmore College, just outside Philadelphia, USA. This errand involved opening the trunk for customs officers and rifling through Sibella's personal belongings. Roger and Sibella had never met. Mission accomplished, Pedder returned to Street, where a few days later he did meet Sibella – and they fell in love. They were married in 1968 in a private ceremony in Bromley Registry Office.

Two years later, Pedder left Clarks. As he describes it:

> Marrying the boss's daughter was always going to cause complications, especially once Bancroft had retired. I had a lot of soul-searching to do – in fact deciding to leave was one of the toughest decisions of my life. I left to join British Home Stores but before doing so I had learned a lot about Clarks. I had worked my way up the retail side of the business and then became a buyer for half the women's ranges. So I understood the business pretty well.

Which would come in handy when Pedder returned to Clarks in 1993 in entirely different circumstances.

The age of management consultants had arrived. In 1963, Tony Clark commissioned McKinsey & Co., which had offices in London's St James's Street, to produce a series of reports on the company. The first was in November of that year. It outlined in detail the responsibilities of each manager, making it clear to whom they were answerable and where their remit began and ended. It was a long, plodding document, which was followed a month later by an even longer one called 'Adopting a Consumer and Customer Oriented Approach to Marketing Branded Footwear'. McKinsey's covering letter to Tony Clark included a short section entitled 'Major Conclusions' which, when read today, appears neither major nor conclusive:

> Opportunities to increase profitable sales volume exist on a variety of fronts. However, there is 'no rabbit that can be pulled out of a hat' to do this. Capturing these opportunities means changing many things. In short, Clarks is going to make marketing the competitive cutting edge of its business.

McKinsey had taken soundings from the trade and included vox pops as part of its Relations with Retail section. 'Clarks is Clarks. They do what *they* want', was one of the comments canvassed. Another was:

> I'm sure they're good craftsmen, but they're living in the 18th century when it comes to realising that retailers are their partners – both of us have to succeed or neither of us will!

'Why don't they stop trying to brainwash us with what they want and find out what the facts really are', was a third.

A main thrust of the McKinsey findings was that if Clarks was to meet its production and sales targets, it would have to consider introducing a second brand name or acquire another branded manufacturer which already had a substantial market share or owned a significant number of retail outlets. The crucial and unresolved question of Clarks expanding upon or limiting its unbranded operations fell outside the scope of McKinsey's study. The report did, however, highlight other areas to be addressed. It was a long list that included:

- Clarks' reluctance to exploit properly the mail order business;
- the urgent need to increase warehouse space;
- a proposal to introduce twice-weekly deliveries by road transport to key customers;
- separating in-stock and forward order inventory records;
- a provision for more flexible handling of orders from large customers;
- a revamped customer inquiries and complaints department;
- improved communications between Street and travelling salesmen (who were in the habit of making over-optimistic delivery promises);
- a greater onus on factory superintendents being held responsible for keeping their word on production dates.

In other words, the consultants were advocating wide-reaching reforms.

It was also suggested that Clarks Ltd should be divided into three separate divisions – women's, children's and men's – a move which Bancroft said would 'release new management energies and powers ... taking the lids off people and letting them get on'. This and several other of the recommendations were acted upon, and within twelve months Clarks had made and dispatched 10 per cent more shoes, with profits up by 20 per cent. The Bullmead warehouse, which had been built in 1954, doubled in size in 1964 and the adjoining Houndwood site in Street was pressed into service, both of which had an immediate impact on the wholesaling and distribution side of the business. In the past, when most of Clarks shoes were made in Street, distribution was mainly by train from Glastonbury station (now defunct), but this had proved far too slow and inflexible for busy retailers. Consumers wanted their shoes immediately and held retailers to account by shopping elsewhere if they could not walk away with what they required.

Clarks itself now had 100 Peter Lord shops, and during 1964 the company paid more than £1 million for the Wolverhampton-based family firm of Craddock Brothers, with a chain of 24 outlets in the Midlands and North West. Reginald Hart, managing director of Peter Lord since 1937, retired and was replaced by Eric Gross, a non-family member, who had joined the company shortly after the Second World War.

The Bullmead warehouse, built in 1954, was doubled in size ten years later as a result of McKinsey & Co.'s reports and recommendations.

Another McKinsey report came out in the summer of 1965, which was circulated to all managers. It emphasised the importance of a proper chain of command, described as 'line-staff relationships'. Bancroft's cover note made the point that 'in all main aspects' the report was as prepared by McKinsey, but, he added: 'I have altered it only as necessary to fit into the organisation structure which we adopted at the end of May in place of the one McKinsey's proposed.'

England won the World Cup in 1966 (with the team's off-field suits designed by Hardy Amies), but there was not much else to celebrate. Harold Wilson's Labour government had been returned to power in March with a slightly increased majority of 97 and was faced with a balance of payments crisis. The pound was devalued, a wage freeze put in place and an unpopular Selective Employment Tax introduced, designed to raise money from the service sectors in order to subsidise manufacturing. James Callaghan, the chancellor of the exchequer, introduced a Corporation Tax at the rate of 40 per cent.

Clarks was not immune to the nation's economic troubles, which were fuelled by the growing restlessness of the trade unions. In 1966, an agreement was reached between the Shoe Manufacturers Federation and the National Shoe Trade Union to reduce the working week further from 41½ to 40 hours, while increasing holidays by seven days to 4½ weeks. This would cost Clarks an additional £250,000 a year – or an extra 5*d*. for each pair of shoes it made.

In the same year, two factories were closed: St Johns in Bridgwater and Northway in Midsomer Norton. And there were redundancies in others: 22 at Minehead, 27 in Street and 51 in Plymouth. A further 150 workers lost their jobs in November across the C. & J. Clark businesses. A spokesman was quoted in the *Daily Telegraph* of 16 August 1966 as saying:

> We have had to cut back our plans for expansion, particularly for women's shoes. We have taken a long and careful look at our overheads and pruned them wherever possible.

The price of raw hides and skins for uppers was rising, but for its soles Clarks was by now using very little leather. In the 1960s, the big breakthrough in soling was the development of polyurethane (PU) compounds, which earned Clarks the respect of – and a considerable amount of money from – the wider shoe-making world. Even back in the early 1950s it had been proposed that the company should appoint a specialist organic chemist to develop PU. This never happened, but fortunately a letter towards the end of 1962 from Michael Mayer-Rieckh, a friend of Peter Clothier, and a member of the founding family of the Humanic Shoe Company in Graz, Austria, galvanised Clarks' interest in PU soling. This letter offered an introduction to Dr Oskar Schimdt Jnr, who had developed a new process for moulding plastic soles on to normal footwear.

A company delegation was dispatched to Austria in January 1963 to investigate the Schimdt process. Its members were impressed. Schimdt then came to Street and the company set in place a formal agreement between him and C. I. C. Engineering, which was part of Avalon Industries. But the clock was ticking, with competitors such as Bata and Wolverine launching their own concerted assaults to exploit the latest technical advances in soling.

A Peter Lord shop interior in Stafford in the 1960s, showing the
sales desk area, with fitting stools in the foreground.

It was not until March 1969 that a prototype PU moulding machine
was commissioned at the Minehead factory, but by 1972 there were
Rotary or what was called In-line machines in six Clarks factories, all using
C. I. C. moulds. Chemical supplies mainly came from Avalon Chemicals
based in Shepton Mallet and specific compounds were developed for individual factories. At one time, twenty different compounds were being
produced, each with subtle differences of colour, texture and flexibility.

Over the next decade, huge investments were made in PU for factories
specialising in casual products such as men's polyveldt and sandals,
women's Clippers and Pop-ons and children's hardwearing shoes for
school. PU was a fundamental factor in sustaining Clarks' image as a
major player both nationally and internationally, and C. I. C. was selling
its compounds to shoe manufacturers around the globe.

The physical properties of PU soles as experienced by consumers were
compelling: lightness, softness, flexibility, resilience (shock absorbency)

Daniel Clark, Bancroft's eldest son, became managing director of Clarks Ltd in 1967.

and durability. In essence, a dream product to market. Some factories with PU machines were working two and three shifts, such was the level of demand for their products.

Bancroft Clark – known always as 'Mr Bancroft' – retired in August 1967 but remained a powerful presence for another quarter century, living just long enough to see Clarks stumble through its darkest hour in 1993. His only official role in the business after standing down was as chairman of Street Estates Limited.

Bancroft had worked in the business from 1919 to 1921 before going up to King's College, Cambridge. After taking his degree, he rejoined the company in 1924 and then succeeded his father, Roger, as chairman in 1942. He occupied that post for 25 successive years, during which he led Clarks through a period of unprecedented growth, both at home and overseas. Comparisons with the period immediately after the war and with 1967, the year he retired, are instructive. Turnover increased from £1.3 million a year in 1946 to £40.4 million in 1967; there were 1,906 employees in 1946 and 14,398 in 1967; Clarks was making 1.4 million pairs of shoes in 1946 and 18.5 million in 1967. There were 175,000 ordinary shares in 1946, compared with more than six million in 1967.

The retirement of Bancroft coincided with that of Arthur Halliday, whose firm in Ireland, John Halliday & Son, had joined forces with Clarks in 1937.

These two high-level departures led to wider changes. Tony Clark became chairman of C. & J. Clark Ltd and Peter Clothier was made managing director. Daniel Clark took over as managing director of Clarks Ltd, the branded shoemaking operation, and Eric Gross was appointed managing director of both Clarks Overseas Shoes Ltd and, temporarily, of the Unbranded Division. Jan Clark, Bancroft's second son, was promoted to the board and made responsible for C. & J. Clark Retailing.

Following Bancroft's retirement, the decision was taken to make Clarks Shoes Australia Ltd an independently managed subsidiary of Clarks Overseas Shoes Ltd. Foster Harrison, who had been factory manager of Alma Shoes, the Australian manufacturer bought by Clarks, was appointed the first managing director of Clarks Shoes Australia Ltd and became a member of the main C. & J. Clark board. The other directors were Stephen Clark (company secretary) and John Frith (financial controller). In 1967, the nine-man board comprised six family members and three non-family members.

Wherever you looked there was change and expansion. Early in 1967, Clarks acquired a 51 per cent interest in Mondaine Ltd, a privately owned company which operated at the high-fashion end of the shoe market, trading under the names of Ravel, Mondaine and Pinet. Altogether,

Mondaine Ltd had some 50 shops in London and the Home Counties, with a turnover of £2 million a year. Four of its stores were in Bond Street and one was in Carnaby Street. Then, less than a year later, Clarks added a Scottish shoe group called Bayne and Duckett to its portfolio, which came with 60 retail outlets in and around Glasgow and Edinburgh, including Baird's, a well-known bootmaker.

In 1968, Clarks acquired the Australian Shoe Corporation and opened a new factory in Melbourne, of which it owned the freehold. A year later, in 1969, a new factory was built in Adelaide expressly for the production of Hush Puppies, a casual shoe made with supple suede uppers and light-weight crepe soles. Created in 1958 by the Wolverine shoe company in Rockford, Michigan, Hush Puppies derived their name from the southern American dish of fried corn balls that were supposedly thrown to barking dogs to quieten them down.

In New Zealand, a new children's factory was opened at the aptly named Papatoetoe, outside Auckland; the minister of customs cut the ceremonial ribbon. A small shoe manufacturer called The Happy Shoe Company was bought in Ghana, making 2,000 pairs of crepe-soled sandals a week. Meanwhile, in America, there was a welcome turnaround in 1969 with the wholesaling company, Clarks of England Ltd, recording sales up by 50 per cent on the previous year. And Clarks' position in rela-tion to the rest of Europe was bolstered by the opening of new offices and warehouses in Denmark and Sweden, in addition to the existing ones in Paris and Zurich.

Back home, at the beginning of 1969, Clarks bought Trefano Shoe Ltd, which specialised in comfortable women's shoes. This company, with 371 employees, operated near Tonypandy in the Welsh Valleys and came with two big advantages: it was in a 'designated development area' that bene-fited from government grants and rebates, and the new Severn Bridge, opened by the Queen in September 1966, made access to and from Wales much easier for heavy goods vehicles.

As Clarks expanded by opening new factories it also sought to increase the efficiency of its operations. Raising productivity and lowing costs were what occupied the minds of factory superintendents and their deputies.

As Eric Saville, who joined Clarks as a management trainee in 1960 after studying classics at Cambridge University, explains:

> I spent a lot of my time with a stopwatch ... The piecework system was central to everything. The harder you worked, the more cash value you had. It was hard work. In fact, it was the closest thing to slave labour that I ever saw.

After completing his training, Saville became head of works study in the Grove factory in Street before moving from one plant to another as a deputy superintendent and then becoming superintendent (factory manager) of the sandals factories in Yeovil and Ilminster. As he describes it:

> I never seemed to stay anywhere long enough to feel I had achieved something. Finally, I said 'no' when they wanted to move me back to Street as a superintendent. Tony Clark tried to persuade me and said: 'I thought you liked a challenge, but clearly you don't.' Eventually, I did what I was told, but left a few months later and joined a management consultancy firm in London. After that, I was offered jobs by other companies but came to the conclusion that I had seen nothing that I liked as much as Clarks.

So Saville rejoined in 1970 and spent the rest of his working life at Clarks, including three years in Australia after Raymond Footwear Components was bought to make heels, soles, lasts, insoles, stiffeners, wedges and other bits and pieces vital to shoemaking.

Saville, who retired in 1995, had nothing but admiration for Clarks:

> Clarks was light years ahead of others in terms of industrial relations ... Each factory had its own factory council and would send representatives to the Company Council in Street, which met two or three times a year. This was a chance to air any grievances direct with members of the board. You could say anything you liked and would be heard.

In 1971, there were further increases in warehouse space at Bullmead, with the provision of an additional 48,000 sq ft built on three levels. The Clarks raw material warehouse at Cowmead also underwent modernisation, and on the Houndwood site a new 10,000 sq ft maintenance garage was opened, complete with automatic car- and lorry-washing machines to service the company's 50 trailers and 100 cars. The improvements to Houndwood cost more than £1 million.

The fifth generation of Clarks was about to take over running the business, but cracks were beginning to appear. A drop in profits in 1972 was described by Tony Clark in his annual Chairman's Report as 'considerably below what we budgeted to achieve'. On sales of £94,169,000, the profit before tax was £4,875,000, down from £5,241,000 on the previous year. And the figures would have been much worse had it not been for the sale of surplus land owned by Street Estates Ltd, whose results were now incorporated into the accounts of C. & J. Clark Ltd.

Competition in the fashion shoe sector was relentless – from Italy, Spain and, increasingly, Brazil – while, at the cheaper end, shoes were pouring into the UK from the Far East, particularly Pakistan and Malaysia. Exports to traditional markets such as Nigeria, Zambia, Malawi, Bermuda, Nassau, Jamaica, Trinidad and Hong Kong were just about holding up, but increases in the costs of shoemaking in the UK were starting to affect Clarks' competitiveness and there was bad news from the Unbranded Division, which, in 1972, posted 'disastrous' results.

It was time to engage the services of another firm of consultants. The Boston Consulting Group, which was based in New Zealand House, in London's Haymarket, spent months examining various aspects of Clarks' business, after which Tony Clark told shareholders:

> We found their reports on various aspects of the business and the opportunities that they saw for growth interesting and stimulating, and certainly helpful in our forward strategic planning.

In truth, some of the Boston Consulting Group's conclusions had made for uncomfortable reading. Its report warned that:

Princess Anne on a visit to Street on 12 May 1970 to open the Street Youth Club.

... although Clarks Limited is an effective manufacturer of shoes in a high income country, in the context of future world supply patterns this will not be a base for future growth.

Echoing publicly what some senior members of staff were thinking privately, the Boston Consulting Group urged the company to 'reduce its involvement in the peripheral activities that neither contribute materially to its strength nor add to its profitability'. Specifically, it described the unbranded side of the business and some of the shoe component operations as 'unnecessary distractions'. Its recommendation under the 'Unbranded' heading, amounted to one word: 'Withdraw'.

This, apart from a small factory in Ireland which continued for a number of years making cheap, unbranded women's fashion shoes, was achieved by the end of 1973. Wansdyke reverted to making branded shoes, London Lane was sold back to its original East End owners and A. & F. Shoes went into voluntary liquidation.

The children's department at the Peter Lord store in Birmingham in 1971.

The Boston Consulting Group went on to suggest that Avalon Engineering should 'phase out of the manufacture and sale of machines' and wrote at length about the pros and cons of Peter Lord operating as an independent multiple. But its most telling observation, and one that would take many years for the company to act upon, addressed the core of Clarks' business – the production of branded shoes. It stated simply: 'Overseas sourcing for Clarks Ltd, from a low labour cost country, or on an owned basis, should be given high priority.'

Any worrying internal reflections on Clarks' future were, to an extent, shared by outside commentators. Prudence Glynn, a fashion writer for *The Times*, penned a long feature in April 1972, which began:

I have always thought of Clarks as the Sainsbury's of the shoe business: equally dedicated to producing best quality for the best price, vastly respectable, family dominated, paternalistic and hung about with an aura of rectitude.

But then she went on to criticise many of the most popular ranges such as Spectrum, Trumps, Nova and Skyline, and concluded how she preferred to have Italian brands in her cupboard. She went on to say:

> I think that right across the British shoe industry there is a need for a much higher standard of design. I should really rather buy native shoes than Italian imports, gentlemen. In the meantime, Clarks gesture to more interesting fashion is very welcome. It is definitely the moment for the carrot, I feel, not the stick.

Peter Clothier, one of those who had striven to make Clarks more fashionable and more appealing to younger consumers, retired in 1973 at the age of 63 and was replaced as vice chairman and managing director by Daniel Clark, Bancroft's oldest son. Clothier had joined the company in 1927 and became a towering figure not just in Clarks but in the wider shoe world, serving as president of the British Footwear Manufacturers Federation and gaining a reputation for his informed lectures on the shoe trade. A special issue of the *Courier* was produced to mark his retirement, including a personal tribute from Bancroft and a long summary of his career by Tony Clark, his friend and colleague of more than 40 years. Clothier, whose two sons, Anthony and John, joined Clarks in the 1960s, said in a farewell message:

> We have to be aggressive and ingenious in creating new products and new wants, and bring these to the public – never forgetting that the customer is the master we must satisfy.

The customer – and the public at large – was given a chance to explore some of Clarks' history when the Shoe Museum opened in Street on 14 March 1974. There had formerly been a museum of sorts, housed in Crispin Hall on the High Street, and not everyone was keen that space should be found for a new one in the main headquarters building. Stephen Clark was firmly in favour and he was largely responsible for overseeing the museum, drawing upon the archives and making sure that a collection

Peter Clothier, a grandson of William S. Clark, worked at Clarks for nearly sixty years, culminating in six years as managing director between 1967 and 1973.

of fossils of ichthyosauruses (extinct marine animals) and a fine selection of stuffed birds were brought safely to their new home, along with shoes dating back hundreds of years. The museum remains today in its prominent place – though the fossils have moved on – and in 2011 was the subject of a news item on *BBC Breakfast* when a group of Chinese tourists included it in their itinerary of Britain, moving seamlessly from the Tower of London to Stonehenge to Street. The archives were relocated to a new purpose-built site in 2012 and are one of the most extensive and well-organised of any company in Britain if not the world.

In 1974, Miss World came to call – not to see the museum but for a special fitting of a pair of Barbarys, part of the relaunched Country Club casual range. 'Gee, they're wonderful and a perfect fit' said Marjorie Wallace, who hailed from Indianapolis, USA, as the Redgate factory manager, David Heeley, slipped the tan and white shoes on to her silky feet.

Miss World was visiting Britain's sixth-biggest private company and now the largest shoemaking concern in Europe. Clarks employed almost half the 8,000-head population of Street and, despite speculation from time to time in the press, there were no plans to float the company, and no intentions to change its family-based management structure. Some sections of the media found this perplexing. An article in the *Observer* towards the end of 1974 spoke of a:

> discernible attitude of caution towards this curious family, which, over the years, had made such a spectacular amount of money in such an unspectacular way.

Grappling with the culture of Clarks became something of a preoccupation for newspapers. The *Sunday Times* was intrigued by the lack of company cars and the way the Bear pub, opposite the head office, was still dry. An article by Allan Hall in that paper's Atticus column on 17 March 1974 carried the headline 'How not to spend a fortune', and was based around a rare interview with Tony Clark who was quoted as saying:

> If you said we were millionaires, I should think we'd all sue you for libel ... I suppose the next generation may be different but I doubt it ... I suppose I'm a bit different from our earlier generations. I have a drink. But I don't smoke in the office until 5 o'clock. We have a rule in here that there's no smoking and it's worth it because we get a reduction on the insurance premiums.

Hall noted that Tony's office was sparsely furnished and had lino tiles on the floor. There was no art on the walls and his desk was 'of the school room sort'. The company car issue was raised during the interview.

'As a matter of fact, nobody has a company car,' said Tony. He went on:

> You see, in a family business where five of the nine directors are all Clarks you have to work and get on together. You avoid situations that create jealousies and frictions. We have always said you should pay people for what they do rather than set up these standards of what kind

of office they have and what kind of car they drive, according to which chair they are sitting in. What do I want with a luxurious office?

Shortly after that interview, and within twelve months of Peter Clothier's departure, Tony Clark himself retired as chairman of C. & J. Clark Ltd at the end of August 1974, giving way to his 41-year-old cousin, Daniel, who decided that, like his father (Bancroft), he would combine the role of chairman and managing director. Daniel had studied engineering at Cambridge University and had joined the company in 1954, taking up his first main job as superintendent of Shepton Mallet four years later. He was interested in matters of the mind, but at the same time was practical, with a passion for how things were made. He was warm, cultured and unfailingly courteous. He was hard-working, well-liked, experienced and greatly respected. But his father was a hard act to follow.

9

Trainers, négligées and selling the brand

ALCOHOL WAS MOST DEFINITELY SERVED at the 150th anniversary celebrations of C. & J. Clark Ltd in June 1975 – and lots of it. There were parties galore to mark this particular landmark, both in Street and in London, where the festivities handily coincided with London Shoe Week. There were three lunches and a dinner in Street alone during the week starting 16 June 1975, all held in a huge marquee erected on lawns in front of the Grange, overlooking the main headquarters building.

The new chairman, Daniel Clark, made four separate speeches, each tailored to his particular audience. The 'Inaugural Lunch', as it was called, held on Wednesday 18 June 1975, was attended by the great and the good from the southwest, including the Conservative Member of Parliament for Wells, the chairman of Somerset County Council, the Mayor of Glastonbury and the chairman of the Street Parish Council. The chairman of Mendip District Council was there, too – Ralph Clark, who was chairman of the Clarks subsidiary, Avalon Industries. Civic leaders were joined by leading lights from the British Footwear Manufacturers Federation, the National Union of Footwear, Leather and Allied Trades and other associated organisations. Clarks' main competitors were included as well. In fact, a senior executive of Startrite, a rival manufacturer of children's shoes, made a speech on behalf of guests, and even Harry Levison from the British Shoe Corporation was asked along.

Daniel Clark became chairman of Clarks in 1974, shortly before
the 150th anniversary celebrations the following year.

The next day, a Thursday, some 500 Clarks pensioners walked into the
tent for lunch and filed out again a couple of hours later, each holding
a little leather wallet containing a cash voucher. The evening do on the
Friday was for all employees with 25 or more years' service under their
belts. Wives and husbands were invited only if they too had chalked up
a quarter of a century at Clarks. Maurice Burt, the factory worker who
had missed the 125th anniversary party because he was unattached
at the time and felt uneasy going on his own, attended this one and,
although now happily married, was perfectly content to leave his wife
at home:

> It wouldn't have done to have the wives there, not at all. It was quite a
> party, I can tell you. I think I must have got home about 4 am and there
> can't have been many steady heads in the morning. Whenever you put
> your glass down or if it was getting near empty someone came along

and filled it up again. There was no dancing or anything, but everyone found a way to let off steam.

The menu was a 1970s classic: 'melon boat' to start, 'dressed Scottish salmon' with mint new potatoes, garden peas and a green salad to follow, rounded off with fresh strawberries and cream. Petit Chablis and Côte de Beaune-Villages flowed liberally. Bill Graves, a non-family member of the board, gave the main address, to which Cyril Gifford, one of the firm's plumbers, whose family had been associated with Clarks for decades, replied on behalf of the whole workforce.

An altogether more sedate lunch took place on Saturday for share-holders. This was followed by a tour of the attendees' choice – either the historic buildings of Street or the churches of Somerset. The former included an inspection of two modern sculptures, *Diamond* and *Steps*, both by Philip King, which had been unveiled earlier in the week on either side of the Grange Road approach to the factory.

Daniel Clark used the anniversary as an opportunity to reiterate some key values. In one of his speeches, he said:

> The Quaker upbringing and tradition of the founders of the company continue to inform the way we think about the business and its prob-lems, and the sort of business we want to be; the conditions under which we employ people; our produce and services, and their integ-rity and usefulness to the community. Whether we think about the product or the way it is promoted, or the people who produce it, we want everyone to be proud to be associated with the company.

In London, Lance Clark, managing director of Clarks Ltd, the branded footwear division, was the host and keynote speaker at two dinners held at the Europa Hotel off Oxford Street, only a couple of days after an IRA bomb had exploded outside the nearby Portman Hotel, injuring three passers-by. At least 1,000 people attended, including the television personality Judith Chalmers (a well-known fan of Clarks), the actress Adrienne Corri, who appeared alongside Peter O'Toole and Richard Attenborough that year in

Key figures at Clarks pose for a photograph to mark the 150th anniversary celebration in 1975. Back row, left to right: Lance Clark, Stephen Clark, Jan Clark, William Johnston and Ralph Clark. Front row, left to right: Foster Harrison, A. W. (Bill) Graves, Eric Gross, Daniel Clark and John Frith.

Otto Preminger's film *Rosebud*, and the actor Patrick Mower, who many years later would become a stalwart of ITV's soap opera *Emmerdale*. A special anniversary exhibition was put on at Clarks' London offices in Berners Street, to which the press was invited, along with those attending the Europa Hotel dinners and others associated with the shoe trade. The exhibition consisted of a visual history of shoemaking set to piped music from the 1930s.

In sharp contrast, there was none of this fanfare and no mood music to mark the closure of Clarks' Yeovil factory four months later in October 1975, when nearly 100 workers lost their jobs. This factory, along with several others, had been operating on a four-day week for a number of months as the country reeled from one economic crisis to another. Cabinet papers released in 2005 under the 30-year rule reveal that the Labour prime minister, Harold Wilson, was warned by his energy minister, Lord

Balogh, that Britain's economy faced 'possible wholesale domestic liquidation' if inflation and unemployment continued to rise. The then industry secretary, Tony Benn, at odds with the chancellor, Denis Healey, pressed Wilson to introduce quotas and higher tariffs on imports, along with cuts in defence spending and selective help to industry – but a cap-in-hand approach to the International Monetary Fund for a £2.3 billion bail-out was the course the beleaguered government took.

Britain was the so-called 'sick man of Europe', limping towards what would become the 'winter of discontent' in December 1978. There was talk of 'lame duck' industries and how the country had been brought to its knees by the 'British disease'. Skinheads in 'bovver boots' threw sharpened pennies at opposition fans at football matches; new 'brutalist' post-war tower blocks became ghettos of antisocial behaviour; and the prospect of public spending being cut by some £3 billion was obscuring any light at the end of the economic tunnel. Many high earners had decamped overseas to avoid being taxed at the top rate of 83 per cent.

While politicians argued and the trade unions stockpiled their options amid escalating labour unrest, housewives took direct action. A Clarks survey in 1976 showed that hard-up mothers weren't bothering to buy back-to-school shoes for their children – and this resulted in a 15 per cent drop in sales for the company. Suddenly, feeling the pinch was a common affliction among UK shoe companies. Workers at K Shoes in Kendal, in the Lake District, were on shortened weeks, as they were at Norvic in Norwich, and at the Down shoe factory in Belfast.

Making matters worse were the imports of cheap shoes flooding into the country at an increasing rate – although this of course was welcomed by independent retailers anxious to keep their buying costs down. Annual shoe imports averaged 80 million pairs between 1971 and 1975, rising to 97.5 million in 1976. This meant that by the end of 1976, 40 per cent of all shoes sold in the UK were made abroad.

There may have been a reluctance to source or manufacture shoes offshore – and certainly it was never given the 'high priority' advised by the management consultants – but there were flurries of activity in this direction. In 1978, a company called Atlas Shoes, in Nicosia, Cyprus, was looking for an investor and Clarks took a 51 per cent share. The plan was for Atlas to produce 150,000 pairs of children's shoes a year, but by 1979 this target had been re-adjusted, with Atlas making around 90,000 pairs of men's sandals instead. John Willets, who was in charge of Atlas, wrote a note to Bernard Harvey, a long-term factory manager back in Street, saying that any other lines at Atlas were merely 'small bits and pieces with heavy development costs, quality problems etc – a formula for disaster'. Atlas closed in 1983.

Closer to home, towards the end of 1975 the company made its first big move into the European Economic Community – which Britain had joined two years earlier during the premiership of Edward Heath – by buying an 80 per cent stake in the French retail chain France Arno, which had 48 shops in major cities, including Paris. It sold mainly women's shoes, but none were from the Clarks range.

Jan Clark, now managing director of C. & J. Clark Retailing, told the *Financial Times* that the acquisition offered scope for further investment and expansion 'and opportunities for the export of footwear from Britain'. Those opportunities never materialised.

A far more significant decision was taken two years later in 1977 when Clarks paid £14 million for the publicly listed Hanover Shoe Company and its subsidiary, Sheppard & Myers, in the USA. The directors felt expansion into America was essential, not least because, according to the minutes of a board meeting in 1976, it was an opportunity to operate without being impeded by 'left-wing policies' in the UK, where Labour had been returned to government in 1974. Clarks had enjoyed some success in America and it was felt that a medium-sized acquisition would consolidate the company's position on that side of the Atlantic, especially one that came with an established retail arm.

Such was the scale of this venture that there was speculation in the media about it being a precursor to a public flotation by Clarks, although, in fact, it led to the removal of Hanover's share quotation on the US Stock Exchange.

The Hanover Shoe Company had been founded in 1899, specialising in high-grade, middle-priced shoes known in North America as 'dress shoes', with proper, welted leather soles. It had shops in some of the best malls in the country and it complemented Clarks, which was known primarily for its casual rubber-soled footwear. The board was impressed by the conservative and honest nature of its way of doing business. Based in Hanover, Pennsylvania, it had three leased factories in West Virginia and ran 240 of its own Hanover-brand shops across the USA.

Clarks had been looking for an opportunity to invest in the USA for some time, and with extra urgency after Florsheim, a retailing giant also specialising in formal shoes, gave Clarks an ultimatum over its prices towards the end of 1974, threatening to renege on its £1 million annual order. Florsheim also rang alarm bells in Street when it began sourcing cheaper versions of Wallabees from Czechoslovakia.

Following the Hanover Shoe Company acquisition, Clarks paid some £3.5 million for the Bostonian Shoe Company a year later in 1979 at a cost of some £3.5 million. Bostonian, a shoe manufacturer and retailer based in Whitman, Massachusetts, was part of the Kayser-Roth Corporation, a subsidiary of Gulf & Western. Jan Clark, who had moved in 1978 from heading up retail in the UK to taking charge of Clarks in North America, was keen to gain more outlets in which to sell Hanover shoes, and the Bostonian deal gave him nearly 100 of them. It was a bold strategy, but one that brought with it a new set of problems because Hanover and Bostonian sold the same kinds of formal footwear at a time when the commercial wind was blowing in the opposite direction, towards more casual shoes. Clarks profits in the USA declined by 10 per cent in 1978 and the position worsened over the next two to three years. But it did mean the company had a presence in America, a commercial base from which it could manoeuvre over the next few decades. Today, the American market is crucial to Clarks, accounting for approximately 40 per cent of its business, and many of the current Clarks stores in the US at one time had either Hanover or Bostonian above the door.

There were, however, some senior directors who worried that Clarks had moved from being a competitive branded shoe manufacturer to an investor in other companies' inferior shoe manufacturing and retailing.

Judging the market in the 1970s was a formidably hard task. Social mores loosened, fiscal budgets tightened. Roy Jenkins, a liberal-minded home secretary in Harold Wilson's last government, had set out to build what he called a 'civilised society' by abolishing the death penalty, decriminalising homosexuality, legalising abortion, relaxing the divorce laws, and reforming theatre censorship. Choices abounded. In the world of shoes, platform soles, as worn by Abba and Gary Glitter, were all the rage, with the likes of David Bowie, Marc Bolan and Elton John doing their bit in the cause of 'glam rock'. But it wasn't all glossy, as Noddy Holder's Slade and the Bay City Rollers clunked around at the top of the music charts in working men's boots and shoes, and on nights out, young men and women were often wearing the same kinds of footwear.

Sporting platform shoes didn't mean you *had* to look like members of Kiss (the American band that was the inspiration for the satirical film *Spinal Tap*) to get noticed. Barbara Hulanicki, the Polish-born fashion designer, produced her Biba-trademark range to great critical acclaim, recapturing some of the elegance of Salvatore Ferragamo's platforms of the 1930s. Clarks' foray into this particular market produced the 1976 Andy Imprint Rangnoddye, with three-inch stacked heels and crepe rubber soles, retailing at £11.99. These were more Barbara Hulanicki than Noddy Holder – but at a fraction of the cost.

Then, just as it was safe to dispense forever with kipper ties and loon pants, along came the punk scene, which did its best to reflect the national gloom. Angry music by the likes of the Sex Pistols and the Clash brought with it ripped clothes held together by giant safety pins, spiky red hair and snarling attitudes utterly at odds with the repressed, genteel culture of *Upstairs Downstairs*, the phenomenally successful London Weekend Television series about an upper-class Edwardian family and their servants, which ran to 68 episodes in the 1970s.

The footwear of choice for punks was Doc Martens, especially the Eight-Eyelet 1460 model, which took its name from the day, month and year of its creation by R. Griggs Group Ltd, a respectable Northamptonshire shoe manufacturer which had bought the patent rights from Klaus Martens and his friend Herbert Funck.

Clarks gave punk culture a wide berth. But a far more perplexing challenge – and greatly more damaging in the long term – was the rise of the sports shoe, or trainer.

In 1895, Joseph Foster, from Holcombe Brook, a small village north of Bolton in Lancashire, founded a shoe company called J. W. Foster & Sons, which eventually ended up as Reebok International Ltd, now a subsidiary of Adidas, the German sportswear company. His big idea was to create a spiked running shoe, which British athletes would wear at the 1924 Olympic Games in Paris, famously captured on the big screen in the 1981 film *Chariots of Fire*. It wasn't until 1960 that two of Foster's grandsons rebranded the company Reebok, so named after a type of African gazelle. Then, in 1979, Paul Fireman, an American partner of an outdoor sporting goods distributor, spotted Reebok at a trade show and secured the North American distribution rights. Within months, Reeboks were selling for $60 a pair, making them the world's most expensive running shoes.

Except that they weren't just running shoes. Like Nike's Waffle trainers, they started as running shoes but ended up as everyday casual footwear and a fashion statement at the same time, a phenomenon that must have astonished their track-suited inventors, Blue Ribbon Sports. Blue Ribbon, the predecessor to Nike, had emerged from the northwest American state of Oregon, where Bill Bowerman, a talented running coach, reportedly poured rubber into his wife's waffle-making machine as part of his search for a comfortable shoe for middle-distance athletes. Along the way he paid an art student $35 for the Nike swoosh, one of the most famous trademarks on earth. Nike, named after the Greek goddess of victory, broke away from Blue Ribbon Sports in 1972 and went on to become a global sensation, helped by its sponsorship of a young Michael Jordan, the American basketball player who had the Nike Air Jordan trainers named after him.

Clarks responded to the trainer revolution by developing a range of its own called 'Clarksport', which included two general training shoes ('Jetter' and 'Jogger'); shoes for squash, tennis and badminton ('Supreme', 'Spin' and 'Service'); shoes for golf ('Golfer' and 'Golf Ace'); a shoe for sailing ('Fastnet') and a shoe for bowls ('Bowler'). Most of these were made in the

Minehead and Weston-super-Mare factories and at Dundalk, in Ireland, one of several factories known for its extensive research and innovative design techniques. Some Clarksport products used the new Polyveldt compound soling that was hard enough to withstand rigorous stresses and strains, but still felt comfortable for the wearer.

On a baking hot June day in 1976, a special men's division sales conference was convened in Street to launch Clarksport. Victor Jenkins, Clarksport brand manager, began proceedings by saying, 'Morning, sports, welcome to the fantastic new world of Clarksport!' and then presented the range, using members of staff as models, who hopped on to the stage carrying accessories appropriate to the shoes they were wearing: a golf club here, a tennis or badminton racquet there. Jenkins reminded everyone that more and more people were joining sports clubs and that the sale of squash racquets was increasing by 12 per cent every year. Watched and supported by Neville Gillibrand, the men's division marketing manager, and by Malcolm Cotton, who was overall head of Clarks men's division, Jenkins pointed out that some Clarks retailers were expecting sports shoes to offset any downturn in the sale of more formal footwear.

'We should be able to produce premium products with our 150 years' shoemaking experience and our expertise in shoemaking in every field,' he said, before handing over to Dr Vaughan Thomas, a leading sports consultant and director of physical education at Liverpool Polytechnic, who extolled the medical benefits of Clarksport. Many golf shoes in the past had contributed to the onset of arthritic knees, he said, by not allowing for the twist in a player's swing. Perhaps letting the occasion get to him, Dr Thomas concluded: 'This is unique in Britain. You are a British company doing this total deal and putting it in the right place – in a specialised shoe shop, with a total back-up behind it.'

That was the problem. The back-up – in terms of a cohesive strategy supported at the highest level and accompanied by a proper marketing campaign – was in fact never adequately put in place, and bitter wrangles ensued about how best to sell the Clarksport range. Should they be on display in dedicated sports shops? Or should they occupy a corner in Clarks' traditional outlets, including Peter Lord?

'The research showed that people wanted to buy sports shoes from traditional shoemakers, but no one really backed the idea at board level,' says Lance Clark, who was himself on the board:

From the start, there was no real commitment, no desire to invest in it and make it work. Then I made the tactical error of concluding that people would buy them in existing shoe shops rather than sports outlets. The fact is that they did initially, but then they didn't.

This is a view largely shared by David Heeley, then manager of the Redgate factory in Bridgwater and the man who earlier had entertained Miss World. Over the course of 40 years at Clarks, he worked in almost every division of the company.

'Clarksport was a real attempt to get into the trainer market, a comprehensive effort,' says Heeley. He continues:

But the fundamental mistake was that they were sold in our Peter Lord stores and in key independents rather than in sports shops. They just did not sit comfortably beside more traditional shoes. The other issue was that the board wanted to see a return on the investment within two years, which was impossible. Profit was demanded too soon. The sad thing to remember is that we were ahead of Reebok at one time and some of our sailing shoes were worn by the crew of Ted Heath's *Morning Cloud* when they were training for the Fastnet race.

Clarksport survived only two years before the range was withdrawn.

'We just didn't think it would come to much,' says William Johnston, a member of the family with broad experience across the company and a specialist in forward planning.

I thought we were already too late to get into trainers and the general feeling at a senior level was that they were part of a phase, like blue jeans. They would go away in time. We thought the same thing about credit cards.

Even forward-planning experts can be caught on the hop, it seems.

Johnston was the son of Priscilla, Bancroft's sister and therefore Daniel's first cousin. He joined the firm in 1962 after coming down from Oxford University and then went to Carnegie Mellon Business School in Pittsburgh, Pennsylvania. In 1974, he was elevated to the main board, and as managing director of Clarks Overseas Shoes Ltd, played a leading role in the purchase of the Hanover Shoe Company, after which, in 1978, he was appointed managing director of C. & J. Clark Retail Ltd.

'The fact is that we were not far-thinking, but you have to remember that some of these things were not blindingly obvious at the time,' says Johnston. 'For example, we should have started importing shoes far earlier – we all know that now.'

There was still an ongoing appetite for trying new ventures, but perhaps at the expense of addressing issues about the core business. For example, Lance Clark and Malcolm Cotton oversaw the introduction of 'Levi's for feet', a canvas casual shoe imported primarily from Korea. In 1977, after many years of negotiation, Clarks obtained a licence from Levi Strauss and Co., based in San Francisco, to sell these shoes on an exclusive basis in Britain and throughout continental Europe, agreeing to pay a 5 per cent royalty on every pair sold. 'Levi's for feet' had been selling successfully in America since 1975 under licence to the Brown Shoe Company, and expectations were high that the same would happen on the other side of the Atlantic. By January 1978, forecasts for estimated sales in Europe were 900,000 pairs. In addition, it was decided to produce a version of 'Levi's for feet' in the Ilminster, Townsend and Shepton Mallet factories, a variant using leather uppers to distinguish them from the all-canvas model. Names for the 'Levi's for feet' range included Chase, Marathon, Dude and Sneak.

'This is a lot of extra business for a lot of people, and for the sake of employment the additional business is worthwhile,' said Lance, speaking at a Clarks Ltd meeting held in the Wessex Hotel, Street, in December 1977.

Lance reported how 'Levi's for feet' had got off to such a 'flying start that at one stage we ran out of shoes'. Sales in Holland and Germany had been strong, getting off quite literally to a flying start when a light aircraft took to the skies in Eindhoven trailing an advertising banner as it circled the city.

In the UK, there were plans to go nationwide with the range in the spring of 1978. This campaign began with 'Levi's for feet' sponsoring a Southern International speedway event at Wimbledon Stadium in south-west London on 26 April 1978 in celebration of speedway's 50th anniversary in Britain. There were reports at the time that speedway had become second only to football as a spectator sport, and on the day a crowd of 7,000 headed for Wimbledon, including invited shoe retailers from the Greater London area, who enjoyed a buffet supper in the stadium restaurant before the twenty-race programme began. Barry Briggs MBE, the acclaimed speedway rider from New Zealand who had won the World Individual Championship four times, was on hand to present the prizes, helped by two Penthouse Pets – centrefold models who had been photographed by *Penthouse*, the magazine widely regarded as a British equivalent to *Playboy*.

John Aram was general manager of the 'Levi's for feet' division. He told the *Courier* that 'what we have got is a long-term agreement between the world's largest maker of casual clothing, including jeans, and Europe's largest shoemakers'. He said the range would be aimed primarily at men and children, focusing on the 14 to 24 age group.

Reflecting on the venture, Aram says:

'Levi's for feet' survived for nearly ten years. During that time, there was some disquiet about it, with several members of the board concerned that resources and effort were going into building up the Levi's brand rather than Clarks, but others thought it was a way of gaining momentum, an opportunity to try something different.

The end for 'Levi's for feet' came in 1987, when the market for trainers and casual shoes suddenly dipped. If you weren't at the epicentre of the trainer revolution you were in danger of withering at the edges. Clarks asked Levi Strauss if it would reduce the agreed 5 per cent royalty paid on each pair sold to 3 per cent. The US company refused and 'Levi's for feet' was discontinued.

Speedway, Penthouse Pets and aerial promotions may have had an

'Levi's for feet' were sold by Clarks in Britain and Europe under exclusive licence from Levi Strauss from 1978 to 1987.

element of gimmickry about them, but they were in keeping with an enlightened outlook when it came to advertising and brand management. In the 1960s, Hobson & Grey, whose clients included Procter & Gamble and General Foods, had taken over from Notley's as Clarks' advertising agency. The agency, which became known simply as Grey, found itself liaising with three different executives at Clarks, one representing children's shoes, another men's and a third women's. The board was aware of this cumbersome chain of command, but it also felt that Grey's was too old-fashioned, and so decided to invite other agencies to tender for the Clarks account, a process from which Collett Dickenson Pearce (CDP) emerged triumphant in September 1974.

Robert Wallace, Clarks marketing director, who had joined in 1971 from Benton & Bowles, the advertising agency, said in an interview in 2006 that Clarks had been looking for an 'agency [that] would if necessary get tough with the client ... large firms [like Clarks] sometimes need tough handling. We did not want an agency that might reflect our own opinions back to us'.

Collett Dickenson Pearce was a breeding ground for talent. Among those who cut their creative teeth at the agency were Charles Saatchi, David Putnam, Ridley Scott and Hugh Hudson. CDP was regarded as sharp and known for its clever slogans, such as 'Happiness is a cigar called Hamlet' and 'Heineken refreshes the parts other beers cannot reach'. Suffice it to say that the worlds of Collett Dickenson Pearce and Clarks were markedly different.

'Collett Dickenson Pearce arrived for their first meeting ... One was in a Porsche 911, one was in a Maserati Bora and one was in a Ferrari,' says Philip Thomas, Clarks advertising manager at the time.

> They came in and they looked the part as advertising people. They wanted to make a statement in this sleepy little town, that we're here to help you as a business and we know what we're doing. They strutted their stuff but also delivered. That was a key mind-set change for us. We'd gone from the Grey days to Collett Dickenson Pearce.

Thomas says that Grey's was in the habit of coming up with four or five creative concepts and 'you'd be sitting there [thinking] which one do you like, not which one is right. But with Collett Dickenson Pearce they'd come down and present one concept and usually it was bloody good.'

One of its first press campaigns featured Long John Silver, accompanied by the line 'There's Only One Clarks'. A television and cinema advertisement showed children running on a beach as if in *Chariots of Fire*, to the accompaniment of music similar to that in the film. This ended up being the subject of legal wrangling which eventually led to action in the High Court, where Mr Justice Vinelott banned the ad in April 1983, ruling that it was 'blatant plagiarism'. On other occasions, some of the advertising became overtly raunchy, such as when, in an ad that showed how Clarks had changed over the years from making strait-laced court shoes to six-inch stilettos, models were seen wearing calf-length négligées for the former, nothing very much at all for the latter.

One press advertisement had eight women standing in a row. The woman on the far left was wearing a knee-length skirt and conservative shoes, the woman on the far right showed a naked leg and wispy party shoes. 'We deserve to be on every woman's black list' read the caption, referring to a woman's guilty pleasures or secret desires.

Another featured four attractive young women in leather boots astride a horse. 'Black beauty. Also brown beauty, tan beauty and black-and-tan beauty' read the copy. And just in case consumers still felt Clarks was rooted in a previous century, CDP came up with an advertisement featuring a group of models in silk petticoats and camiknickers kicking their legs in the air as they danced the can-can. 'Nobody can accuse us of being narrow-minded,' the copy said.

Maybe not, but some thought the pendulum had swung too far the other way. 'Mr Millward, who had twenty or so shops in the South of England, summoned Lance [Clark],' Robert Wallace recalled many years later.

So Lance said, 'This is it, you'd better come and explain yourself,' so we went to Reading and Lance took out a sketch pad and there was a church outside the window of the meeting room. I got absolutely pilloried by these very religious Millwards people ... that it was disgusting and disgraceful and so on. It would encourage pornography and goodness knows what. Lance said not one word and I had to defend it and at the very end they said: 'Well, Mr Clark, thanks for the meeting, what's your view?' And he said: 'There's my view,' and handed over this sketch he'd done of the church. Then we left.

Clarks also placed a growing emphasis on graphic design, engaging in the mid-1970s the services of Pentagram, one of the country's most successful design consultancies, to revamp all its shoe boxes, look at its permanent displays in Peter Lord shops and in other outlets selling

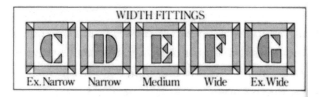

The distinctive lettering designed by Pentagram in the 1970s
for the width fittings on Clarks shoe boxes.

Clarks, and generally coordinate all point-of-sale communication with consumers.

'We had to improve the whole presentation of the brand, but it wasn't easy,' says John McConnell, who was a partner and director of Pentagram.

> Some of those independents were dowdy places that smelled of boiled cabbage. They used to have hardboard signs on the walls and all the stock was hidden behind a curtain or stored downstairs. One of the first things we did was redesign the boxes and then we tried to persuade the shops to have the boxes on display – rather than having a shop assistant go downstairs and return ten minutes later to say she didn't have what you wanted.

A new design policy for children's shoes was a high priority. Any scheme had to look modern but at the same time provide tangible links to the traditional consumer perception of Clarks. Pentagram opted for simple decorative geometric shapes in bright colours, similar to children's coloured blocks. The Clarks logo became thicker and was shown in bright yellow on a green background. In *Living by Design*, published in 1978, the Pentagram partners wrote:

> The need to support the product in the retail outlets required the design of hardware, including shoe display units, footstools, mirrors, a tie-your-own-shoelaces device, in fact almost everything except the boundary of the space.

The Clarks green boxes were smart and authoritative, with the code, style, size and width of the shoes clearly displayed at one end, making it easy for both the shop assistant and the consumer to identify what he or she was looking for. The typeface for the width fitting was chunky, the letters enclosed in a thick square. C represented extra narrow; D was narrow; E was medium; F was wide; and G was extra wide. According to Pentagram:

> The intention is that the shoe boxes will have the additional purpose of creating a brightly coloured wall in the shop, not only promoting the shoes but also enlivening what was previously one of the least attractive aspects of most shoe shops or departments.

Clarks understood that children did not consider shoe shopping the most exciting outing of the school holidays, and so part of Pentagram's brief was to find novel ways of keeping youngsters amused while they had their feet measured and were fussed over by a shop assistant. This led to the introduction in the late 1970s of colourful display panels, moulded in styrene and displayed in bevelled, enamelled frames. Many of these were illustrated by Graham Percy, a New Zealand-born artist who had won a scholarship to the Royal College of Art in the 1960s. He produced a series of pictorial puzzles that quietly promoted shoes while aiming to capture children's attention. One comprised a collage of cartoon characters in which ten pairs of shoes were hidden in the background. 'Can you find them?' read the caption. Another encouraged children to match up footprints to a group of animals walking in desert sands.

Reflecting on those days of branding and advertising, Robert Wallace says his biggest challenge was to make the three divisions of Clarks – children's, men's and women's – 'look as if they actually belonged to the same company' and that he had to work hard to persuade each division head (whom he called the 'barons') to support the advertisements. He recalls:

> At one point, I realised that our ads were much more fashionable than our shoes ever were, but that was the idea. Lance was determined to bring the company up to date and I was there to help him. We had

to set up a clear strategy for the brand and would not deviate from it. Simply put, children's was all about a true fit; men's was about high-tech comfort and durability, and women's was to do with comfort and style – but mainly comfort.

Collett Dickenson Pearce's director on the Clarks account was Geoff Howard-Spink, who went on to become one of the advertising world's elder statesmen. 'The advertising, when it appeared, was unlike any shoe advertising that Clarks, or the shoe industry, had seen before,' said Howard-Spink, writing for *Inside Collett Dickenson Pearce*, an illustrated book about the agency published in 2000. 'The quotes for photographs were staggering. For the price of each press ad you could have shot a television commercial. It was very difficult to explain these prices to Clarks, a Quaker family with a shoe business.'

In 1979, a CDP advertisement for Clarks' 'Cornish pasty' shoe – so named because of its thick, gently curved edges that reminded people of the popular crusty pie – was shortlisted for an advertising award. These shoes had Polyveldt soling and the copy in the advertisement explained how Polyveldt, known in the trade as PV or PU, was made of Contura, a polyurethane exclusive to Clarks.

Apart from durability, Contura gives the Polyveldt sole its flexibility and lightness (Contura is actually half the weight of leather or crepe) ... we hope you're an ordinary man in the street and, having read this far, will rush out in search of a pair of Polyveldt of your own.

Then came the waspish line:

Should you, however, be a rival shoemaker, we'd like to draw your attention to the fact that British and foreign patents and designs are pending or granted. And that Polyveldt are protected by UK Reg Design Nos 967050 and 967051 and Irish Reg Design Nos D3665 and D3664.

Clarks remained with CDP until 1981, when Geoff Howard-Spink and

Clarks new Polyveldts.

First of all, may we invite you to see our new Polyveldts at the Birmingham International Footwear Fair on March 18th, 19th or 20th?

But if you can't make it perhaps we had better tell you a little more about them now.

The styles are more modern than of late and finished in a soft, polished natural hide slighty thinner than before.

As you will see from our photograph, however, it's the soles which show the greatest development.

Do you see? There are two soles, not one.

On the outside there's an immensely durable, solid polyurethane sole, tough as old boots, in fact, tougher.

It lasts longer than crepe, leather or rubber.

Inside there is an inner sole made of low density *expanded* polyurethane.

To touch, it is soft, light, spongy and resilient.

To walk on it is very, very comfortable. Like walking on air, which in fact, you are. There are lots of tiny air bubbles trapped inside.

By combining these two densities of polyurethane, Clarks who pioneered the Polyveldt in the seventies, are making sure it stays your best seller way into the eighties. *Clarks*

A soft sole for comfort.
A tough sole for durability.

Two soles are better than one.

Clarks new Polyveldts – successors to the so-called 'Cornish pasty' shoe.

his business partner, Frank Lowe, left to form their own company, Lowe Howard-Spink.

Developing the Clarks brand was not just down to advertising and graphic design. In the late 1960s, the company hired a market and social research company called Conrad Jameson Associates to advise on Clarks' image and its positioning among consumers. Conrad Jameson was an American living in London who had studied philosophy at Harvard. One of his junior staff was Peter Wallis, who, using the name Peter York, went on to co-author the bestselling *Official Sloane Ranger Handbook* in 1982. When Wallis left to found his own company, the Specialist Research Unit Ltd, with Henry 'Dennis' Stevenson (now Lord Stevenson) in 1973, he reached an amicable arrangement with Jameson, whereby the Specialist Research Unit took on the Clarks account.

Wallis spent the next twenty years advising Clarks, sometimes intensely, sometimes more loosely. He worked closely with Lance Clark,

Robert Wallace and Michael Fiennes, a cousin of Sir Ranulph Fiennes, the adventurer and writer.

Michael Fiennes had joined Clarks as a graduate trainee in 1963 and was universally credited with having a first-class brain. One member of the Clark family says he was 'probably too bright for us'. After graduating from Oxford University with a degree in philosophy, politics and economics, and with the encouragement of Tom Woods, Clarks personnel manager, Fiennes secured a place at Harvard Business School. On his return in 1968, he was fast-tracked into management, working in marketing and then moving to Australia as marketing director in 1971. He returned to Street in 1973 as head of marketing and strategy and became corporate marketing manager of Clarks Ltd, with a seat on the board. However, he was never promoted to the main C. & J. Clark board. He remained with the company until 1982, when, without any warning, he suddenly resigned. 'It was a great shock' says David Heeley:

> He had the brain-power to help steer the company through difficult times, but it must have seemed to him that there was little chance of getting on to the main board because it was top-heavy either with family members or long-term retainers, who had done a great job but perhaps were no longer at the top of their game.

The loss to Clarks was highlighted when, within a few months of his departure, Fiennes set up his own company and won the exclusive UK rights to sell and distribute Ecco shoes, a leading boutique brand from Denmark. This deal lasted seventeen years and was extremely successful, only coming to an end when Ecco launched its own international sales force. In the early 1990s, Fiennes opened Ecco's first shops in Kingston and Bromley and by 1999 there were fifteen such outlets. He and his wife Rosalie, an architectural interior designer, went on to set up the retail shoe and clothes company Shoon.

'Making shoes was part of Clarks heritage and it was difficult for some members of the board to contemplate anything else,' says Fiennes. He continues:

But even if we had thought about bringing in shoes from overseas and concentrating more on wholesaling than manufacturing we were not prepared for it. It was never clear where the company was going long-term and members of the family were pulling in different directions. Even so, I never found another company that I preferred to work for. Clarks was not afraid of looking at new things and always wanted to be at the forefront of change. I used to see Daniel for strategic discussions and I liked him enormously. He was bright and wanted to do the right thing but he didn't have the authority of his father [Bancroft] over other members of the family.

Wallis's experience was similar:

My role was to present the outside world as a sounding point. We did a lot of research that always confirmed the same thing: either Clarks should stick to its core business or, if it wanted to become a fashion item, then it had to do it very well. I argued that you have to find your sweet spot and stick with it. The frustration for me was wanting them to act faster and to understand design better. A great deal of the design came from barmy enthusiasm rather than inspired imagination.

Pride was felt keenly at Clarks over its technological advances. As one former senior manager puts it: 'The genius of the company was that it came across as middle of the road when in fact it was at the sharp end of shoe production and never afraid of new techniques, new innovations.'

The use of computer-aided design (CAD) and computer-aided manufacturing (CAM), developed by Tony Darvill in Street, was a case in point. It offered for the first time the ability to design a shoe from start to finish on screen via an integrated three-dimensional (3D) and two-dimensional (2D) computer software package. The dimensions of a last were digitised and the software allowed the designer to examine and alter the cut of the shoe, its decoration, heel and sole edge, and to see his work from each side, from above or from the back. The designer could also experiment with different colours or colour combinations, effectively doing away with the

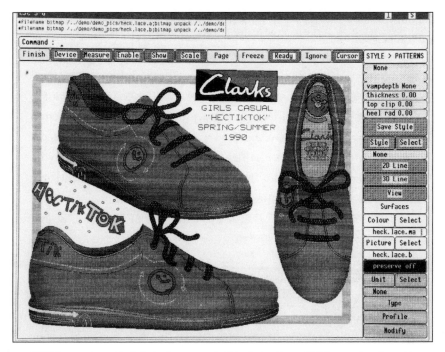

CAD (computer-aided design), as seen in this design from 1990, was developed in Street and widely used throughout the Clarks business from the late 1970s onwards.

old trial-and-error method whereby experimental shoes were made from scratch.

Darvill was working in Clarks' research and development department when he first started developing his ideas in the 1960s, long before the invention of desktop computers. 3D modelling was the subject of in-depth research at Cambridge University's computing laboratory in 1965 and, towards the end of the 1960s, Citroën, the French car manufacturer, made strides in computing complex 3D curve geometry. Darvill was known as a genial eccentric with a forensic eye for detail, who had knowledge of aircraft and car manufacturing and applied his engineering skills to shoe-making. His fascination with footwear sprang in part from wanting to know what kept a straightforward court shoe securely on a woman's foot.

'In my mind, the court shoe is the optimum shoe design,' said Darvill in an interview in 1995. 'It has no laces or straps, it only covers a small part of the foot and yet it fits comfortably and remains on the foot during walking.'

Darvill set about perfecting the design process, providing a capability to flatten the last in a consistent and repeatable manner. This allowed for communication between designers, pattern engineers, component suppliers and production managers, even if they were based in different parts of the world. They were sharing exactly the same information.

'Shoemaster', as Darvill's product was called, was given a boost in 1977 when Clarks collaborated with the Computer Aided Design Centre (CADC) in Cambridge and made a presentation to the Clarks board. Not long after-wards, CAD/CAM teams were assigned to a number of Clarks factories and the software was eventually sold to other shoe manufacturers in the early 1990s.

One of the first companies to show an interest in the product, after seeing it at a trade fair in Germany, was Torielli, an Italian firm southwest of Milan that specialised in shoemaking equipment and had direct contact with shoe manufacturers across the world. Clarks and Torielli joined forces on the Shoemaster project in a 50–50 joint venture, and then in 1996 Shoe-master became independent of Clarks and formed a new company with Torielli called CSM3D. The final Clarks shares in CSM3D were sold to the new management team in 2003 and CSM3D now owns the intellectual property rights. Its UK headquarters is still in Street, and Ian Paris, the chief executive, is a former Clarks employee. CSM3D produces four new versions of its software a year and sells to companies such as Bata, Gucci, Chanel and Bally. Relations between CSM3D and Clarks remain close and Darvill would be a contender to occupy a plinth in Street if the opportunity were to arise.

No one could accuse Clarks of not trying to diversify. Indeed, some would say it tried too hard. The launch of a children's range of clothes in 1979 was a leap too far. Clarks had begun thinking about embarking on this operation in March 1977, with Wallis's Specialist Research Unit producing a favourable report on it six months later. In December of that year, the board agreed that there was an opportunity to sell 'well-designed products ... to those mothers who want something different from chain store offerings but at a price below specialised suppliers'.

Malcolm Cotton held a series of senior managerial roles at Clarks from the 1960s onwards, and was briefly managing director of the company in 1995.

According to the planning department in Street, the aim was to secure 1 per cent of the total market share, which, it was estimated, would generate £4.5 million a year at 1976 trade prices. A children's clothing manufacturer, Pasolds, would be 'approached to assist in development and manufacture'.

The results were sobering. It made losses of more than £300,000 in its first year of trading in 1979, and a loss in excess of £350,000 in 1980, before being withdrawn in 1981. Norman Record, Clarks group economist, sought to explain the failure of what was called the 'Children's Clothing Project' in a document written for Daniel Clark. He said it was

... clearly not well managed ... the combination of entrepreneurial qualities necessary for success in new projects of this kind is likely to be very rare in a largish organisation like ours. Our ability to launch such projects must thus be recognised as extremely limited.

Record went on to say that if Clarks is to 'succeed in a large market we must devote appropriate resources and set our sights sufficiently high. Half-hearted attempts are bound to fail.'

This set-back followed the closure in September 1978 of Silflex, one of Clarks' original factories in Street. To the outside world, this was an inevitable development, softened by the announcement that most of the 230 workers would be relocated to other factories in the West Country – but for Clarks it was an emotional wrench that was hard to bear because it struck at the heart of the company's manufacturing history. The original Big Room, where shoes had been made since the turn of the century, had been silenced.

Most people, even members of the National Union of Footwear, Leather and Allied Trades (NUFLAT), had realised for some years that the sums did not add up. At one time in the early 1960s, some 22,000 pairs of women's shoes were being made each week in Street. By 1978, that number was down to 7,000 pairs. Even so, the closure came as a shock to employees who gathered in the Strode Theatre on a Tuesday afternoon that September to be told the news by Malcolm Cotton, then divisional general manager for women's shoes.

The *Courier* reported Cotton as saying:

This has happened because over the years the needs of our customers have changed, and despite every effort to move with the times, we have not been successful in finding the right products.

At one point in the meeting, a long-term employee confronted Cotton. 'If it wasn't for my father and grandfather you wouldn't have a job today,' he said. Cotton replied:

I do not accept that I sit here today owing my job to anyone's father or grandfather, because if I was not doing this job then I would be doing something else ... I simply believe there is a job to be done, however unpleasant, to try and get the best results for the company and its employees in the long term. We must work for the present, plan for the future and not contemplate the past.

Cotton was not a family member, but he rose to become managing director of C. & J. Clark Ltd in the 1990s. He joined the company in 1965 from Procter & Gamble as an internal consultant and within six months was put in charge of the Silflex factory. In the early 1970s he worked in Ireland, before returning to Street, first as head of the men's division, then of the women's division.

Reflecting on the Silflex closure, Cotton describes it as a 'seminal moment', while Lance Clark, who was managing director of Clarks Ltd at the time, says it was a 'horrible thing to do' that went completely against the Clarks belief in secure employment. But, says Lance:

> ... it was the right thing to do, and looking back we should have closed more factories much faster ... We should have been hard-headed about it. One of the reasons we dragged our feet was because it would cost us £1 million every time we closed a factory. In the accounts the costs of closing factories came out of trading profits so there was a positive disincentive to take the necessary painful decisions.

A combination of rising raw materials, a flattening national economy and changing fashion trends that Clarks was struggling to keep up with began to take its toll. On 22 August 1980, the company announced the closure of Trefano, the factory in Wales, and its satellite unit, White Rose, with the immediate loss of 390 jobs. In addition, there were redundancies at the Dundalk factory, in Ireland, and at the Vennland factory in Minehead. Only a month earlier, there had been job losses in Street, Yeovil and Weston-super-Mare, so that by the end of 1980, the total workforce in Clarks UK factories had fallen by nearly a ninth from 8,500 to 7,700.

Daniel Clark was running the company at a dispiriting time for UK businesses. In 1979, when Margaret Thatcher came to power, inflation was in double figures and unemployment was at a post-war high of 700,000. Government debt required borrowing from the IMF.

Internally, it wasn't easy either. The larger a family business becomes the more complex it is to run, the more onerous to resolve differences among shareholders. The Institute for Family Business says that only 13 per cent of family businesses survive to the third generation, but by the late 1970s Clarks was a fifth-generation family, albeit burdened by many of the inherent disadvantages that come with such a long history. It was only in the 1990s that Clarks started to make the transition from being an owner-managed company to being family-owned but employing professional managers to run the business. The obstacles facing Daniel were immense in comparison to those of, for example, his great-grandfather, William S. Clark, who was the overwhelming majority shareholder with the freedom and authority to make decisions as he saw fit.

Daniel did not attempt to disguise the challenges. When pre-tax profits in 1980 fell to £8.7 million, some 30 per cent below those of 1979, he described them as 'very disappointing'. The *Courier* also was straight to the point: 'The best thing that can be said about 1980 is that it is over.'

Relations with K Shoes – which had been founded in 1842 by Robert Miller Somervell – had always been close, and would become even closer by the end of 1980. Without warning, but operating within the guidelines on mergers and take-overs, Ward White, manufacturers of Tuf, Gluv, John White, Portland and several other lower-priced footwear brands, launched a hostile 'dawn raid' for K Shoes on 21 October 1980, acquiring a 14.85 per cent stake. Ward White paid 60 pence a share, when K Shoes shares had been trading at 47 pence. Clearly, a full bid was in the offing. Ward White was slightly bigger than K Shoes, with a market capitalisation of around £16 million compared with K Shoes' £14 million. It had 100 shops, trading as Wyles, and had recently bought twenty retail outlets in Sweden and 50 in North America.

On the afternoon of 21 October 1980, the K Shoes chairman, Spencer Crookenden, and his managing director, George Probert, met their counterparts at Ward White, who were George McWatters and Philip Birch. McWatters and Birch spoke, Crookenden and Probert listened. The news went down badly in Street. K Shoes was a big brand and the Clarks board did not want it to fall into the hands of competitors. The next day, Daniel Clark telephoned Crookenden to say that Clarks felt compelled to make a counter bid. On 23 October 1980, a meeting was convened at the London offices of Schroders merchant bank, attended by Daniel, Lance and William Johnston, from Clarks, and by Crookenden and Probert from K Shoes. Crookenden stressed how he wished K to remain independent, but if this proved impossible he would rather be in business with Clarks than Ward White, provided K Shoes could maintain its own identity.

'We were much impressed by the character of the Clarks directors, and we particularly admired the quality and total trustworthiness of the chairman, Daniel Clark,' wrote Crookenden in his book *K Shoes: The First 150 Years, 1842–1992*.

The next day, Crookenden issued a statement to all K Shoes' employees, explaining the firm's position and ending with a plea that 'we should all continue to work normally'. Evidently, the one person not working normally was Crookenden. First, he had to appoint a new merchant bank because Clarks and K Shoes shared the services of Schroders. Clarks had been with Schroders the longest, and so it was left to K Shoes to make a new appointment. It was agreed that Kleinwort Benson would take on this role, with Lord Rockley as the senior adviser. Further negotiations ensued with Ward White, after which K Shoes promised to make a definite decision within seven days. That decision was taken on 4 November 1980 in favour of the Clarks bid. As Crookenden explains:

> The K Shoes board decided that Ward White were not the right partners for us ... we gained the feeling that they did not understand the real strengths of K Shoes, and we saw no chance that the two companies would work together in harmony.

But he saw every chance that K Shoes could work with Clarks. On 30 October 1980, Clarks offered 68 pence per K Shoes share, significantly less than the £1 a share K Shoes was looking for. 'George Probert left the meeting in disgust, feeling that they were not really serious in making an offer,' according to Crookenden. There was also concern that the

Monopolies and Mergers Commission (MMC) could scupper any deal, given that Clarks already had around 9 per cent of the total UK shoe market, and K Shoes had 3.5 per cent.

Ward White re-entered the chase after K Shoes published its year-end results on 26 November 1980, showing pre-tax profits of £5.5 million, an increase of 10 per cent on the previous year. The K Shoes share price rose to 78 pence on the back of its results. Ward White submitted a draft of its take-over proposal to K Shoes on 2 December 1980. Meanwhile, K Shoes sent its own terms to Clarks, and on 9 December Daniel telephoned Crookenden to confirm an offer of 95 pence per share, a cash bid of £22.4 million. The deal was done, subject to confirmation from the Office of Fair Trading, which duly came shortly after Christmas, that the bid would not be referred to the MMC.

Crookenden and Probert immediately joined the main C. & J. Clark board, with the former expected to retire in 1983. It was agreed that the K Shoes shops would not have to stock Clarks shoes nor Peter Lord shops be required to sell K branded shoes. Additionally, K Shoes would continue to have its own sales force, its own advertising and marketing department and would negotiate its own terms with the unions. Clarks issued a statement saying that it did not 'foresee any redundancies or job losses, salary or wage reductions' for K Shoes employees.

There are two ways of looking at the purchase of K Shoes. The first is that the two firms were a perfect fit, sharing a shoemaking heritage and a commitment to a wider social responsibility. Clarks had 550 shops and K Shoes had 220. Clarks had 20,000 employees worldwide, K Shoes had 5,700. Clarks produced 15 million pairs of shoes a year, K Shoes made 5 million, and so joining forces made commercial sense. Together, Clarks and K Shoes would provide stiff competition for other UK-based manufacturers and shoe retailers. Both companies would gain from fresh input from their respective senior management executives. Neither brand would be diluted and both companies would continue to negotiate separately with their customers about discounts and other promotions.

As Daniel put it to shareholders:

The Clarks board in 1981 shortly after the acquisition of K Shoes. George Probert, previously K Shoes managing director, is standing at the far left. Others in the back row (left to right) are Jan Clark, Eric Gross, Anthony Clothier, John Frith and Lance Clark. Front row: William Johnston, Spencer Crookenden (previously K Shoes chairman), Daniel Clark and Ralph Clark. George Probert was later managing director of Clarks, from 1985 to 1987, when he made extensive changes to the board.

We now have the major share of the manufacturer branded business in the UK, distributing national promoted brands through our own shops and some 3,000 or so other outlets. We believe that for the future this is the one significant way of competing in the market place with the major national retail multiples.

And indeed there were years when K Shoes made a significant contribution to the profits of the company.

But an alternative view – and one that has gained weight with the benefit of hindsight – was that Clarks had bought a company with very similar problems to its own. Rather than helping the firm to move forward, the acquisition of K Shoes would root it to the past. Indeed, when it came to matters such as sourcing from overseas, marketing and distribution, Clarks was, if anything, ahead of K Shoes. Paying £22 million – money borrowed from the bank and due to be repaid in 1987 – simply to compound your difficulties was a risk.

And so it would prove. Arguably, K Shoes should have followed the Clarks lead and begun closing some of its less profitable factories. Instead, it pushed ahead with the new Millbeck plant in Kendal, which was built by the Eden Construction Company at a cost of £820,000 with a completion date set for June 1982.

'In spite of the overall trading situation, Daniel Clark urged the K Shoes directors not to be too pessimistic about the economic outlook and to continue to invest in order to improve productivity and to expand retailing,' wrote Crookenden.

K Shoes results for 1981 were worrying, but were even worse in 1982, when profits fell from £4.2 million to £2.8 million. A new lightweight walking boot designed in close cooperation with Chris Brasher, the Olympic gold medallist, failed to raise spirits in Kendal, and even a range trading under the name of top fashion designer Mary Quant was withdrawn after less than two years.

In the annual report for the whole group, Daniel confirmed that all chains within C. & J. Clark Retail Ltd had 'failed to meet budgeted sales, in some cases, by a considerable margin'. Furthermore, there had been losses in North America – 'partly by expanding too rapidly' – and in Europe, while Avalon Industries had experienced a 'bad year'. It was also the case that during the recession consumers were 'buying down', unlike in the past when they had tended to stick with brands they trusted.

While telling the K Shoes directors not to be downcast, Daniel seemed a little disheartened himself, saying that prospects in the UK 'do not look very encouraging' and that trading conditions were so unpredictable that 'I am reluctant ... to forecast what the outcome will be.'

The outcome for the first six months of 1982 was a disaster. Net profit before tax for the first six months in 1981 was £10.7 million, falling to a loss of £1.2 million twelve months later.

The successful Flotilla range was introduced in 1954 and was not replaced until 1970. Its sales slogan was 'The City to the Sea', but the nautical theme is not echoed in this 1956 showcard.

Described as 'Desert Casuals' in this 1957 showcard, the Desert Boot was first produced by Clarks in 1949, and its sales reached a peak in 1971. It has remained consistently fashionable and its design has scarcely changed over its lifetime.

In the mid-1970s, Clarks commissioned Pentagram, one of the UK's most successful design consultancies, to overhaul the design of shoeboxes, point-of-sale material and the whole presentation of the brand. The design policy for children's shoes was a high priority. This in-store poster encapsulates Pentagram's colourful, up-to-date approach.

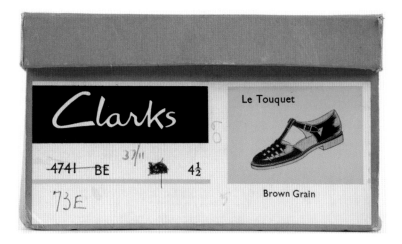

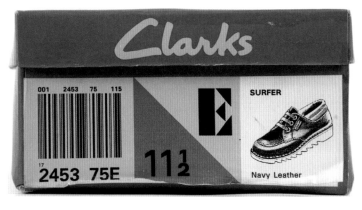

The 1970s Pentagram redesign of children's shoeboxes, using a brighter green, strong colours and bold, geometric shapes (at right), replaced the classic, more muted style of the 1950s and 1960s, such as this shoebox for the classic Le Touquet sandal (above).

Even the footgauge was redesigned by Pentagram, using the same attractive primary colours and building-block shapes in order to appeal to children as much as their parents.

A few years ago, you may recall, we produced our first Polyveldt shoe.

It was supremely comfortable, light and rugged. "What more could any man want?" we asked ourselves.

"A bit more swank and style" came the swift reply. We took the hint and designed a new range of shoes based on our Polyveldt technology.

Something for young groovers as well as their dads. These shoes are still lighter on your feet and longer lasting than ordinary shoes.

The polyurethane soles are still rugged and springy.

But for the uppers we've used a new tough hide that's as soft as glove leather and rather smooth.

And the ankle padding, it's not only a comfort feature, it's a design feature.

In other words, this year we've set out to delight the eye, not just the foot.

Clarks

Hard-wearing shoes needn't be hard to wear.

A 1979 press advertisement for Polyveldt-based shoes – flexible, durable, light and extremely popular. But they came in for criticism in the 1980s and 1990s, when they were perceived as being bland and lacking in style.

The Jack Nano and Daisy 'Magic Steps' children's shoes were introduced in 2010 and 2007 respectively. The vigorous marketing material seen here appeared in 2011.

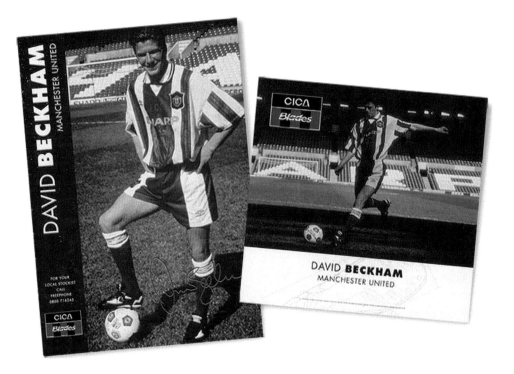

Endorsement by celebrities remains as important as ever. A young David Beckham wears the Clarks Cica Blades range in the mid-1990s (above), while Iain Percy and Andrew Simpson, winners of Olympic medals in 2008 and 2012, were featured heavily in the year of the London Olympics.

The Desert Boot, seen above in a customised Union jack design, is indelibly associated with the Clarks brand, and has been enthusiastically worn by successive generations of style-setters and role models. Below left: Florence Welch, of Florence and the Machine (seen here at the Glastonbury Festival in 2010) wears a pair of Desert Yarra, the Desert Boot derivative on a wedge heel designed by Marijke Bruggink. Below right: Noel Gallagher, formerly of Oasis, is featured on the front cover of the November 2012 issue of Q magazine in a lived-in pair of regular Desert Boots.

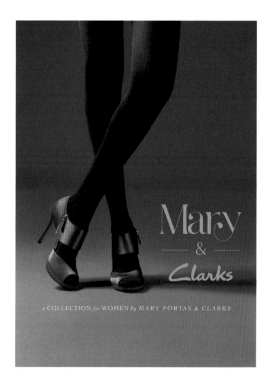

a COLLECTION for WOMEN by MARY PORTAS & CLARKS

Style and elegance continue to be the keynotes for Clarks shoes for women, and also for the design of contemporary Clarks shopfronts and instore displays, as seen in the example below of the 2012 C7 redesign. Above left: a contemporary women's classic, the bestselling Bombay Light, introduced in 2007. Above right: marketing material for the range designed in collaboration with Mary Portas, the 'Queen of Shops', who has been associated with Clarks since the 1990s.

The family-owned and UK-based firm of Clarks has a strong presence worldwide. Turnover in North America is second only to the UK, supported by high-quality marketing: this advertisement ran in US *Vogue* in 2011.

The autumn and winter 2012 UK press and poster campaign, including this widely seen image, was an example of Clarks emphasising itself as a younger, more fashion-conscious brand.

Up-to-date technology combined with enduring values: the Clarks world footgauge uses the latest digital technology to ensure comfort and the right fit.

But there were some happy diversions in the early 1980s. The wedding of Prince Charles and Lady Diana Spencer in the summer of 1981 led to a run on traditional, low-heeled court shoes as worn by the young princess. Clarks capitalised on this by introducing its 'Princess Di' shoe, formally known as the Quiver, which retailed at £14.99. Starting with this one model, Quiver soon became a whole range of footwear. Developed in the Barnstaple factory, Quiver shoes were then produced in bulk in Plymouth, Barnstaple, Exmouth and Shepton Mallet, as well as in Dundalk, where 60 extra staff were taken on to cope with demand.

Meanwhile, the Queen had dropped in to the Peter Lord shop in Staines in March 1980 when she opened the new Elmsleigh shopping precinct. Three years later, the Duke of Edinburgh, in his role as president of the Royal Society of Arts, presented Clarks with the Award for Design Management, an accolade to mark the contribution design makes to the commercial success of an organisation. And just in case Clarks' younger customers were in danger of losing interest, Noel Edmonds, then a leading radio DJ, attended a children's division sales conference to endorse Clarks teenage ranges.

But nothing could disguise the anxiety over the company's overall performance, and there was no attempt to do so in the pages of the *Courier*. In the spring of 1982, the following exchange was printed when Lance Clark was grilled by the company's public relations manager, Ian Ritchie.

'So why have sales been worse than expected?' asked Ritchie.

'The main factor is price,' said Lance. 'In the bad economic times people are paying less for their shoes. We've got to get the price of our footwear down.'

'I think you're blaming outside influences a great deal,' said Ritchie. 'You blamed the imports and you've blamed the consumer for buying the lower price shoes, but surely some of the criticism must be directed inwardly at the management of the business?'

'Yes, I must accept, as managing director, that it is my total responsibility. We have made mistakes. Looking back, had we forecast more accurately the severity and depth of this depression, yes, I should, knowing what I now know, have taken much tougher action more quickly and more aggressively than we did.'

Within months of giving that interview, Lance was replaced as managing director of Clarks Ltd – which was responsible for all UK manu-facturing, wholesaling marketing, advertising, personnel and planning – by 43-year-old Malcolm Cotton. Lance, a major shareholder, faced the prospect of being sidelined when he was given the role of developing C. & J. Clark Continental Ltd. The *Courier* thundered once more, this time with a whiff of mischief, quoting Petronius, a Roman satirist, who in AD 66 observed:

> No sooner did we form into teams than we were reorganised. We tend to meet every new situation by reorganisation, and what a wonderful method it is for giving the illusion of progress whilst only producing confusion, inefficiency and demoralisation.

10

Taking sides

THE GULF between manufacturing and retailing at Clarks seemed impossible to bridge. Manufacturing wanted – and was encouraged – to protect its margins, while retailing wanted – and was encouraged – to buy in shoes at the cheapest possible price. Divisions between the two arms were historic. Manufacturing represented the past: retail was positioning itself as the future – but without the retail experience at managerial level to embrace that future. There were even lifestyle differences. Retailers tended to smoke, manufacturers didn't. As one member of the Clark family recalls:

> Retailers and property people made up the hard core of smokers. They tended to be at the happy-go-lucky, can-do, cup-always-more-than-half-full end of the spectrum. Originally, smokers and non-smokers all mixed together in Street. Then the Human Resources lot got busy and closed the separate senior staff canteen so that all grades shared the same canteen space. However, the canteen was divided into smoking and non-smoking sections, forcing the two cultures apart.

But smoking was the least of the worries. The big question was how Clarks could continue as a profitable manufacturing and wholesaling company. The answer that dared not speak its name was that it couldn't.

This was to consume the minds of senior managers throughout the 1980s and almost consumed the company in the process.

Costs were too high to sustain the factory system and nothing could be done to stem the tide of cheap shoes coming into the country. Daniel Clark said in his annual report for the year ending 30 January 1982 that imports accounted for over half the total number of shoes sold in the UK. And in its 1981 'Strategy for C & J Clark Ltd: Final Report', the Boston Consulting Group had painted a similarly gloomy picture, continually using the word 'disadvantage' when considering the company's position as a UK-based manufacturer. 'Unless Clarks can offer merchandise which is competitive with imports, erosion of its market share may be inevitable,' it said, echoing a refrain in previous consultation documents.

Later in that report, it said: 'Clarks [should] consider importing parts of its product offering. Failure to do so is likely to lead to a gradual erosion of Clarks market share.' In its concluding recommendations, the group called for a halt on manufacturing certain women's lines, including: 'premium fashion courts and dress sandals'; women's 'sporty courts and moccasins'; women's 'warm-lined and fashion boots'; part of women's 'premium and medium price sandals'; and all 'women's slippers'; as well as some 'men's medium price casuals and sandals' and all 'children's warm-lined boots'.

On the high street, meanwhile, the retailing arm of Clarks formed a complicated web of shops that fell under different command structures, encompassing disparate retail names. But Clarks was not one of those names – at least not until 1984. In total, C. & J. Clark Ltd operated some 900 outlets at the start of that year, trading under Peter Lord, K Shoes, Bayne & Duckett, Ravel, John Farmer and James Baker. Flotilla Shoes Ltd was a subsidiary set up to oversee the management and day-to-day operations of the smaller chains such as James Baker, which Clarks bought in 1977, and Bayne & Duckett, both of which operated in provincial towns in Scotland, Wales, the Midlands and north London. There were 290 Peter Lord shops, mainly in prime, rented city-centre sites, stocking Clarks, K and other higher-end brands. Ravel sold no Clarks or K at all, focusing almost exclusively on imported fashion shoes for the teenage and early-twenties market. Ravel shops tended to be close to major fashion retailers.

Three years earlier, the Boston Consulting Group had been scathing about Ravel, describing its performance as 'volatile' and 'sub standard' compared with competitors such as Dolcis, which habitually achieved 60 per cent more sales per shop and had some three times more outlets. 'Ravel presently enjoys little synergy with other CJC [C. & J. Clark] operations', Boston Consulting Group said.

John Farmer was bought in the spring of 1984. It was previously owned by Hanson Trust, which once controlled John Collier, Richard Shoes and Timpson, and had nearly 100 shops in the south of England, pitched at the middle market and selling a wide range of both Clarks and K. In addition, Clarks footwear was available in more than 2,000 independent shoe shops – and the independents accounted for 25 per cent of the UK market. Close ties were maintained with the independents and there were still perpetual fears about the consequences of jeopardising such long-standing links.

David Lockyer was the first-ever graduate trainee to be assigned to the retailing side of the company. Even since retiring from Clarks in 1996 he has continued to keep an eye on the shoe business, recently as a non-executive director of Barratts, the footwear firm based near Bradford, West Yorkshire, which went into administration in December 2011. He joined Clarks in 1968, after which he became a Peter Lord branch manager, then an area manager and finally general manager of Peter Lord before moving into resourcing in the mid-1980s.

When I started, Clarks was a manufacturer and wholesaler, with a small retail sector, amounting to around ten per cent of the whole business. Those of us in retail always thought we should be pushing for the Clarks name to be above the shop door, but we weren't sure that the ladies' brand was strong enough, and it was only when we started resourcing from places like Brazil and Italy and one or two other countries that it became a viable option. Many of us had grown up in the business and we were perhaps too engrained in the idea that we were a manufacturing company and, let's face it, we were good at what we did. I suspect that we needed someone to come along from outside to shake things up a little.

Retailing was expensive, involving the signing of 20- to 25-year 'institutional leases', with five-year upward-only rent reviews of the kind that pension funds involved in commercial property would find acceptable. At the same time, something needed to be done to challenge the British Shoe Corporation, which was still the biggest shoe retailer in the country. Its brands included: Saxone; Curtess; Lilley & Skinner, Freeman, Hardy & Willis; Dolcis; Trueform; and Manfield. Of those, Dolcis was the most fashionable and expensive, while Freeman, Hardy & Willis was regarded as downmarket from Clarks. Manfield, with its base in Northampton, occupied a middle market position not dissimilar to Clarks.

John Clothier, the son of Peter Clothier, was in charge of the retail side of Clarks' business. He had joined the company in 1969 after spending two years at Humanic, a retail-led shoe business in Austria, with which Clarks had close ties. Reflecting on the some of the issues from the early 1980s, he says it was 'quite clear' that the British Shoe Corporation dominated the High Street and it was 'just as clear' that Clarks needed to strengthen its retail position if it were to compete effectively. He continues:

> The costs of retailing were rising fast and we needed to prove that Clarks over the door would work. Then it was a case of completely reorganising our retail portfolio.

Among those pushing for the launch of Clarks 'over the door' and who hoped to see many existing Clarks-owned outlets coming under the one banner, was Robert Wallace, the company's marketing director. He lobbied Howard Cook, Clothier's right-hand retail man and a driving force behind the launch of the first Clarks shops – and finally, in the summer of 1984, four shops opened in quick succession of each other. Called 'The Clarks Shop' rather than Clarks, as they are today, they were regarded as 'concept' outlets that dealt almost exclusively in branded Clarks and K shoes, plus a small proportion of 'Levi's for feet'. The first of these units opened several miles away from London's West End in unfashionable Tooting. This was followed by a second shop in Knowle, just outside Bristol, in a store once owned by A. J. Bull, an independent selling mainly Clarks, and a third in

Until 1984, Clarks shoes were sold through a wide-ranging network of shops trading under many different names. In that year four shops were opened under the name of 'The Clarks Shop' for the first time.

Beaumont Leys, a new shopping centre on the outskirts of Leicester. A fourth shop was unveiled at the end of June in Welwyn Garden City, with a staff of four, two called Julie and two called Jane.

Within twelve months, The Clarks Shop branding had been replaced by just Clarks, and there were eighteen such outlets, located in areas poorly served by traditional retailers stocking Clarks, especially in the inner cities. Brightness and space was what they had in common, with an emphasis on the shop windows displaying as full a range as possible. The consensus was that these shops immediately benefited from not having to feature conflicting brand display cards, but it was also the case that some of the gaps in the Clarks range were exposed. There was a particular under-representation of men's formal shoes, for example.

The overall look of the shops was upbeat and modern. Perspex stands were kept to a minimum and there were zig-zag tiled walkways between the carpeted areas. Most were fitted out by Clarks' own shopfitters – as they are today. The store in Stratford, East London, sought to attract younger buyers, which explained in part why it had a 24-year-old manager and a 20-year-old senior sales assistant, both of whom ensured that one of its better sellers were the Clarks new air-cushioned casuals that had been the subject of a £300,000 national advertising campaign earlier in the year. Building on the slogan, 'Travel with the World's Most Comfortable Air Line', the advertisements emphasised comfort and a degree of luxury and appeared in the national press as well as magazines such as *Radio Times* and *TV Times*, occupying prime positions on their inside or outside back covers. 'With this air line, everyone travels first class'; 'No other air line cruises at our speed'; 'New heights of comfort for air travel'; and 'Only one air line can fly you to the office' were some of the captions, displayed in capital letters above pictures of the shoes.

Alan Devonshire, West Ham United's star midfielder who won eight England caps, was reported to have bought a pair of Air-Comfort shoes from the Stratford store after suffering an injury to his heel and needing a shoe to speed his recovery – and before long, the whole of the West Ham first team squad was kitted out with air-cushioned shoes when travelling as a group to away games. This kind of endorsement was taken a step further and given another sporty twist in the autumn of 1985 when the children's division launched a £500,000 back-to-school advertising campaign starring famous athletes and their mothers. One featured Sandy Lyle, who had just won the British Open Golf Championship at Royal St George's, swinging a club, with an inset picture of him and his mother taken when he was a small boy. 'We looked after his feet from the very first tee' read the copy. Another showed the British number one women's tennis player, Annabel Croft, administering a ferocious forehand: 'She may get tennis elbow but she'll never suffer from foot-faults.'

Any potential surge in sales from Clarks' investment in retail was to be assisted by the new £3 million extension to the Bullmead warehouse, which attracted widespread attention in the media when it opened on 21 August 1984. HTV's *Report West* programme devoted a full ten minutes to Bullmead's computerised conveyor belt system that could sort 400,000 pairs of shoes a week. BBC's *Points West* and the *Financial Times* also

A 1985 press advertisement for the new Air-Comfort shoes. The West Ham United football team was equipped with these for travel to away games.

expressed interest, the latter running the headline: 'Clarks automated shoe shuffle'. Working with a US-based automation company called Rapistan Lande, the system used laser scanners to read barcodes on shoebox labels, sorting up to twelve sizes, four fittings and five colours of shoe and then routing them to the correct van at what was called the 'goods outwards' bays. Speed was of the essence because Clarks operated a by-return replenishment service to its stockists. This meant up to 100 orders could be processed at any one time, with 50 chutes on one level and 50 on another. Productivity at Bullmead increased by up to 20 per cent and the new system meant 50 fewer people were working at the warehouse than there had been three years earlier.

But for all these new shops, advertising campaigns, star endorsements and technological breakthroughs, the business as a whole was in danger of stagnating. Indeed, some members of the board and several senior shareholders felt that stagnation already had occurred. New organisational structures were introduced, but traditional attitudes remained engrained. Daniel Clark, the chairman, appeared to some to be reluctant to bring in managers from outside the family and slow in sourcing shoes from abroad. But some would point to the constraints he faced by virtue of the number of family members on the board and working in the business, and the widely held belief that it was not possible to get the same level of quality from buying-in as you could from producing shoes in factories at home. Others took the view that if the factories in the southwest of England were to be competitive it would require taking out so much labour from the manufacturing process that quality would suffer.

The closure of factories should have happened faster, but Clarks was not alone in grappling with Britain's decline as a manufacturing-based country. As Daniel noted in the 1984 Chairman's Report,

> ... these actions have been difficult to decide on, involving as they do large numbers of people whose employment we have had to terminate, quite often people with long years of service to the Company.

As it was, arrangements were made during 1984 to close Dundalk, in Ireland, where shoes had been made since 1938 following an agreement with the Halliday family to produce Clarks under licence. This was a wrench. Clarks had taken full control of Dundalk in 1972 and relations with the company were close, with Daniel Clark, Lance Clark, Anthony Clothier and Malcolm Cotton all having spent time there as managers. Dundalk was something of a training ground where young executives could cut their business teeth.

In addition to the closure of Dundalk, what Daniel called a 'disastrous year' in America – due in part to the rising value of the dollar – led to the demise of three factories and all Peter Lord shops in the United States and a cutback at Big Sky, a chain of specialist stores selling leisure lifestyle footwear. One of the factories to shut was the original Hanover Shoes plant in Pennsylvania, which had opened in 1910 and at one time had employed 800 people, producing men's formal welted shoes.

Clarks' grip on the North American market in the mid-1980s was so shaky that the British Shoe Corporation expressed an interest in acquiring its retail interests there, but, instead, Clarks began courting Hanson Trust and Ward White, the latter being the company previously thwarted in its bid to buy K Shoes. William Johnston, who had been a prime mover in the original acquisition of Hanover some ten years earlier, was involved in these negotiations, but both approaches came to nothing. The price was deemed not right. Instead, some struggling Hanover stores were closed, while others moved to smaller units where rents were cheaper.

The 1984 shareholders' report showed that the social responsibility component to the company was still very much alive, still central to the Clarks ethos. After being set up more than twenty years earlier, the Clark Foundation now had investments worth more than £3 million. That year, grants totalling some £120,000 were awarded to a variety of good causes. For example, Halfway House Bridgwater, a rehabilitation centre, received £31,000, and £13,000 was given to Nature Conservation. Smaller donations were made to a number of local charities such as Talking Newspaper for the Blind, in Plymouth, and the Somerset Youth Association. Daniel made a point of reminding the family about its Quaker commitment to helping 'charities of a local nature, local that is to places of major employment by us'.

And despite rumblings from some shareholders about the company's overall performance, pre-tax profits for the year ending January 1986 were more than £30 million, 43 per cent up on the previous year, although boosted by property sales and by so-called 'pension contribution holidays' whereby the company did not make any contributions to the pension fund because its assets exceeded the requirements of the pensioners.

This result was achieved on the back of what Daniel called a 'most unsatisfactory situation' in America, particularly in retailing. However, he stressed that of the 20 million pairs sold, all but 6.5 million were made in the company's own factories. 'Our policy is to concentrate our own manufacturing effort on products where we can offer something unique which can command a premium price. The pitfalls of resourcing abroad are legion,' he told shareholders.

All and any changes to the board – and there were quite a few – between 1985 and 1987 should be seen in the context of the rise to power of George Probert, who had joined the board in 1980 on the acquisition of K Shoes. In the spring of 1985 there was a flurry of top-level appointments. Malcolm Cotton was sent to Australia and made a director of C. & J. Clark Ltd, and John Clothier was appointed chief executive of Clarks Shoes Ltd, a new company formed to unite manufacturing and retailing for the first time. He too was given a seat on the board. Of his appointment, Clothier says:

> The thing is that I had always regarded myself as an outsider ... I did not understand the family politics and my father [Peter Clothier] certainly never talked about it. I suppose I just tried to get on with turning a profit – although the fact that sales were good or not so good at that time was neither here nor there. It was the strategy of direction which was not being correctly spelled out.

Clothier's task was exacting. The pressures on manufacturing were such that specification had to be taken out of the shoes to make them cheaper for consumers, but by doing this there was a danger of losing the essence of a shoe made by Clarks. Conversely, sourcing shoes from outside the UK became a growing imperative, but the options available were nothing like what they are today. China had not opened up economically and the Iron Curtain was still firmly in place.

Other new board appointees in 1985 included Alan Mackay, the finance director, along with David Hawkes, from K Shoes, who was made chief executive of K Shoes Ltd, responsible for the company's manufacturing and retailing. At the same time, Probert was given the title of Group Managing Director of C. & J. Clark Ltd.

Jan Clark, Richard Clark and other members of the family remember Probert boasting that he would 'get rid of the family' – and he made a reasonable fist of it. At one point, according to the minutes of a meeting in 1986, he spoke about the 'problems of having [family] board members who were not good enough'. Blunt and outspoken, Probert was not cut from the same cloth as his colleagues at K Shoes, who tended to be public school and ex-army. The son of a miner, he had risen through the ranks at the Kendal company after joining as a graduate trainee in 1948. He had been a shop assistant, a shop manager, advertising manager and then retail manager for the whole company, taking over from the long-serving Stewart Nicoll in 1962.

Probert had been a successful managing director of K Shoes. He insisted that all directors spend time selling direct to customers in the company's shops and decreed that they should participate in any ongoing retail training known as Fitting Weeks. According to Geoffrey Holt, who also joined K Shoes as a trainee in 1948, Probert was a hard taskmaster. 'It was never easy working for George,' Holt is quoted as saying in *K Shoes: The First 150 Years, 1842–1992* by Spencer Crookenden.

Immaculately dressed and always wearing formal, polished welted shoes, Probert found the informality at Clarks infuriating. It was not his style. Neville Gillibrand, while head of the men's division, remembers attending a meeting in Street with Probert and other senior executives. It was due to start at 1 pm. Gillibrand arrived at 1.05 pm to find Probert leaving the room. Gillibrand, who still works as a 'style consultant' and is chairman of Clarks Pension Trustees, describes the scene:

> He was spitting tacks. He said to me: 'I just don't understand the thinking around here.' And I replied that it was the same thinking that showed how K could never make casual shoes and why Clarks could never make formal shoes. We were just completely different. He was from another world and it was hard to get on with him. We had opposing views about everything. George was a serious professional manager but his way of working was at odds with the Clarks culture.

Jan Clark had known Probert for a great number of years before the K Shoes acquisition. 'He was a difficult man,' says Jan. 'He thought we Clarks always got where we were through nepotism – and I suppose we did. He despised privilege wherever he perceived it.'

Probert wasted no time in asserting himself as managing director. At first, he turned his attentions to the United States where he poured scorn on Jan's decision in 1981 to move the US headquarters to new premises in Kennet Square, Pennsylvania, at a cost of $4 million. In a letter to a senior Hanover executive, he likened Kennet Square to an 'ivory tower ... very impressive but very remote'. Then he wrote a candid letter to Ron Mullins, the head of Cegmark International, a New York-based consultancy used by Clarks for issues relating to North America, bemoaning the stock problems in America that he estimated would cost the company $2 million.

Probert said that he would consult the rest of the board about the American operations and then make a decision.

My first inclination is to clear out the lot of them. On consideration, however, that seems impracticable. So I shall be faced with the delicate decision of whom to keep and whom to send packing in a situation where the right answer for every single one of them would be dismissal.

In fact, Jan Clark survived longer than Probert had intended. He was finally removed from his post as managing director of C. & J. Clark America Inc. in June 1986, but remained on the main board as a non-executive director until March 1987. It would seem that Jan was being held to account for the difficulties in North America, where trading losses of 21 per cent were announced by Big Sky in 1985, leading to the board agreeing that 31 of 60 Big Sky outlets would close. There was bad news, too, in South Africa – now part of Clarks Southlands subsidiary, which included Australia and New Zealand – when in January 1985 the factory in Pietermaritzburg closed, leaving 350 employees without jobs. This was blamed on the South African recession and when viewed in isolation was perhaps not too drastic, but retailing in both Australia and New Zealand was also on the slide, with the latter experiencing its worst year in a decade.

On leaving Clarks, Jan remained in the United States and did not set foot in England for five years. 'When you get fired, you're sore. There's no way round that. It meant I had to choose a different course. My mettle was sharpened by the experience,' he says. Jan went on to launch a successful real estate company in Delaware called Land Star Inc. and still lives in the US.

There were a number of proposals floated to change the make-up of the board. One was that Roger Pedder, Bancroft's son-in-law, who had left the company in 1970 and who had wide experience in retailing, be approached to become an executive director, with his exact role to be determined once he had accepted the post. That got nowhere. In the meantime, scheming in the shadows seemed to become a way of life for some members of the family.

Daniel found himself stymied by a poisonous mix of board-level discord, national economic uncertainty and cripplingly high inflation. Even those who disagreed with some elements of his stewardship recognised that he was in an intolerable position. Some men might have walked away altogether on realising that their authority was perpetually being undermined by family tensions and corporate indiscipline. There had been an additional blow when Tony Clark, one of the family's elder statesmen – and Lance's father – died in February 1985. Tony, a former chairman of C. & J. Clark Ltd, was regarded as a stabilising and civilising force. He had been a magistrate, chairman of the local police authority and High Sheriff of Somerset. The death of this decent man was another blow to hopes of reconciliation among the warring factions. Bancroft, in a letter to his son, Daniel, shortly after this sad turn of events, spoke of Tony's 'shrewdness' and described him as one of 'the solid continuing family shareholders' in Clarks.

Daniel needed support. In the autumn of 1985, he telephoned Malcolm Cotton in Australia to explain his predicament. Cotton jumped on a plane the next day – and remembers attending some 'ferocious' board meetings over the next few months. John Clothier, who, like Cotton, was newly appointed to the board, was aware of moves against Daniel, but says he was 'not very clear what the benefits were going to be in replacing him', particularly with Probert still in power.

'Probert's main interest was in driving manufactured shoes through our own shops and we had many heated disagreements about this,' says Clothier.

> His presence was always going to postpone the actions that were necessary. He was a bombastic character who simply did not see that the world was changing.

Daniel, shaken, but determined to battle on, recommended that Clive de Paula should join the board as deputy chairman in November 1985. De Paula was a family member by virtue of his mother, Agnes Clark, the daughter of Frank Clark. As a chartered accountant, he had broad experience in the City and had written a textbook on accounting which remained in print for many years. He was 70 when appointed a director. Daniel hoped he would provide some financial muscle and help sort out the future structure and hierarchy of Clarks.

Board meeting minutes show hostilities breaking out between shareholders and the executive. In June 1986, one minute spoke of a 'total failure of communication between the Board and the family shareholding group ... [causing] complete distrust on both sides'. There was talk of a two-tier board structure which would give shareholders more authority, but this was rejected. Various family shareholder groupings had begun to make their presence felt. A few months earlier, in a document dated 21 October 1985, the Whitenights group – so named because Whitenights was where Roger (Daniel's grandfather) and Sarah Clark had lived on the outskirts of Street – produced a paper called 'Summary on position of shareholders and on manufacturing and trading policies in the UK'. This missive tracked the decline of profits and called for a 'rigorous new management with the highest qualifications and experience ... the urgency of the task requires that this management is brought from the outside as it does not exist within the company'.

The Whitenights group included Stephen Clark and his daughter Harriet Hall, Stephen's brother Nathan, the inventor of the Desert Boot, and Caroline Gould, whose mother was Bancroft's sister. They concluded that the time had come to 'convert our business and trademarks from being primarily manufacturing based to being retail and wholesale led, resourcing from our own factories and overseas'.

Members of the Clark family talk about Probert's 'Night of the Long Knives' during 1986. In fact his cull, carried out with the tacit approval of a majority of the board, stretched over several months, during which he rid the board of three further family members. Officially, they all resigned; unofficially they were removed against their will. First to go was William Johnston in February, followed by Anthony Clothier in May and Clive de Paula in September. Ralph Clark retired as chairman of Avalon Industries, but remained on the board as a non-executive director.

But the biggest change came in September 1986 when Daniel himself finally stood down as chairman and was replaced in a non-executive capacity by Lawrence (Larry) Tindale, the deputy chairman of Investors in Industry Group plc, known as 3i. Richard Clark was instrumental in this appointment after consulting Robert Morison, who had been a partner in KPMG and who had advised companies associated with North Sea oil. Morison recommended Tindale and Bancroft was one of those who strongly supported this appointment – although reportedly he was heard to say many years later that it was one of the worst decisions of his life. Shortly after Tindale's appointment, Morison himself was invited to join the board.

Daniel had endured a torrid time. Shortly after making his announcement to give way, he wrote to his cousin, John H. Clark, who had been working for the company in New Zealand. He was candid about his years in charge.

There was a basic ownership instability in the business arising from the now wide dispersal of family shareholding and the fact that although most family shareholders' wealth is in the business very little of it is involved in a direct management or Board way. A couple of mediocre years allowed this instability to ferment .... I am sad, personally, that the contribution I can make is now so limited but pleased that I can now give more time to other things.

Daniel's father, Bancroft, wrote to his son, thanking him for everything he had done in 'conditions of extreme difficulty.' He said:

Family shareholders are better off at the end of your time than they were at the beginning. That is indeed a solid achievement. They owe you a great deal .... You made bold acquisitions. Some of these have added great strength to the business, some have been harder to master.

Tindale, Daniel's successor, was a seasoned institutional investor who, according to one board member, could 'read a balance sheet with his eyes closed', but lacked any experience or appreciation of the footwear industry. A trained chartered accountant, he had sat on the board of a number of companies, notably Britoil and Caledonian Airways, and been chairman of the British Institute of Management from 1982 to 1984.

'The fact was that he was coming to the end of his career,' says Roger Pedder, who finally was invited to join the board as a non-executive director in 1988. Pedder continues:

He spoke a lot about a return on capital when the issues were commercial not financial. He was the right appointment at the wrong time and his time as chairman delayed further what should have happened. He did not see what really needed to be done and he allowed the internal bickering to continue.

Pedder remembers attending a board meeting some months later when Nathan Clark expressly asked him to take along a plastic bag containing some Chinese shoes with a wholesale price of $10 a pair, almost half what it cost Clarks to make similar shoes in the UK. 'The board meeting started off, as it always did, focusing on the troubles,' says Pedder. 'I'd never seen a shoe on the boardroom table since I'd been back. I said, "Excuse me, gentlemen, I think these are what we should be talking about," as I laid the shoes out across the table. There was a frosty silence and nobody said anything and then we carried on as normal.'

Pedder describes the next few years as a period of endless deliberations and no decisive action. In a 2011 Harvard Business School case study, *Clarks at a Crossroads*, by Professor John A. Davis, Pedder is quoted as saying:

> We were entrenched in the problems of being in uncompetitive, first-world shoe manufacturing and the response to this challenge had been, and continued to be, impossibly slow. The retail side of the business had grown to rival manufacturing, increasingly outsourcing its requirements, and building its own separate management and infrastructure, which created not only a dual overhead but also vituperative internal conflict.

A change at the top coincided with the introduction of a new logo. It was a subtle switch but an important one because it presented a unified corporate image, triggered in part by the need to do away with up to five different shades of green on Clarks' distinctive boxes. The new logo incorporated the Clarks green to represent its heritage and tradition, and a modern grey, which had proved successful in point-of-sale material produced for the shops. This new colour coordination came shortly before an advertising campaign in the spring of 1987 to promote the 'original' Desert Boot, drawing attention to its many imitations by competitors around the world. For a number of years, the Desert Boot was far more fashionable on the continent than it was in Britain. Stylish young Italians were wearing them – though not necessarily the Clarks brand – with their Armani suits, and in Paris they were referred to as 'Les Clarks', even though they were often made by an entirely different company.

By 1987, Clarks was using Boase Massimi Pollitt as its advertising agency. Boase Massimi Pollitt's brief was to do for the Desert Boot what advertising had done for Levi 501s and Doc Martens. Using the strapline 'There is only one desert boot. Clarks. The original', the ads were unquestionably sexual, with the photographs taken by Helmut Newton. One showed a man lying on his back draped over a wall near an inviting blue sea, a woman climbing on top of him, her knee pushed into his groin. Another featured a man leaning against the back of a tractor, his arms behind his head, as a woman stands suggestively in front of him. In both, the man is wearing a desert boot on one foot, nothing on the other.

The ads ran in selected fashion and style magazines such as the *Face*, the *Wire*, *Blitz*, *Arena* and the *Manipulator*. 'The intention was to drop a small pebble in the pond and wait for the ripple to spread out,' Graham Sim, a member of the Clarks marketing department, told the *Courier*. Mission accomplished. Almost all the national newspapers picked up on the ads, with the *Sunday Mirror* running a centre spread headlined 'Hard Sell, Soft Porn'. The *Sunday Telegraph* was more measured, with a piece entitled 'Easily Suede', which concluded that 'the desert boot has all the qualities of the style object ... and a profile just begging to be raised'. The *Today* newspaper – which launched in 1986 and folded in 1995 – must have made for good reading in Street when it said 'Move over Doc Martens, the desert boot is back'.

On another level, Clarks sought to shore up its hold on the children's market, which it had so successfully built up in the post-war years, by launching 'The Foot No. 1', a brochure intended to look like a mini magazine, which was sent out to more than 5 million homes. This was the first time Clarks had tried direct marketing of this nature, showing parents and children up to 26 shoe styles so they could discuss what to buy for school before setting off to the shops. Perhaps prophetically, Clarks could not find a printer in the UK able to deliver the magazine on time and on budget, so went overseas and hired a company in Verona, Italy.

The pressure on the children's division was enormous. It was the biggest earner for the company, maintaining a unique relationship with the consumer that still persists today. In the 1980s, there were some 300 different children's styles at any one time, and of those between 40–50 per cent would be changed each year.

Karl Kalcher moved from Clarks Europe, where he was the territory manager for Germany and Austria, to become marketing manager of Clarks children's division in the autumn of 1984 and later took over as children's director. He was determined that children should engage with the product almost as much as their parents. 'Can I have a pair of these?' is what he wanted to hear children saying, rather than a mother deciding by herself what to buy her offspring.

A case in point was the Magic Steps sub-range for girls and Hardware range for boys. Magic Steps was aimed at four-to-eight-year-olds and was based around the idea of young girls wanting to be a princess. A little diamond appeared on the top of the shoe and when you turned it over there was a secret key encased in a small magnified transparent plug recessed into the heel. A television commercial based around a witch, the magical key and a princess proved hugely effective.

The biggest success for junior boys was the Hardware range, which featured a sole that looked like a computer games console. The styling cleverly combined child-friendly details and splashes of colour, but still within a form that was appropriate to go with school uniforms. The range was dressed up in a concept similar to space warfare video games and was backed by strong television advertising. It was massive in the UK and also proved to be the most successful launch of children's shoes into Europe.

Clarks also re-launched 'First Shoes' (for infants up to two years old) in 1986. This was the bedrock of the Clarks children's brand and where Clarks aimed to win over the hearts and minds of parents and lock them in as customers. The re-launch featured a strong, shrine-like point-of-sale package to give a clear focal point in the shop. The range was expanded to include more premium styles with softer leathers and a greater variety of colours and was a direct response to the leading European brands trying to enter the UK market.

Kalcher insisted on holding regular innovation meetings for his marketing and styling teams, when new ideas could be discussed and advanced. Watching programmes such as *Tomorrow's World* and visiting the research labs at the University of Manchester Institute of Science and

Technology was encouraged as a means of keeping abreast of the latest fastening mechanisms and the introduction of potential new materials.

Andrew Peirce was a product manager in the children's division at that time, working with Kalcher. He remembers those days as both frenetic and stimulating:

> Karl instilled a real sense of purpose. The challenge was demanding but the satisfaction levels were high. The reverberations went beyond the product and marketing departments. Expectations of quality and innovation from the factories [were] raised and the buying office was expected to become much more pro-active. Product was everything – the focus was on excellence and the challenge for a product range manager was somehow to know when to insist that we sacrifice that 'little bit more' so that we could get the shoes ready, at a commercial price, in time for the new back-to-school season.

Children's shoes were central to Clarks' business and to its standing in the minds of consumers. Other initiatives were more peripheral, more questionable – such as the decision to pay some £2 million for a majority interest in Rohan Designs plc. Rohan made outdoor clothing popular with walkers. It was started in 1975 by Paul and Sarah Howcroft, who lived in North Yorkshire, and by 1987 it had thirteen shops and was turning over £5 million a year. When the idea of buying Rohan was first raised, the Specialist Research Unit – the market research company headed by Peter Wallis – warned against it. One of Wallis's partners, Colin Fisher, recalls a conversation when John Clothier told him that Clarks understood brands and that was why it would make a success of Rohan.

'I told Clothier that Clarks did not understand brands – but it did understand Clarks,' says Fisher, who in a remarkable turn of events is now executive chairman of Rohan. Clothier pushed on with his plan, telling the *Courier* that he considered the 'Rohan brand as having the potential to be an exciting complementary business to the mainstream Clarks and K Shoe brands in the UK'. The press picked up on the story with *The Times* quoting Paul Howcroft as saying, in August 1988: 'This will be a big leap forward for Rohan although there is a limit to how big you can get without compromising quality ... I would like to see Rohan doing in its sector what Laura Ashley has done in theirs.'

David Hawkes, managing director of K Shoes, was an enthusiastic walker who already had several Rohan items in his wardrobe. He was made chairman of the company, but it wasn't long before Rohan was wandering around Clarks like an orphan looking for a proper home. In 1996, it was sold on, but changed hands again in 2001, by which time Hugh Clark, Daniel's son, and Fisher had joined Rohan. They found new backers in 2007 and today Rohan has 61 shops in the UK and turns over some £28 million a year. Hugh Clark is no longer involved with Rohan, but sits on the C. & J. Clark Ltd board as a non-executive director, representing family shareholders.

George Probert retired on 30 September 1987, the same year as James (Jim) Power was appointed a non-executive director. Power, who within five years would find himself in the thick of an escalating boardroom feud, had spent ten years with the Burton Group and eight years with British Home Stores, and was the director of finance and planning at Storehouse plc. Probert was replaced as group managing director by John Clothier, leading to another structural tinkering and some short-lived new appointments.

Lance Clark left the company in 1987, but remained a non-executive director. Neville Gillibrand, a popular figure with significant expertise in manufacturing and marketing, became managing director of Clarks Shoes and a director of C. & J. Clark International at the age of 43. Among his responsibilities was to strengthen the retail side of the business by expanding the number of dedicated Clarks shops.

'The problem was that I had no experience of retail,' says Gillibrand, 'and this became quite obvious after a few months.' And, so, in July 1988, Malcolm Cotton returned from Australia – where his responsibilities had expanded to include North America and Avalon – and was given back his

A K Shoes shopfront in 1989 – a familiar high-street sight
throughout Britain until the brand disappeared in 2000.

old job as managing director of Clarks Shoes, with Gillibrand working for
him as head of the Men's and International Division (except for North
America).

In Australia, Cotton had gained considerable knowledge of retailing,
but was at heart a manufacturer. Interviewed by the *Courier* shortly before
assuming his new role, he hinted at the endemic problems between manufacturing and retail and said:

> It seems to me that this complex process of changes associated with
> integrating our manufacturing, resourcing, wholesaling and retailing
> businesses has, not surprisingly, brought about some problems of
> control and balance. This has been affecting the company's results and
> hence morale.

Morale took a further dive when Tindale announced the company's results for the year ending 31 January 1988, which showed no improvement on the previous year, a set of figures saved only from further embarrassment by profits from the property side of the business. 'This is the fourth year of static turnover, which obviously implies a down-turn in real activity,' admitted Tindale. Operating profits for Clarks in the UK were down from £15.3 million the previous year to £7.1 million– although C. & J. Retail showed some gains. Tindale said the outcome was 'well below' what it should have been and promised to 'undertake a major review of strategy', drawing on the recommendations of McKinsey & Co., who, along with the Boston Consultancy Group, had been hired yet again as outside business consultants.

Central to that plan was concentrating efforts on three branded chains: Clarks, K Shoes and Ravel, with Peter Lord gradually being rebranded as Clarks. Lord & Farmer would confine itself to multi-brand retailing, and UK manufacturing would continue, but with the proviso that underperforming factories would close. Avalon Industries would cease trading, apart from some core activities directly affecting shoemaking in the West Country – a bitter blow given the historic links with Avalon going back more than a century. On the continent, France Arno would be disposed of and a close eye kept on North America, where profits were 'unacceptably low'.

The worse-than-imagined results fuelled more bad blood between some family shareholders and the board. This forced Tindale to reassess his earlier position regarding a possible flotation of the company, something that had been discussed privately for many years and which caused concern among many family member shareholders who feared it would lead to a full-scale hostile bid.

As Tindale put it:

Although it should still be possible to obtain a listing for the ordinary shares in the spring of next year [1989], I do not think that it would be in the shareholders' or the company's interests so to do. It would mean going to the general public before the outcome of the major reorganisation had been fully proven and well before the benefits could be demonstrated in terms of earnings per share. The result might well be that the company would get off to a bad start as a listed company, not only in relation to the immediate price of its shares, but also in market understanding. If this were to happen, it would do a substantial disservice to both company and shareholders. I suggest, therefore, that the question of a public listing should be reconsidered when the successful results of the strategy are clear to see.

Tindale received a letter in January 1989 from the Street Family Shareholder Association, a grouping of like-minded shareholders. 'This is the time for plain speaking,' it began, before expressing grave fears for the future of the company. 'We are not saying the value of the whole business will necessarily continue to drop. But we are saying that our members' wealth is at risk. Furthermore we think our members are being asked to take too much on trust.'

Times were hard across the established UK footwear industry as the recession of the late 1980s took hold. Sears Holdings, the high street giant that had some 13,000 shops under the umbrella of its British Shoe Corporation subsidiary, was preparing to close 200 outlets, with the loss of 1,000 jobs, while opting to drop Curtess and Trueform altogether. Meanwhile, the likes of Marks & Spencer, Tesco and other supermarkets were showing a more determined interest in shoes, with Marks & Spencer claiming 6 per cent of the market in 1989, sourcing its entire range from overseas. By the end of 1989, two-thirds of shoes sold in Britain were imported.

'I doubt there are any such firms that would not sooner make more rather than less in the UK, if it was commercially viable to do so,' lamented Geoffrey Marshall, president of the British Footwear Manufacturers Federation, in a letter to *Shoe and Leather News*. But it was evidently *not* commercially viable to do so.

The board agreed that it was no longer possible to keep open Redgate 2, a Clarks closing factory in Street, or Isca, the company's Exmouth factory, which produced women's shoes. Both were phased out in 1988. Nevertheless, there was still no overall policy to stop production in Clarks factories. In fact, some – known internally as Centres of Excellence – were expanding. St Peters added an additional 66,000 sq ft of production capacity to its existing unit, at a cost of £6 million, but never managed to live up to the expectations that followed such a big investment, producing 300,000 fewer pairs than anticipated. St Peters, at one time spoken of in the same breath as the successful Bushacre factory in Weston-super-Mare and the Plymouth factories, closed in 1995.

Closures led to a greater reliance on buying in, something the company had been doing quietly – perhaps too quietly – since the early 1960s. In fact, back in 1975, the men's division had appointed a manager to oversee the importing of formal shoes from Italy, canvas shoes from Korea and slippers from other manufacturers in the UK. By 1990, a third of all shoes – around 6.5 million – sold by Clarks were bought in, mainly from other manufacturers in the UK, Brazil, Portugal, Italy, South Korea and Taiwan. One factory in Italy was producing 600,000 pairs of men's formal shoes for Clarks each year alone. Another Italian company was sourcing shoes from Romania and the Ukraine. Added to that list of supply countries were Spain, France, Hungary, Greece and Hong Kong. At that time, resourcing managers were organised geographically, with one person typically responsible for three or four countries, and Clarks had three offshore offices for this purpose – in Portugal, Taiwan and Hong Kong.

The experience in Portugal was different – or at least it became different. Clarks had seen how German footwear companies such as Ara and Elefanten had pioneered factories near Oporto, following the lead taken by Ecco and Mephisto. With labour costs lower than in the UK and with the Portuguese government encouraging inward investment after it joined the European Union in 1985, there was a strong argument for Clarks setting up a factory on a greenfield site in Portugal, but the board was not prepared to release the necessary capital or increase its borrowings in order to do so. Instead, in 1986, closer links were forged with Pinto de Oliveira, a shoemaking company which was already supplying 8,000 leather uppers to the Bushacre factory at an annual saving of £600,000 a year. This led to a joint venture – with each party having 50 per cent equity – through the formation of a new company called Pintosomerset

Limitada, operating from a 14,000 sq ft factory at Arouca, a hilly farming area about 40 miles north of Oporto.

Two years later, when both Pinto de Oliveira and Clarks needed more capacity, Clarks opted to build a second factory for the sole use of Pinto de Oliveira and K Shoes – and did so to a roll of drums. At a ceremony on 3 December 1988, Mario Soares, Portugal's president, officially opened the new plant at Castelo de Paiva, to the east of Oporto, and a period of training began, with the aim of supplying 30,000 pairs of uppers a week for the factories at St Peters, Barnstaple, Bushacre and K Shoes in Kendal. By June 1990, the factory was employing 600 people, of whom 85 per cent were women and 95 per cent were under the age of 25 .

This was a big commitment for Clarks – and for Portugal. Certainly the powers that be in Portugal must have assumed that Clarks was in Portugal for the long haul. Clarks employees learned Portuguese, the local Portuguese learned English – and the mayor of Castelo de Paiva, Anteiro Gaspargas, clearly had high hopes of an enduring relationship with C. & J. Clark, announcing during a visit in the summer of 1990:

> Clarks came to our region at an important time. Before the factory was built there was work here, but not enough. Many people travelled to Oporto, or even moved abroad to find jobs, but now, since the factory opened, more industry has been attracted to the area, bringing prosperity to what was a very agricultural part of Portugal.

The Clarks general manager in Portugal, Alf Turner, recognised the company's responsibilities towards the region and its people. Speaking to the *Courier*, he said:

> It is important for us to convince all of our employees as well as the community in general that we are serious and committed to our business in Portugal and that in the long run, both they and Clarks will benefit as a result of our work here.

But the Portuguese adventure failed to last. By 2001, it was over and

Clarks was sourcing shoes made more cheaply elsewhere, notably from Vietnam.

Back home, by 1989 there had been ten further factory closures and it became clear that a new factory system was needed if young people were to be recruited in the way their parents and grandparents had been during Clarks earlier years. Piecework had helped workers earn good money, but there was a Dickensian whiff about it, encouraging output rather than quality. In its place, in 1989, Factory 2000 was launched and billed as a whole new system that introduced a flat rate of pay and concentrated more on quality than speed. It aimed to get the product right first time, with minimum waste – a leaner operation to compete more favourably with foreign competition.

Martin Peakman, Factory 2000's project manager, assured employees that the new system would be 'rewarding', referring to both pay and working conditions. Something similar, known as the Toyota Sewing System, was introduced at K Shoes; this came from Japan, where the car colossus Toyota revolutionised the way it cut and stitched the leather seats on quality models. K Shoes discovered the Japanese system through its association with the US Shoe Corporation in Cincinnati and adapted it to its own factories in Kendal. One of its core principles was a move towards self-managed teams of four or five people producing an entire upper, with machinery reorganised into a horseshoe configuration.

'Factory 2000 encouraged people to work in teams, but it turned out to be more expensive and did not improve the quality enough,' says Paul Harris, who from 1988 to 1995 was in charge of the Barnstaple factory, where 20,000 pairs of women's casuals were made each week. As Harris explains:

> It was a desperate move in reaction to the recruitment pressures and the quality pressures, but it was not a magic formula. There was no disguising that manufacturing was becoming very difficult. We were fighting the tide and people sensed that more factories would close, but we also knew that the family had invested so much in those communities. And in any case, buying in shoes from abroad was not as easy as it sounds. Resourcing was not a tap you could turn on overnight.

Nor was restoring order between shareholders and the board. Tindale again stressed in January 1990 that a public quotation would be 'fairer to the majority of shareholders', but everyone knew that since it required a 75 per cent majority, it would never be achieved given the distribution of shares among key family members. Twelve months later, after the company bought in 561,007 ordinary shares at a price of 180 pence per share, Tindale changed his tune. In the Annual Reports and Accounts for the year ending 31 January 1991 he said:

> The success of the buy-in dealt in large measure with the shareholders' requests for liquidity, and market and general trading conditions would in any event prevent a successful share flotation in the near future. In view of the strongly held and expressed views of a substantial minority of shareholders, your Board has decided to postpone indefinitely moves to float the company and the existing method of twice-yearly opportunities to sell and buy shares will be continued.

Tindale also informed shareholders that Lord & Farmer was to close, with most of its shops reverting to either Clarks or K Shoes, and he warned that Ravel was experiencing turbulence. Looking ahead, he warned that things would become 'very tough indeed' for C. & J. Clark Ltd.

He was right – but he would not be around to witness it. By the summer of 1991, he had resigned, a decision taken in part because he was not in the best of health, although those close to him intimated that he was ground down by the wrangling between the board and shareholders, demoralised by the recession and fearful for the future of shoe manufacturing in Britain. He wanted out.

Before his departure, a group of family shareholders including Caroline Pym, Lance Clark, Caroline Gould, Harriet Hall, Nathan Clark and Roger and Sibella Pedder wrote a joint letter to Tindale telling him that it was

> ... in the interests of the management, employees and shareholders of C. & J. Clark that it remains a private family company ... your successor should be someone who has the support of the majority of shareholders.

It went further, leaving him with a plan for the future, which they wished him to recommend to the board prior to his departure.

> The proposal has the full support of ourselves and our Family share-holdings, representing an effective majority of the shareholding in C. & J. Clark. If required we will vote to support them at a shareholders meeting.

It was a radical plan. The proposal called for Lance Clark to be appointed chairman on 26 April 1991 at the Annual General Meeting; Roger Pedder would become vice chairman and John Clothier would be given 'full support' as chief executive, subject to achieving certain fiscal goals by 1993 – 'a profit after interest representing 20 per cent of capital employed'. There were eleven points in total. Under the heading 'Policy' it said, with no apparent irony: 'There is no intention behind these changes to interfere with operational management of the company.'

A record of Tindale's response does not exist. But this audacious manoeuvre came to nothing. Instead, headhunters were deployed to find a successor to Tindale from outside Clarks and they identified Walter Dickson as the man for the job.

Dickson, who was of Scottish descent, might not have known one end of a shoe from another, but he was well versed in the vagaries of working for a family firm with a long history and proud tradition. He was known as 'the man from Mars'. And for good reason, since he had worked for the American-owned confectionery company for 25 years, joining in 1962 from Procter & Gamble as national sales manager and ending up as president of Mars Europe. Along the way, he was variously sales director and then managing director of Pedigree Pet Foods, a subsidiary of Mars, and managing director of Mars Confectionery.

11

Peering over the precipice

WALTER DICKSON arrived in Street in July 1991, just a few weeks after Harrods opened a children's shoe department run by Clarks. The *Courier* of that month reported breathlessly on the Harrods story, running it as a page-one splash. 'We had Diana Ross and Rod Stewart – and the Sultan of Brunei is a good customer. But there is room for ordinary people,' said Angela Holmes, the manager of the Harrods branch.

'Change at the top,' announcing Dickson's arrival, featured on page five and contained an interview with the new chairman by Ian Ritchie, head of public relations, who did not take long in getting to the heart of the ownership issue.

'Mars is a family company. So is C. & J. Clark. What are your views on the contrast between a family and public company?'

'The family business structure is not bedevilled by the short-termism forced on business by the City,' replied Dickson. He went on:

That particular feature was a hallmark at Mars and it seems to me that CJC has the same attitude in terms of time horizons ... There is a marked determination to maintain quality at Clarks ... Although there are differences between family and public companies, both business structures have got to answer to an outside audience ... The difference is that the institutional shareholders are more faceless and uninvolved than are the shareholders in Mars and Clarks. Therefore there is more direct linkage with the shareholding community of a private family company than there is in a public company.

And when that 'direct linkage' turns toxic it is not long before the board is brought to its knees. Just as football managers forever resort to the cliché about how 'at the end of the day it's all about results', it must have been evident to Dickson that only returning the company to sustained profitability – with a healthy dividend paid to shareholders – would keep the peace.

It was never going to be easy when substantial family shareholders continued to agitate in the background.

'The family became a board outside the board and that was always my gripe,' says Malcolm Cotton. 'It meant there were two boards trying to run the company. It was a hopeless situation and it became clear that something major had to change.'

Lance's cousin Richard, one of Bancroft's sons, was about to join the board, and he too had grave reservations about the way the company was being driven, about its range and quality of shoes and about its reluctance to implement the repeated recommendations made by management consultants. Richard had done his own sums and worked out that 25 per cent of profits from 1981 to 1991 had come from selling off assets, such as defunct factories and other properties or disused factories, rather than from the sale of shoes.

One asset sold was a Henry Moore sculpture that Clarks had bought in 1981 for £150,000. In an article composed for the Village Album, a mainly Quaker group that met (and still meets) once a year, and where members read out essays or poems, Ralph Clark recalled how the company had written to Moore asking if the artist might contemplate disposing of 'any rejects'. Moore replied some months later, apologising for having temporarily mislaid the letter and saying that he had no 'rejects', but would be happy to discuss matters further. As Ralph wrote:

The meeting duly took place at his fascinating studio in Hertfordshire, when it was politely made clear that it was not so much a matter of whether we wanted a piece but rather whether Mr Moore thought we were fit people to have one ... the frail and modest 81-year-old artist turned out to be a formidable salesman.

Moore visited Street to inspect the site outside Netherleigh, the original home of James Clark, where it was proposed the sculpture – called *Sheep Piece* – would stand. Moore made approving noises. Clarks would take the work on trial while a price was agreed. Ralph described how two lorries carrying five tons of bronze arrived and the sculpture was assembled on site. Moore then arrived and wanted his creation to be moved six feet to the left.

Sheep Piece appeared to some to depict two sheep fornicating – or at least one sheep climbing on the back of another. According to Ralph's essay, the reception was mixed, with some local councillors describing it as 'obscene'. Several months later, Moore telephoned Street to say that a Japanese company had also expressed an interest in the sculpture. Ralph recalled:

Could we please make up our minds? A nice large and round sum was mentioned. Many discussions took place and finally it was decided to buy – it was, after all, an investment ... I only hope, if ever we have to sell, that the buyer has somewhere to put the piece, but if he does, he will not have half the fun we had buying ours.

The Henry Moore sculpture was sold to PepsiCo in 1991 for around £2.1 million and taken to the American company's sculpture park in Purchase, New York, where it remains today, alongside two other works by Moore.

'I was sad to see it go,' says Richard Clark. 'But it didn't surprise me, because it was another way of propping up the profits. What did bother me was hearing people say that Clarks was selling off the family silver.'

What bothered Richard even more was the idea of floating the company and selling it to new owners. This was an over-my-dead-body option for him and for many other members of the family. Caroline Gould,

The celebrated sculptor Henry Moore visited Street in 1979 to discuss
the purchase by Clarks of his sculpture *Sheep Piece*. Left to right:
Bancroft Clark, Daniel Clark, Ralph Clark and Henry Moore.

an architect, whose mother, Eleanor, was Bancroft Clark's sister, was one
such disaffected director. From 1987, she had been Stephen Clark's alter-
nate on the board, but when he stood down in 1990 she replaced him in
her own right. Gould explains:

> When Daniel was chairman the board was anything but collegiate and
> this continued after Walter Dickson took over. He was a great talker, but
> there was little evidence he was bringing the executive together ... there
> was a lot of working behind the scenes from all sides.

Dickson put in place a new management structure of C. & J. Clark Ltd,
which took effect on 1 February 1992. Its main thrust was that the existing
subsidiaries, including Clarks Shoes and K Shoes, were replaced by a single
company, Clarks International Ltd, with its own executive board.

'The new structure is charged with the management of the strategic and tactical whole,' said Dickson in his first Annual Reports and Accounts. 'Our aim is to become a world class business in terms of product quality, operational efficiency and, as a consequence, in profitability.'

New structures had become something of an abiding theme, normally accompanied by upbeat forecasts for the future. On this occasion, it was John Clothier, the chief executive, who told the *Courier* that this latest new dawn 'represents a real opportunity to transform our business performance and [to] give all of us a truly exciting prospect for the future'.

Certainly, the reshuffled hierarchy had a simpler format. There were five main divisions: brands, under Malcolm Cotton; retail, under David Lockyer; overseas, under Patrick Farmer, who joined the main board in 1990; personnel, under Kevin Crumplin; and finance, under Alan Mackay. Clothier made it clear that transforming the business would not 'fall into our lap' and that 'many difficulties were on the way'. He was proved right on both counts – but the difficulties were of a kind he might never have envisaged.

The environment in which Clarks was operating was not encouraging. Footwear in the UK was in the doldrums, with the market broadly static between 1986 and 1989 and then falling in 1990 and 1991. Out of all consumer spending, that on shoes accounted for 1.23 per cent in 1983, but had dropped to 0.98 per cent by the time Dickson began his part-time, non-executive chairmanship of Clarks. In real terms, spending on footwear fell 4.5 per cent in 1991.

Verdict, a market research group specialising in retail, predicted that even if there were a recovery in the economy it would make little difference to the footwear industry, where the three biggest players were the British Shoe Corporation with an 18.3 per cent share, Clarks with 8 per cent and Marks & Spencer with 5.9 per cent. Footwear prices, said Verdict, had risen at about two-thirds of the rate of retail prices as a whole. It warned that either prices or volumes would have to increase, or else 'a number of companies will cease to function'.

The harsh realities predicted came true in 1992, when Sears – which controlled the British Shoe Corporation – reported an £8.8 million pre-tax loss for the first six months of the year and immediately announced it was closing dozens of Dolcis, Saxone and Freeman, Hardy & Willis shops over the next three years in what became a £32 million restructuring programme.

Clarks' six-month interim results to 1 July 1992 were depressing. The company made a £3.5 million pre-tax loss against a £2.5 million profit in the previous period. The decision was made to halve the dividend from 3.5 pence to 1.75 pence per share. Some 70 per cent of the shares were held by the family, another 10 per cent by family trusts, and 10 per cent by employees, leaving just 10 per cent in the hands of institutional investors.

A few months earlier, in February 1992, it was announced that 300 jobs would go across Clarks and K Shoes. Some 100 of those were back-room staff in Street and in Kendal, but K Shoes' Norwich factory ceased operations immediately and Clarks' Barnstaple factory was reorganised with the loss of 33 jobs.

Kevin Crumplin, the Clarks director of personnel, put out a statement expressing 'very deep regret', adding how he was 'absolutely certain that we will come out of it a leaner, stronger and more secure company'. Two months later, that security looked more precarious than ever when further cutbacks were announced. These included a reduction of 173 jobs in the two Plymouth factories, affecting the cutting, stitching and making departments; nearly 100 job losses at the Barnstaple factory; 67 redundancies at Bushacre in Weston-super-Mare; a down-scaling at the K Shoes Askam factory in Cumbria, and the closure of Avalon Components in Castle Cary, where 89 people worked in last-making.

Walter Dickson's forte was brand management. At Mars, he had come into contact with Larry Light, then chairman and CEO of the international division of Bates Worldwide, the advertising and communications agency. Light, a graduate of McGill University, had been responsible for all Mars Inc.'s advertising and brand promotion and was now to turn his hand to Clarks. During an intensive few months in early 1992, he presided over a number of management seminars, reportedly charging £5,000 a day for his labours.

The company was also paying considerable fees to McKinsey for consultancy services, prompting heated discussion on the board and among family shareholders about the company's resolve to act upon recommendations going back as far as 1988.

Then, when it became apparent that the board was actively seeking approaches from potential outside investors, the mood soured further. One such approach came from two businessmen in Hong Kong, Li Ka-Shing and Chong Hok Shan, with whom Malcolm Cotton had had past dealings in the hope of setting up a joint venture to expand the brand into the Far East. Dickson was excited. China, three years on from the mass protests in Tiananmen Square, was increasingly flexing its economic muscle, with British companies scrambling to be part of the action.

Chong Hok Shan was connected to the Chung Nam Group, the watch and clock movement manufacturers. Perhaps more tantalising was the fact that Li Ka-Shing was one of the richest and most powerful men in the world, with huge interests in retailing.

It emerged that Li Ka-Shing and Chong Hok Shan would provide up to £40 million in cash in return for between 10 and 20 per cent of shares in C. & J. Clark Ltd. Lance Clark and the other dissenting voices on the board – including Richard Clark, Roger Pedder and Caroline Gould, who were dubbed the Gang of Four by some sections of the press – were furious about this development.

The situation came to a head in September 1992, when Clarks announced that an extraordinary general meeting (EGM) had been requested by the so-called Gang of Four and that it would be held on 16 October 1992 at Glastonbury Town Hall. The resolutions requiring a vote at that meeting called for the removal of both Dickson as chairman of C. & J. Clark Ltd, and Jim Power, one of the non-executive directors. It was proposed that they would be replaced by, respectively, Michael Markham, a businessman known to Lance, and Hugh Pym, Lance's 32-year-old nephew, then a television news reporter with ITN based in Scotland.

In a letter to shareholders, the board – or, at least, a majority of the board – struck back, describing Dickson as 'an agent of change whose record in brand marketing is well known, and whose leadership in developing the new strategy outlined in the 1991/92 Annual Report has been invaluable'. It went on to say that 'these proposals represent another chapter, but no solution, to a long-running history of ownership, control and management issues which have bedevilled the Company for many years ... Your board believes that the requisitionists' proposals would:

- result in the loss of valuable, known talent and leadership to the Board and the Company;
- fail to provide the necessary balance on the Board required for the successful implementation of the business strategy of the Company outlined in the Annual Report;
- fail to add relevant experience to the Board;
- result in control of the Board by certain family groups without offering shareholders who wish to realise their investment the opportunity to sell their shares at a fair price.'

Included with the letter was an appendix in the form of a statement from Dickson and a separate statement from Power. The first was entitled 'Resolution to remove me from the Board', the second, 'Resolution to remove me as a Director of the Company'. Dickson pointed out that in January 1992 he was offered an improved financial package tying him into Clarks until June 1994 and therefore it was absurd suddenly to seek his resignation.

Shortly after the sending of this letter, Clarks confirmed that discussions had opened with Electra Investment Trust, a venture capital group, which was keen to make a 'friendly' bid for the company, thought to be in the region of £100 million, or just over 125 pence a share.

'The whole thing is tentative at the moment. We are not a contentious organisation,' Michael Stoddart, chairman of Electra, told the *Daily Telegraph* on 4 October 1992. 'We will not proceed if there is any opposition, but we expect to be able to offer support to the people who want to carry this deal out.'

The next day, the 'requisitionists' as they were called formally – the rebels, informally – wrote to all shareholders explaining their reasons for calling the EGM, as follows:

For some considerable time we have been greatly concerned about the Company's performance and its future direction. We fully appreciate that such a measure is a recourse of last resort, and we would not be taking this action unless all other avenues to protect the interest of shareholders and employees had been exhausted. We have tried through Board representations and in meetings with the chairman to have our concerns addressed, but without success.

The letter quoted the McKinsey report of 1988 on improving the company's performance: 'Successful execution of this strategy should, on best estimate rather than optimistic assumptions, lead to returns on capital employed of just over 20 per cent by 1992'. But, the requisitionists said, 'on 13 August 1992 the Company issued a profit warning. Clearly things have gone very wrong in C. &. J. Clark Ltd'.

On 9 October 1992 the board responded – and the tone was distinctly less polite:

The requisitionists want control but have no strategy ... their use of the McKinsey strategy is farcical: McKinsey have stated that, if market conditions had not changed, the company would be on track ... they [the rebels] have damaged the Company and disregarded the interests of shareholders. If they have done this as requisitionists, how would they behave if they controlled the Board?

The credentials of both Markham, who was 40, and Pym, who did not have a business background, were questioned, their experience contrasted with that of Dickson and Power. 'What do Hugh Pym and Mr Markham add, other than Board control for the requisitionists?' retorted the board. Markham had been described by the rebels as an 'experienced businessman specialising in corporate turnaround' who was involved in a 'Special Project on running a group of leasing companies'. Supporters of Dickson and Power were forthright in their response:

Our difficulty is that the requisitionists have persistently refused to provide the Board with any details of his career or qualifications. This remains true to this day. What is his career history? What are his qualifications? What is the factual basis of this 'outstanding record in corporate turnarounds?' What has leasing to do with branded footwear? We wish to know, and so should you.

With the EGM scheduled and the voting forms printed, the requisitionists realised that the stakes were dangerously high. They had a change of heart. Rather than calling for a vote to oust Dickson and Power, the meeting at Glastonbury Town Hall would ask shareholders to agree to an adjournment, with a view to holding another meeting later. But there would still be a chance to debate the future of the company.

On the morning of the EGM, *The Times* reported that Markham had issued further details of his career. Since 1982, he had undertaken a number of projects for Banque Hunziker, a Swiss bank, and was currently engaged in restructuring Product Finance, a leasing subsidiary of DG Bank, for the Co-operative Banks of Germany. Perhaps more pertinently, *The Times* added that he had advised a group of rebel shareholders during an acrimonious eight-year battle for boardroom control at Southern Resources, an Australian gold-mining company. The rebels felt that although Markham did not have experience of the shoe business he had the expertise that was needed. They also felt his credentials were no less worthy than those of Dickson, who came to Clarks from a confectionery firm.

The Glastonbury meeting was open to the media. This was another late decision. Originally, John Clothier wanted it to be for the ears of shareholders only and asked Eric Dugmore, who worked for C. & J. Clark Properties, to find a firm that would search the premises for listening devices. Dugmore sought advice from a London company and was told that the sophistication of modern surveillance technology was such that it could be operated from outside the town hall. 'I do not feel therefore it would be worthwhile having a search, at a considerable cost,' he reported back to Clothier in a memo.

It was an overcast morning on Friday, 16 October 1992. Almost every seat in the 480-capacity hall was taken. On stage, the board sat behind a long table, with Caroline Gould at one end, Roger Pedder at the other. Judith Derbyshire, the company secretary (and daughter of Ralph Clark), occupied a seat behind the board, alongside Nigel Boardman, from the company's solicitors, Slaughter & May. A photograph of the Queen looked down from one wall, a ticking clock from another.

Dickson tried to break the ice. 'If we had sold tickets for this meeting we might have made a bit more money than we are making from shoes at the moment.' There was a nervous titter. No one seemed in the mood for levity. After several minutes explaining the current state of trade, Dickson said there was full recognition that Clarks 'products must be improved' and that both sides realised the 'marketability of shares is a pressing problem and has been a problem for some time'. Then he paused, before continuing, his voiced raised: 'So how on earth have we managed to get into this contentious impasse?'

He outlined the key disputed areas over ownership and control, and then confirmed that on 18 September 1992 the board had received a letter from Colin Fisher – representing Electra – with a view to making an offer to shareholders. If the EGM agreed to an adjournment, that offer, and any others, would be considered in an orderly way over the next few months, leading up to the annual general meeting (AGM) in the spring. He proposed establishing a special bid committee, which, he stressed, would work in the interests of all shareholders and remain independent of any warring factions.

Then, before asking for a show of hands to agree or disagree on the adjournment, he opened the meeting for questions from the floor. There was no shortage of takers.

Frederick Terry, a former employee, pleaded with the board 'not to be at one another's throats'; Grant Bramwell, who had previously worked at K Shoes, said Clarks was in danger of becoming the 'laughing stock of the shoe trade'; and Michael Fiennes, who had left Clarks to work with Ecco, said the meeting would not be happening if an 'effective international strategy' had been put in place fifteen years earlier. Specifically addressing the original resolutions, David Edwards, a shareholder married to John Clothier's sister, poured scorn on Markham's credentials.

Edwards ended by calling for Lance Clark's resignation. Lance responded, chronicling the deterioration of company profits in the previous six years, which, he said, now valued shares at 90 pence. He added: 'We were also concerned that the proposed investment of considerable sums of money behind the company's brands was inappropriate until the quality of the shoes had been considerably improved and that it was a waste of money until that had been done.' Lance welcomed the adjournment, but reminded the meeting that 'as a major shareholder you inherit not only considerable advantages but a responsibility and a duty' and that it was 'wrong to sit back and do nothing'.

Daniel Clark, by this time the treasurer of Bristol University but still a non-executive director of Clarks, was seated next to his brother, Richard. He said:

> ... no company can run under a divided board and I think we have to realise that, whatever the outcome, if the resolutions before the EGM were voted, the board would remain divided. So what is the solution? The only one that I can see is that there must be a change in ownership and I have to say I am extremely sad to have to come to that conclusion. It is our business. I am the fifth generation of the family in the business and I know that many of you share that feeling. But we cannot live in the past.

Three away from Daniel was Pedder. He wished to speak and wanted to do so from the lectern in front of Dickson. Centre stage. Dickson moved behind into the second row. Pedder announced:

> We have a situation where this company is not profitable, has declining profitability and we need to pull it up by its bootstraps. If I don't see that happening then it is right I should object.

Then, in what amounted to a declaration of intent, Pedder said he had an independent track record in turning round another business and suggested that he was 'the only one in this hall to have done that'. He added: 'I believe you need a vigorous and entrepreneurial management.'

Following comments about the damage the meeting had caused to the morale of those who worked in the business, there was a show of hands in favour of the adjournment. The meeting was closed.

The Bid Committee that was formed to explore options for selling the company at the highest possible price was chaired by Jim Power. Its other members were Daniel Clark and Roger Pedder from within the company, and Sir Maurice Hodgson, the former chairman of ICI, and Andrew Laing, the managing director of Aberdeen Trust plc, from outside. Hodgson was a former chairman of the Civil Justice Review Advisory Committee reporting to the Lord Chancellor between 1985 and 1989 and was a serving member of the Council of Lloyds. Laing, aged 40, had experience as a commercial lawyer and had advised several private companies about their futures.

Dickson had warned at the October 1992 EGM that Clarks would experience a 'dangerous' six months while soliciting bids. His prediction was correct. For the year ending 31 January 1993, pre-tax profits were down by nearly a third to £19.7 million compared with £28.8 million twelve months earlier.

By the beginning of March 1993, three potential suitors had come forward: Electra Investment Trust, the company which had identified itself as an interested party prior to the October EGM; F. I. I., a rival shoe manufacturer, which made footwear for, among others, Marks & Spencer; and Berisford International plc, a properties and commodities group that was in the throes of rebuilding itself and actively seeking investment possibilities.

On 21 March 1993, Monty Sumray, chairman and managing director of F. I. I., went on record saying that his company would make a good fit with Clarks. 'We are strong in more formal footwear and Clarks is strong in more casual shoes,' he told the *Sunday Times*, confirming that the figure of £150 million was, more or less, common to all three bids.

Two days later, Clarks announced that Berisford had been selected as the party to proceed to the next stage of negotiations and that the two companies' respective merchant bankers, Schroders and Baring Brothers, would begin working together to this end. Berisford's due diligence investigations triggered six weeks of intense speculation as rival factions began preparing themselves for what would be Clarks' 'high noon', an EGM on 7 May 1993 to decide the future ownership of the company.

Finding itself in the spotlight was not something that sat easily with Clarks, but both sides of the argument tried to conduct themselves with dignity. The *Daily Telegraph* said shortly after the news of Berisford's intentions that 'so far the Clarks boardroom has been as leak-proof as its shoes'.

Berisford became a public limited company in 1982 when it diversified from its commodity-and-food-based activities into property and financial services, achieved mainly by a high degree of leveraging. The property crash of the late 1980s and falling commodity prices had rocked Berisford and led to a refinancing package conditional upon a programme of disposals and cashing-in of assets.

John Sclater, a trustee of the Grosvenor Estate and a member of the Council of the Duchy of Lancaster, was appointed its chairman in March 1990. He oversaw the selling off of Berisford's largest asset, British Sugar, for £880 million a year later.

The company's chief executive, Alan Bowkett, who was 42, had only begun his job a few weeks before the proposed Clarks deal made it on to the negotiating table. Bowkett arrived from United Precision Industries Ltd, where he had led a management buy-in and where he oversaw a £200 million turnover, with 4,000 employees in ten countries.

Sclater wrote to Walter Dickson on 1 April 1993, assuring him that Berisford saw Clarks as a long-term core business and that 'the sale or breakup' of the company 'forms no part' of the plans. He said he hoped there would be as 'few compulsory redundancies as possible, consistent with the need to improve the profitability of the business'. Twenty-four hours later, Kevin Crumplin circulated Sclater's letter widely among Clarks employees and confirmed that the EGM on 7 May 1993 would be held at the Royal Bath & West Showground outside Shepton Mallet. Battle lines were drawn and within days a group of shareholders calling itself

Shareholders Opposed to Enforced Sale (SHOES) had sprung into action, bringing together various strands of the family. It outlined its position in a letter to shareholders dated 7 April 1993:

> It is important that our company is not sold at a low price which reflects the problems of the past, rather than the future potential ... we believe that Clarks has a good future. Family ownership has proved responsible in the past and has considered the long-term view. The sale at this time and in this manner would seem to be short-sighted and destructive.

SHOES was careful not to exacerbate the rifts at board level, saying it recognised the effort that had gone into maintaining Clarks' position through a difficult period. 'Whatever differences there have been, they can and should be resolved by reasonable negotiation,' but it warned that if the board persisted with a sale, 'it will be essential to coordinate opposition'. The letter was signed by Harriet Hall, Stephen Clark's daughter; Sarah Clark, Daniel and Richard's sister; Charles Robertson and Benjamin Lovell, both grandsons of Roger Clark; and Hugh Pym, Lance's nephew.

On 19 April 1993, an official 30-page document summarising Berisford's proposals was sent to all shareholders, valuing ordinary shares at 239 pence, a price that was 'fair and reasonable', and confirming that if the resolution was defeated 'there will be no transaction', but that if the resolution was passed, Berisford would 'in the absence of unforeseen circumstances, acquire Clarks'.

On page sixteen of the document, under the heading 'Views of other Clarks Directors', an open letter from Lance Clark, Richard Clark and Caroline Gould was printed in full. It made the point once again that with a strengthened management team and appropriate changes to the board, Clarks could turn itself around:

> The problems that have faced the Company can and should be solved from within and this is in the best interests of shareholders, employees and the Company as a whole.

Roger Pedder, one of the so-called Gang of Four who initiated
the eventful Extraordinary General Meeting of October 1992,
later served as chairman of Clarks from 1993 to 2006.

Roger Pedder, the fourth member of the Gang of Four, chose not to
put his name to this. Instead, his own personal statement was published,
stressing that he believed the Berisford bid amounted to a 'full and fair'
price for the company and that he was in favour of putting it before shareholders, but that, rather than recommend a particular course of action,
he believed shareholders needed to weigh for themselves the prospects of
remaining in private ownership against realising their investment.

SHOES addressed the problems that had beset the previous decade, and
offered solutions. Firstly, the adoption of corporate governance within
one year, so as to establish a clearer division of responsibilities between
directors and shareholders, including fewer Clark family members on the
board, and representing the interests of Clarks shareholders on an elected
Shareholder Council with defined powers. Secondly, full implementation
of the existing three-year plan. And thirdly, support for a public flotation of

Clarks at a time to be determined by the board within five years, assuming the general economic conditions were favourable.

Pym took a month's unpaid leave from ITN to campaign against the sale. Normally the one asking the questions, on 28 April 1993 he found himself in the interesting predicament of facing the media himself. 'There is a Clarks alternative,' he told the *Daily Telegraph*. 'This is the implementation of a plan for a new board structure with a shareholder council. This, combined with a flotation, provides an inherently better structure on the road to success for Clarks.'

Berisford's chief executive, Alan Bowkett, thought otherwise. 'I see a shareholders' council as a way of increasing conflict ... the promise of a flotation is an empty promise,' he told the same paper.

And so it continued. Almost every day in the run-up to Friday, 7 May 1993 there were stories in the press chronicling the twists and turns, the latest jibe from one side or the other.

The closer the vote came, the straighter the talking.

Flotation of the company within five years could not be contemplated, said the board, because institutional investors would not want to put their cash into a company 'fraught with internal' wranglings. SHOES then denounced Berisford as a 'hotch-potch of small businesses, most of which are for sale'.

For almost two months, SHOES engaged the services of Bracher Rawlins, a London firm of solicitors, which in turn brought in Brian Coultas, a corporate finance adviser, to work on the campaign. One issue exercising the legal team was how the board had determined that only a 51 per cent majority would be required to win the vote, rather than 75 per cent, as some people had thought likely under the terms of Clarks' articles of association. If the board were selling the company rather than the business then it would indeed have required 75 per cent of the vote.

'We looked into this and went as far as instructing counsel, but it turned out that the 51 per cent ruling was perfectly legitimate for what the board was trying to do,' says Alan Bracher, a partner at the firm.

A week before the EGM, senior staff gathered in the Orchard Room in Street to hear the Berisford people make their case. Dickson began proceedings by reminding everyone that Clarks had been damaged by 'compromise and fudge' and by a board that was divided. He said the situation had become 'intolerable'. The Berisford bid was 'fair and reasonable,' and its board was 'talented, seasoned and cohesive, which is more than we can unfortunately say about our recent board history at Clarks'. He added: 'We have to change the ownership or stay where we are with all the tension.' The response from the floor was more evenly balanced than at the Glastonbury meeting.

'I understand what we can do for Berisford,' said David Hillcox, head of children's sales, 'but I haven't a clue what Berisford can do for us.' Unlike at Glastonbury, Pedder did not wait until the end to speak. 'I have tried to remain independent and I care as much as anyone,' he said. 'I don't believe us to be weak. I don't find dissent to be weak. It is not weak to point out the deficiencies of the company.'

Malcolm Cotton's contribution made for a withering indictment of the recent past.

I have observed the total undermining of a very competent family chairman [Daniel Clark], the selection of a second chairman [Tindale] by the rebels who undermined him and attempted to remove him within a month of his arrival and I have seen another man, Walter Dickson, brought to public examination in Glastonbury Town Hall. The solution has to be clarity of ownership.

After nearly an hour, the Clarks board swapped places with the Berisford board to answer further questions. David Heeley asked Bowkett to explain his methods of working with a company such as Clarks, to which the potential in-coming chief executive responded with a story about visiting a businessman in Japan who told him to 'get the software right' before doing anything else. It was not a convincing contribution. At one point, the SHOES reaction to the take-over was discussed, prompting James Lupton, a member of the Berisford contingent, to say that the tone adopted by those against the sale was 'disappointing' and that the only concern he had was that Berisford 'might be paying too much for Clarks'.

By now, the Clarks story was no longer confined to the business pages.

'Out of Step' ran a headline on 2 May 1993 in the *Mail on Sunday*, with the sub-head: 'The bitter feud that threatens the rule of a family dynasty'. This unedifying double-page spread included a Clarks family tree with pen portraits going back to James Clark (1811–1906). It ended by saying that whatever happened on 7 May 1993, 'the six-generation family dynasty is almost certain to lose control'.

Almost every other paper and media organisation came to the same conclusion. The *Daily Telegraph* predicted that Clarks' fate would be the same as 'the Lloyds and the Barclays, the Cadburys, Frys, Rowntrees', all of whom had either gone public or been bought out. In an editorial, the paper said that Berisford's 'solution would allow a management to manage in a way that the existing shareholders have prevented, and brought the company to crisis. If the bid is rejected today, Clarks future looks grim.' Ian Ritchie, Clarks' long-standing company spokesman, was quoted by the *Telegraph* as saying: 'One of the Quaker mottos is that pride is a sin and people who start shouting about themselves are going against that. It is very hurtful that this has gone into the public domain'.

It was a fresh, clear morning on Friday, 7 May 1993 as the gates to the Royal Bath & West Showground swung open. The meeting was held in the Showering Pavilion, named after the Showering family from Shepton Mallet who had founded the drinks company behind Babycham, the sparkling perry ('I'd love a Babycham') that had been popular in the 1960s and 1970s. A huge, cavernous building normally occupied by cattle during agricultural shows, the pavilion could easily seat 1,000 people. Television crews jostled for prime position, journalists bagged their places on fold-away chairs hired especially for the occasion. The last time Shepton Mallet had seen such excitement was when it was identified as the town supplying the silk for Queen Victoria's wedding dress.

And the meeting was not the only significant event that day at the showground. In a hall next door, the police were holding a day of riot training for officers attending the forthcoming Glastonbury Music Festival.

Pym remembers arriving in the hall 'quietly confident' that the votes would go SHOES' way. He had talked the night before to Harriet Hall, who had done her sums; she too was optimistic. Hall sat next to Alan Bracher, the solicitor. Richard Clark also had been working out who would vote which way – and was nervous. Pedder and his wife, Sibella, thought it too close to call. Sibella's father, Bancroft, did not attend. Aged 91, he was confined to his wheelchair at home in Street. Prior to the meeting, a family member had distributed various quotations in response to the shareholders' proxy votes. One of these was from Oscar Wilde's *The Ballad of Reading Gaol*:

Yet each man kills the thing he loves.
By each let this be heard.
Some do it with a bitter look,
The coward does it with a kiss,
The brave man with a sword!

Dickson opened the meeting at 11 am by saying he had received a letter from a shareholder recommending he look at Proverbs, chapter 14, verse 1 ('Wisdom builds her house, but folly with her own hands tears it down'). Dickson said he had taken the shareholder's advice and suggested others might wish to do likewise. Then he outlined the position of the majority of the board and said it would be 'tragic' to turn down the Berisford offer. The meeting then went on to reveal the passionate commitment of family shareholders to the company, whichever side of the argument they were on.

Lance Clark articulated the well-rehearsed case against a sale and then accepted that in the past he had 'made mistakes' and been 'clumsy' in some of his protestations against the management of the company. He reiterated his total commitment to floating the company and then asked Richard Clark and Caroline Gould, two of the leading rebels, to make similar pledges. 'I can completely agree with what you have said, Lance, and I commit myself,' said Richard. 'I have no hesitation in committing myself likewise,' said Caroline.

Lance reminded the meeting that Britain was emerging from a deep recession and that Clarks was in a good position to prosper when the economic wind changed direction:

It is an idiotic time to sell, absolutely idiotic ... you've got the best brands in the trade, you've got a strategy and a plan to deliver shareholder wealth. You've got the commitment to float so that you can realise that wealth as and when you want. Please do not hand that over to somebody else. I ask you passionately to reject the bid and keep Clarks independent.

Pedder spoke early, acknowledging that the price Berisford was offering was acceptable, but insisting it was not an offer he wanted to accept. Pauline Clark, Daniel's wife, spoke forcefully about how those who wished to sell 'cared passionately' about Clarks, certainly just as passionately as those who wanted to keep the company in private hands.

The *Daily Telegraph*'s leader of that morning was bandied about at some length – and used by both sides. Dickson said he agreed with the prognosis that the future was 'grim' for Clarks if it did not accept the offer. Pym stressed the complete reverse:

A good deal for Berisford must by definition not be a good deal for us, that's what deals are all about. I ask you to think hard about that, a good deal for them is not a good deal for us ... I urge you very, very much to think hard along those lines and to reject this resolution.

There were some touching contributions from employees. Les Gay, who worked in the St Peters factory, said there were still people on the Clarks board who 'know how to make a pair of shoes', but that when he looked at the Berisford people he could see 'no one that has any concept at all of what this industry is all about'. Gay added that he was due to retire in September and that 'Mr Daniel has taken good care of my pension, but there is also the problem of the people's jobs, and to be quite honest the old saying is, better the devil you know than the devil you don't.'

John Clothier, the Clarks chief executive, stood by his earlier position that only a change of ownership could deliver an improved performance, while Daniel Clark questioned the rebels' motives in changing their minds about offering shareholders a market for their shares by agreeing at the eleventh hour to a flotation:

It is only in this last week that this group has been willing to make that move ... and they still say that they would have preferred to remain private, but they now recognise the overwhelming desire of shareholders to have a flotation. Now, why have they suddenly been converted that way? In my view, it is that they have become frightened.

Daniel finished by declaring how the alternative to a sale was 'just too appalling to contemplate'.

Malcolm Cotton did not intend to speak. Reflecting on this, he says it was because he felt badly torn. 'I did not like the Berisford people and I never thought it [selling] was the right thing for the business, but I believed it was the right thing for the shareholders. Emotionally I hated the idea. My support [for selling] was based on a cold, calculated look at the company.' But he did speak, coaxed to his feet by Pedder, who wanted him to recall a conversation they'd had 24 hours earlier about Berisford's visit to K Shoes in Kendal. Cotton queried whether it was relevant, but spoke about it anyway, saying that Berisford 'had a lot to learn about a labour intensive industry' and suggesting that Berisford 'were surprised and perhaps a little awed by what is, in fact, required'.

Cotton did not then sit down, however. Instead, he spoke at length about why, after nearly 30 years at Clarks, he was exasperated and not convinced by SHOES' 'scanty' plans. But he fell short of recommending a sale.

Please, if you decide to reject Berisford's proposals, and it's well within your power, and if that's your decision we will work to make this company happen and grow as we want it to. But please make sure you deliver corporate governance, a proper council of shareholders and proper flotation. Otherwise, this will never end.

Richard Clark made a personal plea:

It has been said that we shouldn't allow our hearts to rule our minds and I agree with that. But my heart is in this company. I live in Street. I want the company to prosper. I live in the house which James Clark [the founder] was born in and all descendants who are shareholders here today are descendants of his ... I think it isn't our hearts that we have to worry about, it's our minds, and it's our minds which have got to make up the judgement ... I expect the bid to be voted down and I do not want to be called a rebel again.

It was now 1 pm. Dickson said it was time 'to press on'. He formally proposed the resolution that Clarks be sold to Berisford International. Daniel Clark seconded the motion. Then, in accordance with Article 63 of the Articles of Association of the Company, voting began, supervised by National Westminster Registrars, with KPMG acting as scrutineers. The result would be declared at 3 pm.

For the next two hours, shareholders did their best to look relaxed. Some gathered in small groups and shared picnics in the spring sunshine. A reporter from the weekly Mid Somerset Series did the rounds with his notebook. One young Clarks employee told him: 'The last time I was here was to watch Gary Glitter. This is as much theatre as that, I suppose.'

Shortly after 3 pm, the EGM resumed. 'We have the results,' said Dickson:

Total votes cast for the resolution: 34,115,455 – 47 per cent of the vote. Total votes against the resolution: 37,819,7818 – 52.57 per cent of the vote. Therefore, I declare that the resolution has been rejected. Thank you very much for attending. The meeting is now over. I wish everyone well.

12

Shoes for 'Mr and Mrs Made It'

THERE WERE NO RECRIMINATIONS. No gloating from the winners, no sulking from the losers. Polite handshakes were exchanged between rivals on the board. Barings, the merchant bank representing Berisford, issued a short statement expressing its regrets, and Alan Bowkett said he was 'saddened' by events. Walter Dickson promised that the board would 'work towards achieving agreement on how best to take advantage of the great strengths of its [Clarks] brands'. On a personal level, he would consider his position.

Hugh Pym's wife, Susan, was in tears. Harriet Hall simply turned to Alan Bracher, the SHOES group's legal adviser, and said, 'I'm going to give you a kiss, Alan.'

At the time of the vote, Clarks was over two thirds owned by the family, with the remainder owned by outside institutions, the Clarks pension fund, employees and ex-employees. A comfortable majority of the family had voted against selling the company, while the vast majority of the non-family had voted in favour of selling.

An agreement had been made that whatever the result both sides would observe a two-week cooling-off period. The less said the better was the implication – although those involved in what would become a new corporate governance structure began work immediately. Even the media seemed subdued, but perhaps that was simply because a long-standing Quaker family company being sold would have made a better story.

On 18 June 1993, Dickson wrote his final letter to the Clarks shareholders, confirming that an independent chairman would be appointed in due course as his successor, plus two non-executive directors. In accordance with the SHOES commitments, he said a family shareholder council would be established by 31 October, and that this council would appoint two family members to sit on the main board as non-executive directors by the end of the year at the latest. It was agreed that the board of C. & J. Clark Ltd would not only have fewer family members but would be smaller in general. He confirmed that Harriet Hall was to serve as the shareholder council's first chairman.

In addition, and as promised, the company would prepare itself in 'an orderly way' for a Stock Exchange listing within five years 'dependent on a range of factors'.

Two days later, Dickson announced his resignation.

Roger Pedder was made non-executive chairman while a new chairman was recruited. Norman Broadbent, the firm of City headhunters, was commissioned to find suitable candidates and arrived at a shortlist of names drawn from the City. None met with the approval of family members on the appointments committee. They did not want a Walter Dickson Mark II and argued strongly in favour of their preferred candidate, Roger Pedder. Then, on 6 November, it was announced that Pedder, who was 52, had been offered the job – and had accepted. Upon his appointment, Pedder stood down as managing director of Pet City, the company he had jointly founded and which went on to be bought by the US group, PetSmart, for £150 million in 1997.

'We knew he had experience as a chief executive and was good at running things, but he had never been a chairman and so it was a risk – a risk we were willing to take,' says Richard Clark.

Shortly after Pedder's appointment, Daniel Clark stood down as a non-executive director after 26 years on the board. He went on to pursue his interests in academia, deriving great pleasure from his research and writing. He gained a Masters in Archaeology (Environment) from London University (Birkbeck) and followed up with a doctorate at Bristol University, where the title of his thesis was 'Insular Monument Building: A cause of social stress? The case of pre-history Malta'.

Earlier in 1993, on 23 July, Daniel's father, Bancroft Clark, had died at the age of 91. Bancroft had always said he hoped there would be no obituaries in the national press following his death, but obituaries duly appeared. *The Times* called him 'the Grand Old Man of the British Shoe Industry' and a 'giant of a man in all respects' who would wander the factory floor in a white coat 'pouncing on the smallest error and ripping up defective shoes with his bare hands'. The *Financial Times* credited him with developing the famous Clarks foot gauge and said 'if the shoe fits, wear it' would be a suitable epitaph for the man who led the company for 25 years.

Meanwhile, there were no major changes to Clarks' senior management – not yet, at any rate. John Clothier remained group managing director and Malcolm Cotton was made deputy managing director. In his first Annual General Report, for the year ending 31 January 1994, Pedder announced that despite the ructions earlier in the year, results were an improvement on 1992, with profits before tax of a little over £20 million compared with a virtually break-even position for the previous year.

Clarks was still a shoe manufacturer, wholesaler and retailer. It had fourteen factories in the UK, five in Australia, three in North America and two in Portugal, and in the UK it had shops trading under the Clarks, K Shoes and Ravel names. But no one was under any illusion that the structure of the company could continue much longer in its current form. Indeed, there was a question mark over Clarks' whole raison d'être, not least because in Britain there were 25 per cent fewer shoe retailers than five years earlier and the buzz word was 'discounting'. UK discount stores were claiming a 4 per cent market share, a frightening figure for a quality shoemaker such as Clarks with high overheads, and which itself could only boast 5 per cent of the market, the same percentage at the time as one of its main rivals, Marks & Spencer. But this was nothing compared with what was going on in the USA, where discount and outlet stores were growing at an alarming rate, seizing 8 per cent of the overall shoe market. No wonder, then, that Bostonian, the US business owned by Clarks, recorded profits of under $5 million on sales of $110 million for the year ending January 1993.

'We simply were not competitive,' says Pedder. 'It was obvious that the whole notion of the company had to change and become retail-marketing led.'

But there was one area in which the company *was* competitive: Clarks Village, the outlet store in Street that was opened in August 1993. John Clothier was the driving force behind this venture – the first of its kind in Britain – assisted on the ground by Chris Pleeth, who worked for Clarks Properties. K Shoes had opened factory shops in Kendal and Doncaster in 1992 and everyone had been pleasantly surprised by the results. This was confirmed when Clarks commissioned a survey of holidaymakers in Cumbria, showing that 66 per cent of those polled put shopping at the top of their list of preferred activities, way above fell walking.

The factory outlet experience in Street was to be on a bigger scale than in Kendal, and Clothier says his determination to push it through was born, in part, from a moment of frustration.

'I came out of a board meeting one day in a rage over something or other that had been said. I thought the best thing to do was light a cigarette and go for a walk around the block. I passed by the abandoned factories and it was clear we should use them to sell certain lines at discount prices.'

Both Clothier and Pleeth went on fact-finding tours to the USA, where factory outlet villages often occupied up to 300,000 sq ft of space in vast business parks or dedicated malls. During one of these trips, Pleeth attended what was billed as an 'Outlet Conference' in New Orleans, after which he recommended that Clarks Village in Street should have more of a rural atmosphere about it, replete with a sit-down restaurant, outdoor play area and various picnic spots. Shopping at Clarks Village offered a family day out in a rustic environment. The number of visitors predicted for the first year was 850,000 – but this target was reached within just four months.

Plans were then immediately put in train to expand Clarks Village. The Next to Nothing store was joined soon afterwards by Laura Ashley, Benetton, Thornton's and Black & Decker, paying no ground rent but giving Clarks a percentage of their takings. In 1995, Clarks Village won an Award for Innovation from the British Council of Shopping Centres.

Such was its success that the board realised it needed to be run by a

Clarks Village, the first retail outlet centre of its kind in Britain, was opened in August 1993 and is now one of Somerset's most popular tourist attractions, containing nearly 100 high-quality stores.

management that specialised in such businesses. And it was also agreed that selling the village made financial sense. MEPC, a publicly quoted property company, was the favoured buyer, but the disposal of what was officially called The Factory Outlet Centre Business required an EGM of shareholders. This was held on 21 May 1997 at the Wessex Hotel, within walking distance of Clarks headquarters. In the past, Clarks EGMs had not always been happy events, and on this occasion too there was some opposition to the sale, but in the end it went through with a 75 per cent majority. MEPC paid £80 million for the three factory outlets in Street, Kendal and Doncaster.

Some commentators speculated that the sale was part of a Clarks strategy leading up to a stock market flotation, given the commitment to float within five years of the 1993 EGM if conditions were right. However, during an interview with the *Financial Times* a month earlier, Pedder had said Clarks would continue to concentrate on its core business and was not focused on going public:

The family shareholders are happy, and it is not a subject of debate. We would consider it if market conditions came right and if we felt it was the right time to raise funds for expansion. At the moment we don't need to.

Today, Clarks Village is visited by four million people a year and is one of Somerset's most popular 'free' tourist attractions. Marks & Spencer was a new addition to the village in 2002, occupying the former Grove factory, since when the number of stores housed in various buildings just off the High Street has reached nearly 100, with parking for 1,400 cars and 10 coaches. The village is now owned by Hermes and managed by Realm Ltd.

The sale of Clarks Village was a good example of the newly formed family shareholder council – known officially as the Street Trustee Family Company (STFC) – working effectively. The council takes the form of a company limited by guarantee. Joining involves giving the council power of attorney to vote on behalf of the shareholder's shares – a block vote, in effect, subject to various safeguards, rather than family shareholders voting individually. Before using the proxies it holds, the council informs all members of the way in which it intends to vote on any issue, allowing members to withdraw their proxy if they so wish.

Members of the STFC board are elected every four years by the shareholders, with each member of that board requiring the support of shareholders owning 4.5 per cent or more of the equity of C. & J. Clark Ltd. The council's two nominees on the board of C. & J. Clark Ltd serve as non-executive directors, and communication between the boards of C. & J. Clark Ltd and STFC is channelled through the Clarks chairman, with meetings held four times a year. The shareholder council has its own secretariat paid for by the company.

'I saw my job as keeping the shareholders united and off the management's back, but at the same time the shareholder council was and is a way of holding the management to account,' says Harriet Hall, STFC's first chairman.

There were family members at the time, however, who feared the shareholder council would be a licence for the different factions to carry on squabbling. This did not happen. Hall says it was 'immediately encouraging that all those who wanted to sell the company opted to join the council rather than staying outside and sniping. Some people thought that

The family shareholder council held its first meeting on 5 February 1994. Back row (left to right): Jan Gillett, Tom Clark, Adrian Little, Hugh Clark, Sibella Pedder, Gloria Clark, Ben Messer Bennetts. Front row (left to right): John Aram (secretary), William Johnston, Charles Robertson, Harriet Hall (chairman), Ben Lovell, Sarah Clark, Caroline Pym, Nathan Clark, Cyrus Clark.

once things had settled down councillors would stop attending, but this has never been the case. In fact, numbers have increased through allowing younger family members to attend so they can gain experience of looking at the company's performance.'

Indeed, in a 2012 survey of family shareholders, one question asked was 'How long do you intend to be a shareholder of Clarks for?' The response of 89 per cent of those polled was 'My lifetime.'

Hall brought to the role knowledge of family members and a clear focus honed by her legal training. She had been a key figure in the group that had kept the company independent, and so had a lot to lose if the council did not do its job.

John Aram, who had worked at Clarks for more than twenty years, was chosen as the STFC's first secretary. He is unstinting in his praise for Hall, saying that 'many people thought the council was doomed to fragment', but that she 'somehow kept all the factions working harmoniously together – an extraordinary achievement'.

From the council's inception, it was important that the past bickering among and interference from family members did not obscure the fact that serious and legitimate concerns about the future of the company had to be addressed – and quickly. 'I knew that the board and management must be clear that shareholders as a united force required action to restore the company to profitability,' says Hall.

Family firms on the scale of Clarks were thin on the ground in Britain by the mid-1990s – a theme that had been picked up by BBC Radio 4's *In Business* programme on 1 May 1994. Pedder was invited to the studio and was asked by the presenter, Peter Day, 'Don't you find this family company a difficult one to manage?'

Pedder replied, 'I think it obviously can be because of the troubles we've had. But if you look on the positive side, it has tremendous dedication, both from the family and from the workforce, and has an identity of many years of dedication which other companies probably don't enjoy.'

'Yes, but if you're trying to manage a company like this then the family tends to get in the way,' suggested Day.

'Not necessarily,' replied Pedder. 'I think it is a misapprehension to think the family's always in the way ... I think the difficulty is to both own and manage directly. And it's that which we've sorted out over the last year.'

Sir John Harvey Jones, the businessman well known at the time for his *Troubleshooter* TV series, was asked to contribute to the programme and pronounced that 'the transformation of family firms in this country is the key to our economic revival'.

In the case of Clarks that transformation was still to come, and perceptions of the company remained unflattering. For example, Janet Street-Porter, then head of the BBC's youth programming, was quoted as saying that the corporation for which she worked was in danger of becoming the 'Clarks shoes of the multimedia world, something that your mother would buy for you but you'd never choose for yourself'.

Meanwhile, Pedder, who had always taken the view that poor management was as much to blame for the Clarks slump as rising costs and general market conditions, found himself telling shareholders that 1994 had been a 'real disappointment', with net profits before tax down on 1993. But he was also able to assure them of moves that were aimed at arresting the slide.

Two factories – St Peters in Radstock, Somerset, and Marlinton, in West Virginia, USA – were to be closed, and further cuts were planned in 1995 to make the company 'better focused and highly cost effective'. The St Peters factory had been the largest single employer in the town (population 5,000) for almost forty years, its closure representing a dark day for the local community. The decision was also taken to close the K Shoes offices in Kendal and merge the operations of Clarks and K in Somerset. This meant the arrival in Street of Peter Bolliger, who had been appointed managing director of K Shoes in the summer of 1994.

Bolliger was a big beast in the shoe jungle. Born and raised in Basel, Switzerland, his CV included a period with the respected Swiss shoe business Bally, before he moved to South Africa to join a footwear company associated with Carvela shoes, now part of the Kurt Geiger stable. It was while in South Africa that he crossed paths with Mohamed Al-Fayed, the owner of Harrods, who wanted to bring him to London as his new managing director.

'He told me he liked the Swiss and that a lot of his money was in Switzerland,' says Bolliger. 'He also said he liked shoe retailers.'

Bolliger stayed at Harrods five years, eventually falling out with Al-Fayed in spectacular, but not unusual fashion. When he announced he was leaving, Al-Fayed's then director of public affairs, Michael Cole, put out a statement stressing that Bolliger's departure was 'not voluntary'. Then, referring to Al-Fayed's unique proprietorial style, Bolliger was quoted by the *Mail on Sunday* on 24 April 1994 as saying: 'You simply can't have two kings in an organisation like Harrods ... I'm confident I will get another job ... I know President de Klerk [of South Africa] and he'd be grateful for my skills.'

When he came to Street from Kendal, Bolliger was initially put in charge of the women's division and was 'quite anxious because nothing in Street seemed to have changed,' he says. 'The old guard was still there and there was a lot of talk about what we should do but not a great deal about how to go about it.'

Pedder was about to make moves to change that. He realised only too well that the issue of Clarks' competitiveness had still not been properly addressed – and he knew that tinkering at the edges was not the answer. He was well aware that the wage gap between Clarks' employees and their Third World counterparts could not be bridged. A Clarks factory worker in the West Country made on average £15,000 a year; a worker in India made £300. This glaring disparity became all too evident when Pedder and Dudley Cheeseman, the Clarks production manager, flew to India towards the end of 1994 looking at factories in Ambur, the capital of India's shoemaking, in the south of the country. In one factory, they noticed men's shoes with Marks & Spencer labels in the footbeds. Pedder asked what was the factory price for the shoes and quickly worked out that if Clarks were to produce something similar in the UK, it would have to charge customers £34.99 a pair to stand any chance of covering its costs and making a small profit. M&S was selling them at £29.99. The owner of the factory then asked if they wanted to see another factory nearby, which was using equipment inspired, as it happened, by machinery used by Clarks back at home.

'Who are you making these for?' asked Pedder, on seeing rows of well-made casual shoes.

'Marks & Spencer, of course,' said the owner.

The Indian trip convinced Pedder of the need for change at the top of Clarks, and so, with a view to bringing in a new CEO, he stood Clothier down as chief executive with effect from January 1995, bringing to an end the Clothier family's long day-to-day association with the company.

'I had been in the thick of it for seven years and I knew what was coming,' says Clothier. 'Some people can take the task of sacking large numbers of people lightly. I wasn't one of those. I did not want to sack the people my father [Peter Clothier] had hired – even though I knew it was necessary. In the circumstances, it was the right time for me to go.'

He was replaced by Malcolm Cotton on an interim basis, who was given the title of Managing Director (operations). Pedder became executive chairman.

The search for a new CEO gained impetus when Pedder was reading a magazine on board a flight to Boston. The article was about up-and-coming British managers who were all under 40. One of these was Tim Parker, who by then had led Kenwood's management buy-out from Thorn EMI before grooming the company for a flotation in 1992. He was described as 'young, brash, well-educated and known to stick his neck out'.

Contact was established and he was appointed on 29 September 1995, although he would not start until January 1996. Kenwood's shares fell 10p on the announcement.

'I met Tim in Salisbury and he said there was not going to be room for both of us at Clarks and I accepted that,' says Cotton. 'I realised the advantages of bringing someone in from outside.'

Parker was still only forty when he eventually got his feet under the desk at Clarks. But he had packed those years with experience. Educated at Abingdon School and Pembroke College, Oxford, where his degree was in philosophy, politics and economics, he had toyed briefly with the idea of a career in politics, chairing the Oxford University Labour Club and later working at the Treasury as a junior economist when Denis Healey was chancellor. But it was not long before he swapped the public for the private sector, taking an MBA and moving seamlessly towards supporting the Conservatives.

As part of the 2011 Harvard Business School case study, Parker said:

I was looking around for a new challenge. I felt this was a really interesting opportunity, not least because I quite liked shoes and I thought, well, if I can go and work in this company and help them to make more shoes that I would actually like to buy, then that would be good.

Regarding the task at hand, he said:

Clarks had market share. There are two key determinants for room to manoeuvre. One is scale and the other is relative scale. So, if it's big,

Tim Parker, recruited from outside the company by Roger Pedder, radically restructured the business as chief executive from 1995 to 2002.

it means there's a lot you can change. If it's bigger than its nearest competitor, it means that you're in an even stronger position. And Clarks had both of these things in retail.

Pedder said in the same Harvard study that Parker's personal situation was ideally suited to a family firm such as Clarks:

He wasn't of the family, wasn't of the area, didn't come from the shoe business. He didn't have any alliances. He didn't have any people to protect. He wasn't in debt to anybody. All positives, because he didn't bring any baggage with him. What he brought was an objective mind about what needed to happen in an economic situation.

Parker had done his homework, and within six weeks presented his first report, 'Strategy, Structure and Management'. It was a plain-speaking, no-nonsense critique of the company with some far-reaching conclusions. And not always easy reading:

> The main reason for Clarks failure in recent years has been, frankly, management incompetence on a massive scale, leading to, at best, inertia and, at worst, bad decisions. The answers to these problems are to be found in the culture of the company and its personnel policies ... the location of the business in a relatively isolated part of the West Country, with a very pleasant lifestyle for those of middle-class income, has fostered a comfortableness and a cloister-like sense of detachment reminiscent of an Oxbridge college.

Parker railed against what he called the 'civil service mentality', whereby pay and benefits continued to rise and 'incompetence' was rarely tackled. He admonished the company for the way it had allowed parts of the business to 'deteriorate into baronies', fostering a culture whereby 'high individual interests' had ranked above those of the business. 'Compromises over control mean that no one is really responsible for anything: marketing can always blame the factories; the factories can always blame Indian uppers and retail can always blame poor results on non-delivery,' he said.

What must have stung the management and the workforce most was how he used the company's values as a stick with which to beat it.

> What is quite incredible is to hear the well-intoned mantra of 'integrity'. What integrity is there in a management which looks after its own, fails to grapple with the key strategic issues facing the business, and, as a result, saddles the company with a huge cost burden and horrendous results?

Parker laid out some key strategic goals and outlined what would be required to achieve them. Clarks must become a retailer for 'middle England' at home but a premium casual brand overseas. This would require a lot more 'sparkle' going into the research and design side of the company and then, once the product had improved, there would be an investment in advertising, focusing on one or two specific markets. Some 'really original thinking' was required to address the 'pedestrian' children's business, with a view to making it a creditable international brand.

On manufacturing, he said it was not clear how many factories were viable but he stopped short of calling for their complete closure. 'If alternative sources are available at considerably lower cost we must consider closure. It is doubtful whether we will end up with anything other than a handful of plants in the UK.'

Within ten years of Parker taking over as CEO, every single Clarks-owned factory in the world was to be closed.

Parker's changes were comprehensive. He issued a decree that jackets and ties were not strictly necessary in Street and he pressed for more flexible working hours, keen that staff should not always feel duty bound to clock off at 5 pm precisely.

Putting his new management team in place, he made Bolliger his most senior lieutenant as UK operations director. Among others in key roles were Neville Gillibrand, who became international brands director, and Royston Colman, who was made manufacturing director.

For many long-serving managers, Parker's withering indictment of the past was hard to swallow. Those who found it hardest were the professional shoemakers who had risen through the ranks; in many cases they had been employed by Clarks all their working lives and they took pride in the product.

Kevin Crumplin, who, as director of personnel and a member of the main board, had been keen to recruit Parker, experienced mixed emotions. 'I did not like Parker personally. I did not care for his arrogance and lack of respect for what the shoemakers had achieved,' he says. 'But I accepted that the transformation had to happen. Sadly, you sometimes need a person like him to do what is required. My position was that I had helped deliver what the board and the shareholders wanted, but I didn't want to stick around any longer.'

Crumplin resigned in February 1996, just days after Parker produced his damning report.

Royston Colman's appointment as manufacturing director effectively meant he was in charge of closing down the factories – and by the end of the process had made himself redundant.

'Tim used to tell me that I had the worst job because everyone else was building while I was destroying,' says Colman, adding:

And the speed with which we stopped manufacturing increased as confidence in resourcing grew. It wasn't always pleasant, but I hope I did it with as much sensitivity as possible. I suppose over the years I helped to get rid of 5,000 people, many of whom I knew personally.

Colman was one of those who went with Parker to inspect shoe factories in China during 1997. Pedder, Bolliger and Mark McMenemy, who was hired from Marks & Spencer to succeed Alan Mackay as finance director, were among others on that trip.

'We saw some state-of-the-art machinery and some very professionally made shoes produced at a fraction of the cost,' says Colman. 'It was obvious to me from that moment that my role was to tick off our factories by closing them down as fast as possible.'

Colman himself left in 2000, although Parker brought him back briefly on a part-time basis to shut one of the Portugal factories in 2001. After that, he threw himself into charity work.

The first factory to close under the Parker regime was in Bridgwater, followed by those in Shepton Mallet, Plymouth and Askam, Cumbria, in July 1996. In Australia, the factory in Preston was shut down, along with Marlinton in the USA, where profits for the year ending 31 January 1996 had 'effectively collapsed' due to a 'combination of over-optimism, poor marketing and a failure to control the sales function', as Pedder put it in the annual report.

The situation in North America was dire. To address this, Bob Infantino, who had been recruited in 1992 from Rockport, the Boston-based footwear company, was put in charge of the whole North America operation – Clarks of England, Bostonian and Hanover – and slowly the business on that side of the Atlantic started to improve. The entire North American operation now came under the title of Clarks Companies North America

(CCNA). In the USA, more so than anywhere else, consumers perceived the Clarks brand differently from their British counterparts. Parker was happy to allow this, and he gave Infantino considerable freedom to manage the North American operation in his own way.

Encouragingly, a year later, in 1996, Clarks of England was named winner of the Company of the Year award by *Footwear News*, a specialist industry publication in the USA, and twelve months later the North American operation posted trading profits of $16.7 million, more than double what was achieved in the previous year. This was mainly as a result of improvements in the wholesale side of the business, and although retail was still disappointing, Parker felt the prospects in North America 'had never been stronger'. He was proved right. From 1995 to 2001, sales increased by 57 per cent, with operating profits up five-fold, achieved in part by introducing highly competitive discounts to attract new consumers, a strategy that caused difficulties for some of Clarks' weaker competitors.

Back home in Street, a quarter of the Clarks workforce in the town (more than 500 people) lost their jobs, largely as a result of the brand and retailing buying teams working as one unit. Parker was unequivocal:

> If you want to make things happen in a business with problems, you have to accentuate the sense of crisis. Stress that there is no alternative. It is fear that normally drives people to take action and to change things. There was a hope [on the board and in the Council] that you might be able to retain a portion of the business in the United Kingdom, but slowly it dawned on everybody that it wasn't commercial. Our pricing was completely wrong. But more critically, we couldn't make the shoes the market really demanded.

Old perceptions of Clarks persisted. In September 1996, the *Independent* ran a feature with the unfortunate headline: 'Do we need Clarks shoes?' To which the answer, some 1,500 words later, came as a resounding 'no'. Perhaps in a spirit of mischief, the journalist, Jonathan Glancey, then the paper's architecture and design editor, wrote:

To my eye, most Clarks shoes are ugly, bland and unstylish. Clarks are not to be taken seriously by adults. And what about the sort of schoolteacher who used to wear Clarks Polyveldts? How could any schoolboy aspiring to zip-up leather boots from Elliots, Toppers or Kensington Market take seriously a teacher who wore omelettes for shoes?

He had some ammunition left strictly for Parker:

Clarks may well survive and even prosper with new professional, business-school-educated management, and good luck to it. But, if you are a grown up, save up for a decent pair of leather shoes (wear bin-liners tied with string if you have to whilst doing so), learn to polish them and enjoy their patina and comforting natural smell.

His advice went largely unheeded, as results for 1997 across the whole group finally began to reflect Parker's restructuring of the business. Profits were up to £39.4 million from £33.6 million the previous year, the best figures since 1987.

Parker called it a turning point, and said a crucial difference was that Clarks was making shoes its customers wanted to buy rather than the shoes 'we wanted to make them'. It was also abundantly clear that Clarks shoes were too expensive to make in England. Cost-cutting not only affected the production process but meant there was less money to create new styles. This cemented Parker's objective to change the company from being a manufacturer and wholesaler with some retailing to becoming a retail-led business with some wholesaling. Never knowingly understated, Parker told shareholders at the start of 1998:

We have three very clear objectives: to be the No. 1 shoe retailer in the UK; to be the No. 1 children's shoe brand in the UK by a factor of at least two over our nearest competitor; and to be the world's No. 1 shoe brand outside the athletics arena.

His cause was helped by the collapse of the British Shoe Corporation. Ten years earlier, one in four pairs of shoes bought in Britain was sold in a BSC store. By 1997, that figure was less than one in ten as the late Sir Charles Clore's chain of high street shops began to unravel. Freeman, Hardy & Willis, Mansfield and Saxone were all no more. In fact, the only recognised BSC names still trading were Dolcis and Stead & Simpson.

Parker's commitment to increased advertising paid dividends – despite a tricky episode in April 1997 when the company was forced to abandon a campaign showing children walking on a railway track and then sitting on the lines. There had been several recent deaths involving children and trains, and the Royal Society for the Prevention of Accidents took a dim view of the posters. Clarks claimed that the line in question was disused because weeds were growing through the sleepers, but admitted an 'error of judgement' and withdrew them.

In the autumn of 1997, Clarks' cutting-edge advertising agency, St Luke's, came up with the strapline 'Act your shoe size, not your age' for a series of TV ads that ran for six weeks. Sections of the media immediately picked up on Clarks' efforts to shed its old-fashioned image, with the *Financial Times* making the point, correctly, that Clarks was regarded as considerably smarter and more fashionable overseas than it was in the UK.

Parker told the paper:

If you go for a conventional campaign attempting to look younger, you're in danger of losing a large chunk of people at the older end of the market. We wanted something with broader appeal that says you can buy our products without any residual feeling of buying into something institutional.

A stroke of good fortune came Clarks' way when Richard Ashcroft, frontman of The Verve and not exactly the institutional type, wore a pair of Wallabees – first launched in 1966 – on the cover of the band's massive-selling 1997 album, *Urban Hymns*. And it could have done no harm that Parker, with his shock of curly hair and propensity for wearing jeans and no tie – and who played the flute in his spare time, and drove a Porsche – was something of a dashing figure.

Profits rose and factories closed. By the end of 1999, there were only four UK manufacturing plants left – Ilminster, Barnstaple and Weston-super-Mare in the West Country, and one in Kendal in the Lake District. By 2005, there would be none.

Re-organisation continued apace. Ravel, which had been struggling, was incorporated into the main retailing division based in Street, and more than 40 per cent of Clarks and K Shoes stores were fitted out in new designs aimed at dealing with what Parker called the 'dowdy image'. He felt there was too much green associated with the Clarks logo and its shops. The idea was to introduce white and beige, a brighter, cleaner and sharper presence in the High Street.

At board level, Harriet Hall, who had been central in establishing the new governance structure following the Berisford bid fall-out, became a non-executive director of the board in 1999, replacing Caroline Gould. Lance Clark, meanwhile, one of the longest-serving C. & J. Clark Ltd board members, was replaced as the second family director by Ben Lovell, Roger Clark's grandson. William Johnston, a former director and family member, took over from Hall as STFC chairman.

A year later, in 2000, it was announced that all K shops would close, marking another end of an era. On some high streets, K and Clarks were practically neighbours and, more to the point, were selling almost the same kinds of footwear. This duplication clearly was absurd, involving two separate advertising campaigns, two sets of accounts and two similar shop fronts. But for K to cease trading in its own right was still a blow for a brand with such an illustrious history. Some K shops became Clarks, others were sold off, and the K Women's shoe range was incorporated into the Clarks shops.

During 2000, the issue of whether Clarks should be floated was discussed once more. The board had held consultations a year earlier with

Dresdner Kleinwort Benson, resulting in the strong advice that it was not in the best interests of the company to float. It was thought that stock market conditions weren't right and that the company would not command its true value. This recommendation was duly passed on to the shareholder council, which had already agreed that in the event of the board opting to float the council would vote on it. No such ballot was required – and as of 2012 the flotation issue has not been aired again.

Parker produced another of his strategy documents in 2000, this time for general circulation among the workforce. Although it was called 'The Road Ahead', much of it concentrated on the changes that had already been made both culturally and commercially. It stressed how 75 per cent of the 38.6 million pairs of Clarks shoes sold each year were now sourced rather than manufactured by the company, and he predicted that turnover would reach £1.1 billion by 2004, with profits in excess of £100 million. In fact, this landmark wasn't achieved until 2010.

'The key in the long term is product,' he said. And he continued:

> The shoes that we create for our customers are what will make or break our business ... globalisation is the force that shapes the shoe industry and we must make the transition from what is essentially still a British company, to a global business ... in order to succeed we must search relentlessly for the best creative and technical skills around the world ... change is not just part of life these days. Change *is* life.

Results for 2001 were particularly heartening – a fourth consecutive year of record returns. Even Ravel, which had been flat for those four years, increased sales by 6 per cent, against an industry average of 1.5 per cent. Overseas, Clarks saw a drop in business in the USA following the 11 September terrorist attacks on the World Trade Center, but still saw operating profits for the year as a whole rise 31 per cent to $30 million.

Much of this success was down to more than £5 million spent on advertising. In addition, a new range for crawling babies performed well, and so too did Clarks winter boots on the back of a return to fashion for footwear of this style. A particularly strong poster ad targeted the young and the young at heart, with the copy saying: 'Feel like an adrenalin charged finely tuned trained to the max pumped up top level athlete. On his day off.'

Towards the end of 2001, Parker gave an interview to the *Daily Telegraph* during which he reflected on some of the changes he had introduced:

> One of the things I don't like is people feeling they are entering an institution [in Street headquarters] ... When I turned up here, everyone was in cubbyholes, and we've pulled down the partitions. Some people don't like open-plan, but you can never please everyone.

Asked about Clarks' growing international reach, he said,

> Half a million people in Hong Kong buy a pair of Clarks – that's one in ten. And we make 25 per cent of our sales in America, where they call it 'Euro comfort'. Apart from Reebok and Nike we are the biggest shoe brand in the world.

The interviewer noticed Parker was wearing a pair of Clarks Desert Boot Originals, the famous range that had reinvented itself over and over again. Then came a question about his future, especially since it was now unlikely there would be a public flotation.

'Aren't you bored?' he was asked.

'When I was young I thought a great objective would be to retire early,' replied Parker, 'but the question is: retire to what? Who wants a husband at home?'

Parker didn't retire, but when it became clear that Clarks was indeed not going to float – not now and not even sometime in the near future – he took himself off in August 2002 to join Kwik-Fit, which three years later he sold to a private equity firm, PAI Partners, for £800 million. He subsequently ran the Automobile Association and oversaw its merger with Saga. At the time of writing he is chief executive of Samsonite, the luggage company, after a brief three-month stint in 2008 working as a deputy to the London mayor, Boris Johnson.

He is quoted in the Harvard case study saying:

There are points in a business career when you go in to work in the morning, and it's all fresh and you're really getting traction. If you have strong esprit de corps on the team, you're having fun, everybody's making a bit more money and it's a positive vibe. Post-restructuring, those early days are exhilarating because you can see things really taking off. And of course they can't stay that way for ever. In shoes, you're only as good as your last season. I tend to get a bit bored, and that's not good for anyone.

Parker was replaced by Peter Bolliger. This amounted to a 'handing over of the keys', as Bolliger puts it, because he and Parker had worked closely to forge a powerful partnership. The only other serious candidate to succeed Parker was Bob Infantino, but he ruled himself out and remained in charge of CCNA.

Building on Parker's achievements, Bolliger concentrated on developing Clarks as a global brand rather than, as he describes it, overseeing a 'collection of shoes'. Under Bolliger, the company finally completed the transition from being a manufacturing company to being a wholesale and retail branded business, sourcing its shoes from abroad. He set the goal of doubling the business in the USA and substantially strengthening the workforce in the Far East, where by now some 30 million pairs of shoes were made a year, primarily in China and Vietnam. In his first annual report, for the year ending 31 January 2003, he was able to tell shareholders that operating profits in North America were up just over 40 per cent on the previous year. This trend continued during 2003, with Clarks going through the 10 million pairs a year sales barrier in North America for the first time.

The business in North America was primarily a wholesale operation, but there were now 143 Clark-owned stores. Sales of Bostonian 'dress shoes' had slowed – in keeping with a trend away from formal footwear in the USA – but there was excitement and anticipation about the launch of two new brands developed jointly by CCNA and the Clarks design team in

Street. Privo was a range of men's and women's sporty casuals, and Indigo was a collection of contemporary ladies' fashion shoes. Both were aimed at filling a gap between formal shoes at one end of the spectrum and trainers at the other. Privo was targeted at the unisex athletic and leisure markets, while Indigo was seeking to attract young, stylish American women. These two sub-brands exceeded expectation in their first full year of trading, with combined sales of more than half a million pairs.

Closer to home, Bolliger – with the full support of the board and the shareholder council – moved to close the Elefanten children's shoe business that was based in Germany. Clarks had bought this firm in February 2001 for £23 million, making it the first acquisition that the company had made for 20 years. Elefanten was the leading children's shoe brand in Germany, with a strong reach in both the Benelux countries and in the USA. In 2000, it recorded sales of just under £56 million, but with a profit of only £600,000. At the time, Tim Parker justified the takeover by saying the Elefanten brand had 'exciting prospects for growth', but he also conceded that some people might find the acquisition 'surprising'. He said the alternative – pushing the Clarks name in Germany – was not feasible: it 'would take a long time and considerable expenditure to convince mothers of young children [in Germany] to try a new brand, even Clarks'. Elefanten would provide the 'critical mass immediately on which to build an exciting business in the future'. This did not prove to be the case, however, and Elefanten ceased trading in the autumn of 2004.

In the UK, planning for the new Westway Distribution Centre, next to the Bullmead Warehouse site in Street, followed Bolliger's appointment. This extraordinary £50 million building would be fully functional within three years of its ground-breaking, capable of receiving and shipping some one million pairs of shoes a week and with capacity to stock five million pairs at any one time. There was some resistance to the building from people living near it and because of related traffic issues, but the employment it offered was welcomed locally.

For those not used to seeing a 21st-century warehouse where computerised cranes fetch and carry stock with unfailing accuracy and astonishing speed, it's a revelation. Containers arrive from the docks at Southampton

The Westway Distribution Centre, completed in 2005, is packed with state-of-the-art technology and dispatches Clarks shoes all around the world.

or Felixstowe, whereupon bar codes on each box are read and the goods whisked to their allotted place before later being dispatched.

Knapp, an Austrian logistics company, was responsible for the equipment (stacker cranes, rollers, conveyors and a Beumer double-stack sorter), while Arup was hired as the building engineers, and the computerised warehouse management system was created by Manhattan Associates.

The Westway building has a clever aesthetic. It looks a great deal lower and leaner than it really is because of its gentle curves and metallic grey/blue colour scheme that blends with the sky above and the busy Street bypass below. There are nearly two miles of aisles inside, but retrieving a carton from the furthest location takes less than sixty seconds, with the cranes accelerating faster than a Ferrari. Westway dispatches Clarks shoes via 600 chutes to everywhere in the world except North America, where construction is under way on an even more advanced warehouse than the one in Street.

Roger Pedder always made it clear he would step down when he reached the age of 65. This he duly did in May 2006, after twelve years as chairman.

Circumstances dictated that the man who did so much to rebuild Clarks after the travails of 1993 found himself presiding over a difficult last year as chairman. Increased competition from discount stores and super-markets, plus the launch of new fashion outlets such as Oasis and New Look, both of which added shoes to their product list, saw Clarks' core UK market fall by 3.8 per cent. Then, shortly after Pedder's retirement, Ravel was closed, with some but not all of its shops taken over by Clarks.

Pedder was characteristically upbeat. 'Look how far we have come,' he said in his final annual report. 'Look how we have grown and how profit-able our business has become. The platform we have and are building for the future delivers even in a bad year an operating profit of £82.4 million.'

There is no doubt that Pedder over this period oversaw a remarkable turnaround in the company's fortunes. During his chairmanship, his team had to cope with the £80 million cost of closing factories in the UK and North America, and the £28 million cost of writing off Elefanten, partially offset by the sale of assets worth £70 million, including Clarks Village. However, annual turnover increased 40 per cent from £655 million in 1994 to £921 million in 2006, and pretax profits were up nearly three and a half times, from £20.8 million to £71.9 million.

Pedder, a member of the family by marriage, was replaced by Peter Davies, previously chief executive of Rubicon Retail Ltd and the non-executive chairman of Crew Clothing. Davies had held senior finance posi-tions at Avis RentaCar and Grand Metropolitan before joining the Burton Group in 1986. For the first time in its history, Clarks had a non-family-member chairman in Davies, and a non-family-member chief executive in Bolliger. Not long afterwards, Charles Robertson replaced William John-ston as chairman of the shareholder council.

Bolliger's goal of transforming Clarks into what he called a 'genuine global brand' coincided with the so-called 'credit crunch' that led to a global financial crisis. Even so, results for the year ending 31 January 2008 showed growth of more than 8 per cent, amounting to sales of just over £1 billion for the first time. Vindicating the company's strategy to raise Clarks' profile in Asia, sales across China, Hong Kong and Korea increased by 19.6 per cent, and Japan enjoyed substantial growth, up by 25.1 per cent. In North America, turnover reached a new record during a year when department stores and independent retailers were having a torrid time. Clarks increased its retail outlets by eleven in the USA, making a total of 221. And Privo was the star performer.

The global financial crisis that kicked off in 2007 and gathered steam in 2008 hit consumer spending hard. Nevertheless, Clarks opened a further 68 stores worldwide during 2008 and launched a new multi-channel, retail capability via its website. This new site – offering consumers a choice of direct next-day home delivery or a 'click and collect' option at any shop or Clarks franchise – made an encouraging start, generating £3.4 million of additional sales, a figure that would rise to £20.7 million a year later and £32.2 million in 2010.

Bolliger retired on 31 March 2010, after sixteen years with the company. During that time, Clarks had become the market leader on the High Street, with more than 400 own-brand shops. But his achievement went far beyond that. Peter Davies, Clarks chairman, told shareholders that Bolliger had 'overseen the transfer of manufacturing operations from the UK; the transformation of our UK retail operation; the investment in the modernisation of our infrastructure and systems and the launch of the vision for Clarks to become a global brand'. Davies added something else – that Bolliger had been 'instrumental in helping develop a strong internal candidate as his successor'.

That successor was Melissa Potter, who had joined the company as a graduate trainee in 1989 after reading English at Cardiff University. Her appointment was made following a global search using Egon Zendor, a firm of headhunters, but no outside candidates were felt to be her equal. As tradition dictated, Potter spent her first week learning to make a pair of shoes and then a year working in retail, notably in Clarks shops in Marble

A Clarks web page from the new retail website that was launched in 2008.

Arch in central London and in Kingston upon Thames. She had risen to be managing director of Clarks UK division and then of Clarks International, and had joined the board in June 2006.

Potter became chief executive of C. & J. Clark Ltd in March 2010, aged 42. The following year, Clarks recorded its highest-ever results. Total sales grew 9.2 per cent to £1.28 billion, with operating profits increasing by 13.9 per cent to £110.9 million, the first time profits had ever exceeded £100 million. The North American business was especially successful, with profits jumping spectacularly by 82.7 per cent to $85 million, 'well in excess of our best expectations and almost a third more than the previous highest result of $64.7 million recorded in the year ending January 2008,' Potter told shareholders.

There was a change of command in North America. Bob Infantino left the company at the end of 2010 and was replaced as president of CCNA by Jim Salzano, an internal appointee. Since then, business there has continued to flourish, with Clarks selling 20 million pairs for the first time during 2011, with a record turnover of $839 million, representing a rise

Melissa Potter, appointed chief executive of Clarks in 2010, has worked for the company since joining as a graduate trainee in 1989.

of more than 14 per cent over 2010. There are currently 290 stores in the USA and Canada, with a further 130 planned to open by 2016. As part of Potter's integrated worldwide strategy, they are to be fitted out almost exactly like Clarks shops in the UK and the rest of the world.

Meanwhile, Clarks has established a joint venture in India with the Future Group, one of the country's largest retail businesses, divided 51 per cent/49 per cent in Clarks favour. A new company was formed for this purpose, Clarks Future Footwear Ltd, based at Gurgaon, near Delhi, and there are now 20 dedicated Clarks stores in India. Clarks shoes are also sold widely in third-party shops and department stores in India.

Worldwide, Clarks sells more than 52 million pairs of shoes a year from a total of 1,156 shops – which include its wholly owned stores, concessions, factory outlets and franchises. There are some 15,000 employees, of whom 12,000 are based in the UK. In the financial year ending 31 January 2012, turnover for the whole group was nearly £1.4 billion, with operating profits of £115.8 million. The regional breakdown of turnover was £601 million in the UK, £536 million in North America, £162 million in Europe and £99 million in the rest of the world.

During 2012, Potter set about establishing Clarks as a global business with four regional divisions: the UK and Republic of Ireland; the Americas; Europe, including Russia; and Asia Pacific.

In seeking to develop a universal image for the brand, Potter says there are two crucial components. First, that some things never change – such as the 'integral values' of the company. And, second, that the company will thrive only by continually adapting to change.

It is certainly true that Clarks has remained remarkably aligned with the values of its Quaker foundations. Clarks talks openly about 'caring for people' both within and outside the company, and in 2012 launched the Clarks Code of Business Ethics, the aim of which is to highlight the company's ethical values and principles, ensuring the highest standards of behaviour and integrity wherever Clarks has a presence and in everything that it does. To support this, an independent Speak Up service was launched at the same time, which enables employees worldwide to voice concerns about inappropriate activity in strict confidence.

In addition, and underpinning the company's commitment to integrity, the Clarks Code of Practice sets standards for the company's suppliers. This code requires full compliance with all local and regulatory requirements and supports the core principles of the International Labour Organization, the United Nations agency responsible for developing and overseeing international labour standards.

Charitable giving by Clarks amounts to some £500,000 each year, through a combination of cash donation and value of goods donated. The company supports a range of organisations, including UNICEF education projects funded from worn shoe returns, and Soul of Africa, which trains unemployed and unskilled women to hand-stitch footwear. Each sale of a pair of Soul of Africa shoes helps provide sustainable employment, with the profits from these sales being donated to initiatives aimed at children affected by Aids. In 2012, the company started to support projects by Miraclefeet in India, where children with clubfoot are treated without surgery, using plaster casting and bracing.

Over the years, various members of the Clark family have set up trusts, which also own shares. Together with the Clark Foundation, these support wide-ranging interests such as education, international aid, historic building repair, conservation and the empowerment of women in the developing world, particularly in the Middle East and Africa, and also support present or former employees experiencing hardship. Clarks' First Step Programme in the USA provides six-month paid internships to people with disabilities. The scheme involves challenging work and is aimed at giving the internees confidence to find full-time employment.

True to its commitment to housing in Street, when the warehouses on the old Houndwood site became redundant on the completion of the new Westway distribution centre, the company, encouraged by family members Tom Clark, Caroline Gould and Richard Clark, who are all Street residents, and with the support of the shareholder council, developed an imaginative proposal.

The shareholders worked with Chris Pleeth of the company's property department to commission architects Feilden Clegg Bradley to develop a layout for the site and a design for the first phase of building, which was then adhered to by the developers, Crest Nicholson. The layout aimed to improve the balance between cars and people and to provide a variety of open spaces occupying 40 per cent of the site, including public squares and boulevards.

All of the first phase houses and flats, completed in 2010, were built to EcoHomes 'Excellent' standard to achieve a substantial reduction in carbon emissions. A sustainable urban drainage system created a network of swales and reed beds. This both deals with surface water run-off and provides a habitat for native species. Mechanical heat recovery units were also incorporated.

Historically, these unchanging values have sat comfortably with Clarks' ability to change, on which the company's very survival has depended. As has been described earlier, the company has changed dramatically over the years: it is now strictly a wholesaling and retailing business, sourcing shoes mainly from China, Vietnam, Cambodia and Brazil, and it is governed in a very different way to how it was before the rejected Berisford bid in 1993.

Clarks' track record in pioneering innovation goes back to William Clark's introduction of machinery into the manufacturing process during the second half of the nineteenth century. Later, the company was quick to experiment with soling made from artificial materials; it exploited the idea of width-fittings to acclaimed commercial success and became universally recognised for measuring children's feet properly; and it was quick to adopt computer technology.

A long way from hand-stitched sheepskin slippers: a resin model of a classic shoe produced by 3D printing technology direct from CAD data.

Today, true to its heritage of embracing modern technology, Clarks has added digital 3D additive prototyping to its shoemaking armoury. This technique, more widely known as 3D printing, creates a physical form direct from CAD data produced by a designer. A prototype model of a shoe can now be produced and assessed without the need for costly moulds, and in a tenth of the time taken by previous methods. And as well as allowing design ideas to be developed faster, this innovation also makes it possible to evaluate a wider range of variations within each style. Alongside this new 3D technology, Clarks has also pioneered the use of digital data to improve its service to customers by creating a fitting gauge for use on digital tablets and touchscreen devices – a whole new way for consumers to connect and interact with a familiar brand.

Any shoe business has to be adept at responding to fashion and seeking to shape it. Clarks' record for this has been patchy over the years, at times taking a lead in determining fashions, at others trailing and appearing old-fashioned. Not so long ago, many consumers regarded Clarks as dowdy – safe, good value but still dowdy – but today those same consumers increasingly have a different view of Clarks.

Potter acknowledges as much:

It's true that in the past we became polarised between young people and older people, rather than appealing to the 30–45 bracket. But that has changed. We are all about real fashion for real people with a sense of energy and fun about it. And the commonality between the average 65-year-old and 30-year-old is closer than ever before. Everyone wants to look stylish, whatever their age.

In Street, there are 60–70 shoe designers, who work up to two years in advance of any particular sales season. There is also a 'Trend Department' consisting of four people who look even further ahead at socio-economic developments on the one hand, and colour, form and texture on the other. A shoe spends 3–6 months in the product development stage before samples are made, and in any season Clarks produces some 80,000 pairs of samples.

Some sections of the media have picked up on the changing profile of Clarks customers.

'Suddenly, the 186-year-old business [Clarks] has acquired street cred,' announced *The Times* towards the end of 2011. The paper reached this conclusion by reporting that there were waiting lists for the company's mid-calf suede boots, known as the Majorca Villa range, and that the Neeve Ella boot, a cross between a Spanish riding boot and a traditional British Wellington boot, was selling out in Clarks stores across the UK.

Clarks has been working in collaboration with Mary Portas, the so-called 'Queen of Shops', who first worked as a consultant to Clarks during Tim Parker's time as chief executive. Since then, she and her agency, Yellow Door, have produced a series of magazine ad campaigns, culminating in 2011 with 'Where our heart is: the spirit of Clarks', featuring images set in the Somerset countryside against a backdrop of honey-coloured Georgian houses with honey-skinned young male and female models.

'I wanted to bring the brand back to where it belonged,' says Portas, who was commissioned in 2011 by the prime minister, David Cameron, to conduct an independent review into the state of the British high street. 'Everyone steals heritage, but Clarks oozes it from every pore, and then when you add that to something modern and sexy you've really got reason to shout about it. To me, Clarks represents the best practice of British quality and comfort at a decent price.'

The 'street cred' reference in *The Times* touched on Clarks' ongoing involvement in the music scene through its Clarks Originals association with live bands such as Little Dragon, Bo Ningen, The Rassle and Louise and the Pins. 'Clarks Originals are of the moment. Always have been. Always will be', reads the copy in the *Clarks Original Live* magazine that supports bands starting out on their quest for success.

Towards the end of 2012, a book called *Clarks in Jamaica* chronicled the perhaps surprising association between Clarks and the reggae scene on the Caribbean island. Written by Al Newman (aka Al Fingers), the book waxes lyrical about singers such as Dillinger, Ranking Joe, Little John, Super Cat and, more recently, Vybz Kartel, all of whom have incorporated Clarks into their music. It was the Desert Boot which began this love affair, finding favour in the late 1960s with Jamaica's so-called 'rude boys'. Newman quotes a Jamaican producer as saying, 'The original gangster rude boy dem, a Clarks dem wear. And in Jamaica a rude boy him nah wear cheap ting.'

Historically Clarks has tended to have its greatest influence on fashion at the times when it has advertised most effectively and creatively. Its early showcards – often endorsed by stars of stage and screen – had a homely, comical edge to them. And its first national campaign in 1933 employed the services of the American artist Edward McKnight Kauffer, who at the time was regarded as an avant-garde figure and who quickly gained a reputation for elevating advertising to a high art.

Investment in advertising continues. The successful 'Act your shoe size not your age' campaign from the Tim Parker era was followed by 'Life's a long catwalk' and then 'New shoes'. More recently, 'Stand Tall. Walk Clarks' tapped into a younger, more fashion-conscious market. 'Kids love the look and parents appreciate the quality that means (good) value for money,' read the copy in an advertisement feature that ran in the *Sunday Times* in July 2012.

The importance of advertising is now ingrained. Similarly, the Clarks hold on the children's market remains as strong as ever. 'First shoes' and 'Back to school' options are displayed prominently, supported by reminders that 'little feet need the best of care,' a consistent theme going back many decades. Much is made of a toddler's first pair of shoes, with staff on hand to catch the moment in a photograph which is then presented in its own cardboard wallet. The back-to-school market is as important to the company as Christmas is to many other retailers. The abiding policy is still based around the idea of attracting the child to the brand as much as his or her parent. In the UK, out of a total of almost 29 million sales by Clarks, 10 million are children's shoes.

Because Clarks has always stressed the importance of children having their feet properly measured and their shoes properly fitted, until 2012 the company did not sell any children's shoes via its online channels (which in 2011 accounted for nearly 11 per cent of total retail sales). But the demand was there, prompting the company to offer customers the chance to buy either a Toddler Gauge (for £6) or Junior Gauge (for £8) for themselves so they could measure their children's feet at home, order online and then choose between home delivery or collection at a store of their choice. Both gauges come with a set of guidelines, and there is an online video instruction.

Having put the design flair back into shoes, the company is now making sure they are displayed to best advantage, and so the stores themselves are changing. Over the next few years, the 'white global format', as it is known, is being phased out and replaced by the C7 format, which is warmer and more welcoming, with brown and green as the dominant colours. C7 takes inspiration from Clarks history, with shoes sitting on top of upturned wooden crates with 'Street, Somerset 1825' printed on them, and in many branches five lasts are secured to a panel above the main cash desk, with 'Master shoemakers since 1825' written underneath.

Well-designed shoes and well-appointed shops need good staff. Engaging with customers is central to Clarks retail and marketing imperatives. During 2012, a team of Clarks' best and most experienced store managers travelled the country carrying out what the company calls 'Leap Training', designed to give shop assistants greater confidence on the sales floor.

'The best people we have are those with strong outside interests who like to talk to customers,' says Richard Houlton, Clarks Director of Channels, whose responsibilities include retail shops, franchise stores, the wholesale business and online sales. 'We are trying to reinvigorate the shopping experience, which means you are properly greeted and feel that someone understands your needs. And a good sales person will always bring out a second choice for the consumer.'

Visitors to Clarks get a taste of the company's purposeful informality, particularly if they are invited to the Cowshed café on the first floor. Office workers and department heads dress casually and conduct meetings at tables scattered about the room. Talking and listening are encouraged.

In the wider business world, the Clarks shareholder council is seen as a model for other family firms, with the Institute for Family Business (UK) habitually using the company to demonstrate proper family governance. The structure allows for longer-term thinking and balances profit reinvestment with dividend pay-outs.

'The Clarks board has a clear understanding of what the owners want and in turn the owners leave it to professional managers to run the business,' says Grant Gordon, director general of the Institute for Family Business. 'Crucially, the owners are putting the interest of the business before their own liquidity and this sense of long-term responsibility is bound to trickle down throughout the workforce.'

Harriet Hall, the first chairman of the shareholder council following the failed Berisford bid, says that the three non-family chief executives of Clarks since that time have all 'recognised that as a family we have an attachment to how the company is progressing that goes way beyond an interest in the figures'.

Explaining the relationship between family and management further, she continues:

If we were shareholders in a public company we would not get anything like the detail of information we are given. Questions about the minutiae of what is going on in Street are answered. There are times when we may get close to stepping over the line in trying to influence management, but on the whole I believe that they take this in the spirit in which it is meant – as an expression of our commitment to the future of Clarks.

Peter Davies, the Clarks chairman, regards the family council as an 'effective bridge' between the shareholders and the board. He says:

When I joined the company I was told that one of the strengths of Clarks was its passionate shareholders – and that one of its weaknesses was its passionate shareholders. In a company that has evolved as far as Clarks has in separating ownership from management, it would be easy for the lines to get blurred. The council is well informed on the company's strategy and performance, and has regular opportunities to question the chairman, chief executive and finance director on any issues that concern them. In parallel, the shareholders can channel queries and concerns effectively through the council.

Clarks goes about its business in its own determined but quiet way and does not seek media exposure. Potter, with Davies's backing, declines interviews with the financial press, and the Clark family – several of whom still live in Street – recoils from publicity. They come together once a year at the AGM to hear Potter and the board explain the latest set of figures and outline plans for the future, after which sandwiches and soft drinks are served in the former canteen at the back of the main headquarters building overlooking the Quaker burial ground.

Around 80 per cent of shareholders are family members or family trusts, including charitable trusts. The remainder are mainly employees, ex-employees and trusts associated with the company, including the Clarks Foundation. The total dividend paid for the year ending in January 2012 was £21.7 million.

The woollen slippers created from off-cuts by James Clark soon after 1828 were a clever idea. James was not content to live in the past and, crucially, he came up with something people wanted to buy. Today, the growth of the business still depends entirely on people wanting to buy Clarks shoes. Potter likens a brand to a promise. And the promise is that comfortable shoes can be stylish, and stylish shoes can be comfortable – and stylish and comfortable shoes can be bought at affordable prices. It must help that Clarks enjoys a brand awareness of which many of its competitors can only dream, and implicit in that awareness is a sense of trust, even though many consumers may know little about the company itself.

An insurance company recently carried out a survey to identify the profiles of what it called 'Mr and Mrs Made It'. It found that they have an average of four bedrooms, off-street parking, a power shower, and they go on holiday abroad most years, often to far-flung destinations. They eat out at restaurants at least once a fortnight. And they wear Clarks shoes.

Surveys, like opinion polls, aren't always reliable. What they conceal can be just as interesting as what they reveal – but you don't need a survey or an opinion poll to determine that C. & J. Clark Ltd is a redoubtable British institution striding purposefully towards its 200th anniversary.

Appendices

Appendix I
A Clarks chronology

1801 Cyrus Clark born.

1811 James Clark born.

1821 Cyrus Clark forms partnership with Arthur Clothier in woollen business.

1825 Partnership dissolved; Cyrus sets up on his own making sheepskin products.

1828 James Clark apprenticed to his brother Cyrus and soon after makes slippers from sheepskin offcuts.

1833 James enters partnership with Cyrus.

1842 Clarks rescued by loans from local Quakers.

1851 Clarks exhibits at Great Exhibition.

1855 William Stephens Clark joins business, aged 16.
First last-making machine acquired; by this date all Clarks ladies' boots were available in a range of sizes and widths.

1856 Singer sewing machine introduced on trial.

1858 James Clark imports machine to cut soles.

1863 Trust deed signed by Quakers who had lent the company money. William Stephens Clark put in charge of the business as a condition of the loan, aged 24.

1866 Cyrus Clark dies.

1870 Clark, Son & Morland founded to continue the sheepskin business.

1871 Most loans made in 1863 repaid.

1873 New partnership between William and James.

1880 All-out strike over implementation of use of new machines, key to profitability of company at this time.

1884 John Bright Clark joins the company.

1888 Roger Clark joins the company, aged 17.

1889 James Clark retires. New partnership between William and his brother Frank Clark.

1891 Appointment of sales agent in South Africa.

1893 Alice Clark joins the company.
Carton-making department set up; shoes sold in boxes.

1896 Opening of the 'big room', an open-plan room in the factory for all shoe-making processes.

1897 First joint venture in retailing with McAfee in London's West End.

1903 C. & J. Clark becomes a limited company; first step in process of splitting management from ownership.

1904 Hugh B. Clark joins the company.

1906 James Clark dies.

1908 John Walter Bostock joins Clarks from Northampton as production superintendent.
W. S. Clark 1908 Trust created by William Stephens Clark for benefit of employees, providing education, relief in need, etc.
First London showroom in Shaftesbury Avenue.

1912 Wilfred Hinde sent to USA to study the 'factory system'.

1913 Formation of Street Shoemakers Provident Benefit Society.

1914 More than 1 million pairs of shoes made.
Day release for children between 14 and 16 agreed.

1919 Formation of Factory Committee or Works Council.

1924 New library built for Street.

1925 William Stephens Clark dies.
Centenary pension fund created for benefit of employees; pension provision for employees continues to be developed.

1933 John Bright Clark dies.
First national advertising campaign.

1935 First purchase of chain of retail shops.

1936 Clarks handwritten logo introduced by Bancroft Clark.

1937 Peter Lord chain of branded shops started.
Opening of Greenbank swimming pool in Street, funded by a legacy from Alice Clark.

1938 Frank Clark dies and Roger Clark becomes chairman.
Joint venture with J. Halliday and Sons of Dundalk, Ireland, to make shoes for Clarks.

1942 Bancroft Clark becomes chairman.

1943 Clarks makes wooden-soled shoes because of wartime shortage of leather.

1945 First wholly owned Clarks factory outside Street opened in Bridgwater.

1946 Footgauges introduced in shops.
Fact-finding visit to USA to examine shoe production.

1947 Princess Elizabeth and Princess Margaret seen wearing Clarks shoes on South African tour.

1949 First Desert Boot sold.

1950 First range of shoes for teenagers.

1953 CEMA (for moulding rubber soles to uppers) production started.

1956 First IBM computer acquired, allowing better control of sales and stocks.

1959 Bancroft Clark goes on fact-finding mission to Russia.
Clark Foundation established.

1960 Peter Lord opens in Oxford Street, London.

1963 Management consultants McKinsey hired.

1964 Clarks TV commercials with James Bond theme.

1967 Bancroft retires; Tony Clark becomes chairman and Peter Clothier managing director.

1973 Clarks ceases making unbranded shoes (except for small amounts in Ireland).
Peter Clothier retires as managing director.

1974 Clarks shoe museum opens in Street.
Tony Clark retires as chairman and Daniel Clark become chairman and managing director.
Collett Dickenson Pearce (CDP) hired as advertising agents.

1975 150th anniversary celebrations.
Appointment of manager to source shoes made by other manufacturers.

1976 Clarksport launched (ended 1978).

1977 Purchase of Hanover Shoe Company, manufacturer and retailer, in USA.
Clarks start making 'Levis for feet' under licence (until 1987).

'Shoemaster' CAD/CAM software installed.

1978 Closure of Silflex factory (the 'big room') in Street.

1980 Purchase of K Shoes.

1984 First Clarks branded shops opened.

      £3 million extension to Bullmead warehouse, Street.

      Closure of Dundalk factory, Ireland.

1985 Tony Clark dies.

      George Probert appointed group managing director.

1986 Joint venture with Pinto de Oliveira to make shoes in Portugal (until 2001).

1987 Daniel Clark retires as chairman, replaced by Lawrence Tindale, first non-family chairman.

      George Probert retires as group managing director, replaced by John Clothier.

1988 Purchase of Rohan (sold 2007).

1990 One-third of Clarks shoes made abroad.

1991 Lawrence Tindale retires as chairman, replaced by Walter Dickson.

1992 Extraordinary General Meeting in Glastonbury to appoint new chairman (adjourned).

1993 Offer for the company by Berisfords rejected.

      Walter Dickson retires as chairman, replaced by Roger Pedder.

      Bancroft Clark dies.

1995 Tim Parker appointed as chief executive.

2002 Tim Parker stands down as chief executive, replaced by Peter Bolliger.

2005 Last pair of Somerset-made Clarks shoes produced at Dowlish Ford on 15 March.

      New Westway distribution centre opened.

2006 Last pair of UK-made Clarks shoes produced in Cumbria at Millom works (closed in August).

      Roger Pedder retires as chairman, replaced by Peter Davies.

2008 Start of multi-channel retailing (including internet selling).

2010 Peter Bolliger retires as chief executive, replaced by Melissa Potter.

Appendix 2

The Clark family
(showing family members named in the text)

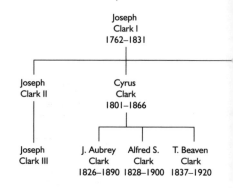

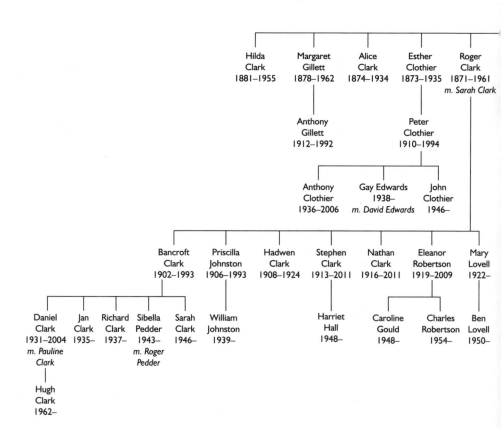

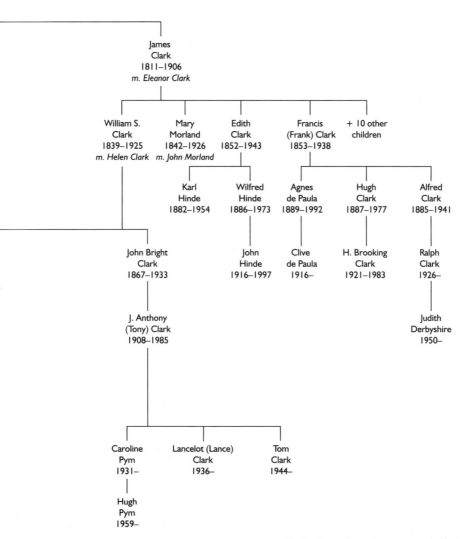

This family tree does not attempt to include all members of the Clark family. Members of recent generations not named here and who have worked at Clarks or served on the shareholder council are listed in Appendix 3.

Appendix 3

Other Clark family members

Current members of the Clark family who are not shown on the family tree in Appendix 2 but who have worked at Clarks or served on the shareholder council include:

Tim Campbell – son-in-law of Lance Clark; shareholder council; family non-executive director.

Adrian Brooking Clark – son of H. Brooking Clark; worked at Clarks.

Alice Clark – daughter of Stephen Clark; shareholder council.

Asher Clark – grandson of Tony Clark; shareholder council.

Cyrus Clark – son of Tony Clark; worked at Clarks; shareholder council.

Galahad Clark – grandson of Tony Clark; shareholder council.

Gloria Clark – daughter of Daniel Clark; worked at Clarks; shareholder council.

James Clark – son of Richard Clark; shareholder council.

Jan Clark – son of Jan Clark; worked at Clarks.

Joey Clark – grandson of Tony Clark; shareholder council.

John Clark – son of Richard Clark; shareholder council.

Peter Clark – son of Jan Clark; shareholder council.

Alex Clothier – grandson of Peter Clothier; shareholder council.

Gay Edwards – daughter of Peter Clothier; shareholder council.

Sebastian Edwards – grandson of Peter Clothier; worked at Clarks; shareholder council.

Bevis Gillett – grandson of Margaret Gillett; shareholder council.

Helen Gillett – great-granddaughter of Margaret Gillett; shareholder council.

Jan Gillett – grandson of Margaret Gillett; shareholder council.

Eleanor Gould – daughter of Caroline Gould; shareholder council.

Matthew Hall – son of Harriet Hall; shareholder council.

Adrian Little – son-in-law of Peter Clothier; shareholder council.

Martin Lovell – son of Mary Lovell; works at Clarks; shareholder council.

Ben Messer Bennetts – grandson-in-law of Hugh Clark; shareholder council.

Geoffrey Pedder – son of Roger and Sibella Pedder; works at Clarks.

Irene Pedder – daughter of Roger and Sibella Pedder; worked at Clarks; shareholder council.

Hester Pelly – granddaughter of Tony Clark; shareholder council.

Roger Pym – grandson of Tony Clark; worked at Clarks; shareholder council.

James Robertson – son of Eleanor Robertson; worked at Clarks; shareholder council.

Robert Robertson – son of Eleanor Robertson; worked at Clarks.

Roger Robertson – son of Eleanor Robertson; worked at Clarks.

Martha Stewart – granddaughter of Mary Lovell; shareholder council.

Roger Sylvester – grandson of Bancroft Clark; shareholder council.

Tamzin Trickey – great-granddaughter of Hugh Clark; shareholder council.

Alice Wakeford – daughter of Daniel Clark; worked at Clarks; shareholder council.

George Wakeford – grandson of Daniel Clark; shareholder council.

Roger White – grandson of Stephen Clark; shareholder council.

Appendix 4

An exceptional resource: the Clarks archive

THE REMARKABLE AND EXTENSIVE HERITAGE collections associated with the Clark family and C. & J. Clark Ltd are looked after by the Alfred Gillett Trust. Under the care of a team of professional archivists, who manage and provide access to the collections, this unique archive is now largely open to the public for the first time in its history.

An innovative new building has recently been constructed by the Trust at The Grange in Street, adjacent to the historic Clarks factory building, to house the collections. Accessible as never before, and providing fascinating opportunities for social, historical and business research, this archive represents an exceptional resource of real value and interest. As a major employer, the high profile and presence of Clarks within the locality is reflected in a rich collection which encompasses business history and the history of the Clark family, as well as Quaker history and many aspects of local history.

The business archive is extensive, containing records relating specifically to the commercial activities of C. & J. Clark Ltd and its subsidiary companies, including financial records, annual reports and papers relating to family and non-family directors. Papers of acquired companies such as K Shoes Ltd (Kendal) and John Halliday & Sons (Dundalk, Ireland) are also represented, as well as allied concerns such as the Avalon Leather Board and Clark, Son & Morland. Reflecting Clarks' position as a major landowner in Street, a significant collection of plans documents the development of the town itself (including workers' cottages and civic buildings such as the Crispin Hall) as well as factories elsewhere in the southwest and beyond.

The heritage holdings relating to shoes are comprehensive. A full range of Clarks shoe catalogues dating back to 1848 gives an invaluable insight into the development of shoes by the company up to the present day.

Similarly, a rich collection of point-of-sale advertising materials illustrates trends in advertising and retail merchandising, with strong holdings from the early 20th century. Over 500 shoemaking machines also form part of the archives, with the earliest dating to the late nineteenth century.

The historic shoe collection forms a focal point, with a small fraction (some 1,500 items) on permanent display in the firm's Shoe Museum at 40 High Street, Street, including a nineteenth-century facsimile of the firm's earliest shoe, the 1829 'Brown Petersburg'. The Alfred Gillett Trust is responsible for the remainder of the collection held in store, which provides a unique record of Clarks shoes up to the present day. Shoes from elsewhere within the UK and around the world are also represented, with the earliest examples dating from the Roman period. In all, the shoe collection contains nearly 20,000 single shoes, making it one of the finest collections in the UK.

The heritage collections also include a large photographic archive, which documents the history of the Street factory site as well as other Clarks sites across the southwest of England and the development of Street itself. Also available is a rich selection of photographs relating to the Clark family, together with a sizeable collection of nineteenth-century Quaker costume from former family members, as well as family artworks, artefacts and furniture.

Paper-based archive collections include the papers of John Bright MP (1811–89, father-in-law of William Stephens Clark), as well as members of the Clark family and related branches, including the Pease, Hinde and Gillett families. Those branches who lived at Millfield and Whitenights in Street are especially well represented. One unusual part of the family's papers is *The Village Album*, compiled by the Clark family literary society. This family group was begun by James and Eleanor Clark in 1856–7, and met several times a year to read wide-ranging 'Album Pieces', covering poetry, stories, history, comedy, description, travel writing, philology, satire and natural, family and local history. The tradition still continues in Street to this day and the set of albums now contains nearly 100 volumes.

The Trust also looks after an extensive reference library, which covers the history of Quakerism, Street and environs, fashion and shoemaking.

The heritage collections are open to members of the public by prior appointment. Please contact the Trust for further details:

Alfred Gillett Trust
The Grange
Farm Road
Street
Somerset BA16 0BQ
archives@clarks.com

The Shoe Museum is open during usual office hours, and is situated next to the High Street entrance of C. & J. Clark Ltd:

Shoe Museum
C. & J. Clark Ltd
40 High Street
Street
Somerset BA16 0BE
(01458) 842243

Bibliography

Autumn in England, Street, C. & J. Clark Ltd, 2011.

Blakeway, Denys, *The Last Dance: 1936, The Year of Change*, London, John Murray, 2010.

Bossan, Marie-Josephe, *The Art of the Shoe*, Rochester, Grange Books, 2007.

Braithwaite, William C., *The Beginnings of Quakerism*, London, Macmillan, 1912: reissued, Cambridge University Press, 1961.

Braithwaite, William C., *The Second Period of Quakerism*, London, Macmillan, 1919: reissued, Sessions of York, 1979.

Brooke, Iris, *Footwear: A Short History of European and American Shoes*, London, Pitman, 1972.

Cadbury, Deborah, *Chocolate Wars*, London, Harper Collins, 2010.

Carlock, Randel S., and John L. Ward, *When Family Businesses are Best*, Basingstoke, Palgrave Macmillan, 2010.

Corley, T. A. B., *Quaker Enterprise in Biscuits: Huntley & Palmers, Reading 1822–1972*, London, Hutchinson, 1972.

Clark, Roger, *Somerset Anthology*, York, William Sessions, 1975.

The Clarks Desert Boot: Fifty Years of Style, Street, C. & J. Clark Ltd, 2000.

Clarks of Street, 1825–1950, Street, C. & J. Clark Ltd, 1950.

Clutterbuck, David, and Marion Devine, *Clore: The Man and his Millions*, London, Weidenfeld & Nicolson, 1987.

Crookenden, Spencer, *K Shoes – The First 150 Years, 1842–1992*, Carnforth, Mayoh Press, 1992.

Czerwinski, Michael, *Fifty Shoes That Changed the World*, London, Conran Octopus, 2009.

Ferguson, Niall, *Empire: How Britain Made the Modern World*, London, Penguin, 2003.

Gordon, Charles, *The Two Tycoons: A Personal Memoir of Charles Clore and Jack Cotton*, London, Hamish Hamilton, 1984.

Hannibal, Alfred, *Last Fitting and Pattern-cutting*, 1885.

Hudson, Kenneth, *Towards Precision Shoemaking*, Newton Abbot, David & Charles, 1968.

Jenkins, Simon, *A Short History of England*, London, Profile Books, 2011.

Kynaston, David, *Austerity Britain 1945–51*, London, Bloomsbury, 2007.

Lehane, Brendan, *C. & J. Clark, 1825–1975*, Street, C. & J. Clark Ltd, 1975.

Lovell, Percy, *Quaker Inheritance*, London, The Bannisdale Press, 1970.

McGarvie, Michael, *Guide to Historic Street*, Street, C. & J. Clark Ltd, 1986.

McGarvie, Michael, *Bowlingreen Mill*, Street, Avalon Leatherboard Co. Ltd., 1979.

McGarvie, Michael, *Street in Old Picture Postcards*, Someren-Eind, Holland, European Library, 1995.

Morrison, Kathryn A., and Ann Bond, *Built to Last? The Buildings of the Northamptonshire Boot and Shoes Industry*, London, English Heritage, 2004.

Pedersen, Stephanie, *Shoes: What Every Woman Should Know*, Newton Abbot, David & Charles, 2005.

Quaker Faith and Practice: The Book of Christian Discipline of the Yearly Meeting of the Religious Society of Friends (Quakers) in Britain, London, The Yearly Meeting of the Religious Society of Friends, 1995.

Steele, Valerie, *Shoes: A Lexicon of Style*, New York, Rizzoli, 1999.

Sutton, Barry, *C. & J. Clark, 1833–1903: A History of Shoemaking in Street, Somerset*, Sessions of York, 1979.

Swann, June, *Shoemaking*, Aylesbury, Shire Publications, 1986.

Thomson, Ruth, and Chris Fairclough, *Making Shoes*, London, Franklin Watts, 1986.

Walford, Jonathan, *The Seductive Shoe: Four Centuries of Fashion Footwear*, London, Thames & Hudson, 2007.

Walvin, James, *The Quakers: Money and Morals*, London, John Murray, 1997.

Wilson, A. N., *The Victorians*, London, Arrow Books, 2003.

Wilson, A. N., *Our Times: The Age of Elizabeth II*, London, Hutchinson, 2008.

Worshipful Company of Cordwainers, The, *The Boots and Shoes of Our Ancestors*, London, 1898.

Index